KILDARE

*For nurturing my early interest in Irish history, I dedicate this book*
*to the memory of my father Jimmy Cullen (1902–95)*
*who shared with me his memories and involvement in the Irish Revolution.*

# *Kildare*

# The Irish Revolution, 1912–23

Seamus Cullen

FOUR COURTS PRESS

Set in 10.5 on 12.5 point Ehrhardt for
FOUR COURTS PRESS LTD
7 Malpas Street, Dublin 8, Ireland
www.fourcourtspress.ie
*and in North America for*
FOUR COURTS PRESS
c/o IPG, 814 N. Franklin St, Chicago, IL 60610.

A catalogue record for this title
is available from the British Library.


ISBN 978-1-84682-837-9

Printed in England
by TJ International, Padstow, Cornwall.

# Contents

# Illustrations

*Credits*
2 *Clongownian*; 21 Collins family and *Leinster Leader*; 28 Máire Cruise O'Brien and O'Brien Press; 8 Gerry Cummins and Éanna de Burca; 12 Alice Curran; 16 Delaney Archive Trust, Carlow College Archive; 19 *Garda*

*Review*; 23 Irish Labour History Society Archive; 30 *Journal of the Kildare Archaeological Society*; 5 Deirdre Lawlor; 24 Charles Lillis; 29 Conor McHugh; 20 Eoin McVey; 13, 26 The National Archives, London; 4, 9, 11, 17, 22, 25 National Library of Ireland; 3, 15, 18 National Portrait Gallery, London; 6 Edward O'Kelly; 14 Éamon Ó Modhráin collection; 1 Parliamentary Archives, London; 10 The Royal Lancers Museum Trust; 27 Fr Christopher Walsh; 7 White/Nealon collection.

## MAPS

# Abbreviations

| | |
|---|---|
| AOH | Ancient Order of Hibernians |
| ASU | Active Service Unit |
| ATIRA | Anti-Treaty IRA |
| BMH | Bureau of Military History |
| Cd. | Command Paper (British parliamentary papers) |
| CI | County Inspector, RIC |
| CO | Colonial Office, TNA |
| CSORP | Chief Secretary's Office Registered Papers |
| DORA | Defence of the Realm Act |
| *EH* | *Evening Herald* |
| *FJ* | *Freeman's Journal* |
| GAA | Gaelic Athletic Association |
| GHQ | General Headquarters |
| GOC | General Officer Commanding |
| GPO | General Post Office |
| *Hansard* | House of Commons debates |
| HO | Home Office |
| IAPL | Irish Anti-Partition League |
| IFS | Irish Free State |
| IG | Inspector General, RIC |
| IGC | Irish Grants Committee |
| *IHS* | *Irish Historical Studies* |
| *II* | *Irish Independent* |
| IMA | Irish Military Archives |
| INAA | Irish National Aid Association |
| INAAVDF | Irish National Aid and Volunteer Dependants' Fund |
| IPP | Irish Parliamentary Party |
| IRA | Irish Republican Army |
| IRB | Irish Republican Brotherhood |
| *IT* | *Irish Times* |
| ITGWU | Irish Transport and General Workers' Union |
| IUA | Irish Unionist Alliance |
| IVDF | Irish Volunteer Dependents' Fund |
| IWM | Imperial War Museum, London |
| *JKAS* | *Journal of the Kildare Archaeological Society* |
| KCoA | Kildare County Archives |
| *KO* | *Kildare Observer* |
| *LL* | *Leinster Leader* |

| MS    | Manuscript                                       |
|-------|--------------------------------------------------|
| MP    | Member of Parliament                             |
| MSPC  | Military Service Pensions Collection             |
| NAI   | National Archives of Ireland                     |
| NLI   | National Library of Ireland                      |
| *NLT* | *Nationalist and Leinster Times*                 |
| O/C   | Officer Commanding                               |
| RDC   | Rural District Council                           |
| RDF   | Royal Dublin Fusiliers                           |
| RIC   | Royal Irish Constabulary                         |
| SF    | Sinn Féin                                        |
| TNA   | The National Archives, London                    |
| UAPL  | Unionist Anti-Partition League                   |
| UCDA  | University College Dublin Archives               |
| UDC   | Urban District Council                           |
| UIL   | United Irish League                              |
| UVF   | Ulster Volunteer Force                           |
| WO    | War Office, TNA                                  |
| WS    | Witness Statement to Bureau of Military History  |

# Acknowledgments

I would like to extend my gratitude to Professor Mary Ann Lyons and Dr Daithí Ó Corráin for inviting me to contribute to this series and for their continuous support and advice. This study of the Irish Revolution in County Kildare is the culmination of a lifetime of interest and research and I wish to acknowledge with thanks some of the many people who encouraged and assisted me with this work. The book is based on a doctoral dissertation completed in the School of History and Geography at Dublin City University. I am deeply indebted to my supervisor Dr Daithí Ó Corráin who provided expert advice, guidance and work beyond the call of duty. His vast knowledge of the Irish Revolution and his enthusiasm for the Kildare project was an inspiration to me throughout the lengthy period of research. The staff of the DCU School of History and Geography deserve my gratitude, in particular Professor James Kelly, Dr William Murphy and Dr Leeann Lane. I am grateful to my fellow PhD students, Dr Mary MacDiarmada, Dr Gerry Hanley and Martin Ryan, for being so generous with their time and advice. A very special thanks to Dr Karina Holton for the many hours of assistance at every stage. Her keen eye for proof reading, ideas, encouragement and discussion were immeasurable and are much appreciated. For their encouragement and assistance, I wish to acknowledge the support of Dr Anne Dolan, Mary Cullen, Professor Raymond Gillespie, Dr Noel Murphy, Fergus White, Dr Anne-Marie McInerney, Dr Joseph Quinn and Gerry Kavanagh. I am grateful to Dr Mike Brennan for his skilful production of the maps herein and Tony Murray for photo restoration. I wish to thank the staff of various research libraries and archives where the research for this book was conducted: the Cregan Library, DCU, Trinity College Library, John Paul II Library, Maynooth University, the National Library of Ireland, the National Archives of Ireland, the Military Archives, UCD Archives, the Irish Labour History Society Archive, the Irish Railway Record Society Archives, the Guinness Archives, Dublin Diocesan Archives, the General Records Office, Clongowes Wood Archives, the Delany Archive, Carlow, Kildare County Archives, Louth County Archives and Mayo County Archives. In the UK great courtesy was extended to me in the National Archives, the British Library, the Imperial War Museum, Parliamentary Archives, the National Army Museum, London, the Bodleian Library, Oxford and the Churchill Library in Cambridge. I was fortunate to have access to a number of collections in private hands. In particular, I wish to thank Adhamhnán Ó Súilleabháin and the late Edward O'Kelly for granting me access to the papers in their care. I would also like to acknowledge the many people I interviewed, too numerous to list here. My thanks go to all who provided photographs used in the volume especially relatives of individuals connected to the revolution in Kildare. My greatest gratitude is to my family. To my sons, James and Bryan, for taking on the burden of my day job when necessary and for technical and IT assistance. Finally, my wife, Fiona, for her unfailing patience, and, in particular, second opinions on my work.

# The Irish Revolution, 1912–23 series

Since the turn of the century, a growing number of scholars have been actively researching this seminal period in modern Irish history. More recently, propelled by the increasing availability of new archival material, this endeavour has intensified. This series brings together for the first time the various strands of this exciting and fresh scholarship within a nuanced interpretative framework, making available concise, accessible, scholarly studies of the Irish Revolution experience at a local level to a wide audience.

The approach adopted is both thematic and chronological, addressing the key developments and major issues that occurred at a county level during the tumultuous 1912–23 period. Beginning with an overview of the social, economic and political milieu in the county in 1912, each volume assesses the strength of the home rule movement and unionism, as well as levels of labour and feminist activism. The genesis and organization of paramilitarism from 1913 are traced; responses to the outbreak of the First World War and its impact on politics at a county level are explored; and the significance of the 1916 Rising is assessed. The varying fortunes of constitutional and separatist nationalism are examined. The local experience of the War of Independence, reaction to the truce and Anglo-Irish Treaty and the course and consequences of the Civil War are subject to detailed examination and analysis. The result is a compelling account of life in Ireland in this formative era.

*Mary Ann Lyons*
*Department of History*
*Maynooth University*

*Daithí Ó Corráin*
*School of History & Geography*
*Dublin City University*

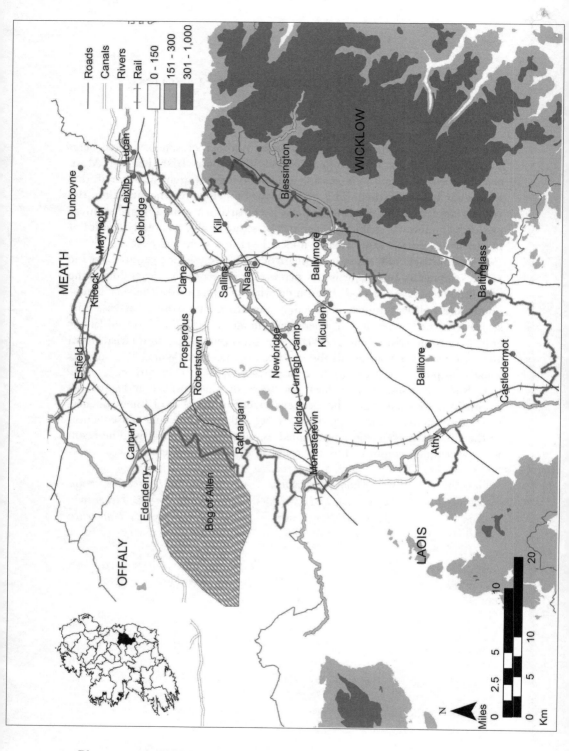

1 Places mentioned in the text

# 1 Kildare in 1912

On 16 May 1922 the British army stationed in Kildare packed their bags and evacuated the remaining barracks in the county, including the Curragh camp, the second-largest military base in the United Kingdom. It took the final party of evacuating military personnel and more than 100 vehicles one hour to pass through Naas in what the *Derry Journal* described as 'a bloodless victory', the surrender to the IRA of England's greatest stronghold in Ireland. Eight years earlier, when British army officers in the Curragh effectively mutinied rather than obey government orders to assist in the implementation of home rule in Ulster, the idea of an evacuation would have been deemed a fantasy. Kildare's long established status as a garrison county differentiates it from all others. The Irish Revolution (1912–23) had a substantial impact on Kildare, which was central to some of the most significant episodes of this tumultuous decade: the Curragh incident (1914), the British army's response to the 1916 Rising, the intelligence war during the War of Independence, and the Irish Civil War when Kildare's military barracks were occupied by National army personnel and its prisons held the highest proportion of republican prisoners in Ireland. Kildare was also unusual in swiftly returning to its peaceful and largely law-abiding Redmondite roots after 1923, though under a pro-Treaty label.

In January 1912 the RIC county inspector (CI) for Kildare described the county as 'peaceable and free from crime, [with] no agrarian trouble, no boy-cotting or intimidation'.[1] Subsequent reports continued to convey the county's political tranquillity and relative prosperity. A key theme of this study is how Kildare's status as a garrison county helps explain its law-abiding nature during the early years of the revolution. The substantial resident population of military personnel significantly aided the local economy, which was based mainly on agriculture. The first twelve years of the century witnessed important political and socio-economic change. The Local Government (Ireland) Act 1898 effectively ended landlord control of local government by produc-ing democratically elected representatives from among the ordinary people. Great strides had been made to resolve the land question under the land acts of 1903 and 1909, and to alleviate poverty with the introduction of the Old Age Pensions Act of 1908. There was also in this period a greater cultural awareness of being Irish, which had an important impact on nationalism. But the dominant political issue facing Kildare and all other Irish counties in 1912 was the third home rule bill introduced in April. The crisis generated by this tested the noted tranquillity of the county between 1912 and 1914.

Kildare is roughly triangular in shape with its apex to the south. An inland county, it is the fourth-smallest county in Leinster with an area of 654 square miles occupying a mere 2.1 per cent of the area of Ireland. As shown in map 1, Kildare borders Wicklow to the east, and Dublin and Meath to the north, Carlow to the south and Offaly and Laois to the west. Regarded as the flattest land in Ireland, it is only in the extreme east, where the county boundary meets the Dublin–Wicklow mountain range, that the terrain reaches 305 metres above sea-level. There are a number of important physical features in the county. In the centre lies the open pasture of the Curragh. Comprising 4,870 acres, it is the largest unenclosed area of fertile land in Ireland.[2] The Bog of Allen occupies a sizeable area towards the west and north-west. The main river, the Liffey, meanders through the county in a semi-circular course from the Wicklow mountains in the east to the Dublin county boundary at Leixlip. The south of the county is drained predominantly by the River Barrow, while an area of west Kildare is drained by the River Boyne.

Historically, all communications from Dublin to the south and west passed through County Kildare. In the early twentieth century the principal road to the west, corresponding with the present M4, entered the county at Leixlip and exited at Clonard in the north-west. The main road leading to the south, today the M7, proceeded from Dublin at Rathcoole, through County Kildare as far as Monasterevin. The route to Waterford (now the M9) branched off this road at Naas and cut through the south of the county as far as Castledermot. Not only was Kildare well served with its road network, the Grand Canal and the Royal Canal, the two most significant canals in the country, passed through it. In all, over seventy miles of canals extended throughout Kildare, a greater quantity than any other county. As map 1 indicates, Kildare was also particularly well served with railways. The Midland Great Western Railway line, connecting Dublin with Galway and Sligo, ran through the county almost parallel to the Royal Canal. The Great Southern & Western Railway, linking Dublin with Cork, Limerick and Waterford, also passed through. With its extensive communications network, it is unsurprising that all land traffic, both passenger and commercial, from Dublin to much of the west and south of the country, passed through Kildare.

Demographically, the 1911 census indicated that Kildare was unusual in many respects. With a population of 66,627, it ranked fourth in Leinster. However, due to the sizeable presence of the British army, a significant proportion of that population (7,668 individuals or 11.5 per cent) was born in Britain. By comparison, in Dublin, the centre of British administration in Ireland, only 5.53 per cent of the population was British-born.[3]

There were four significant garrison towns in County Kildare in 1912: the Curragh camp, Naas, Newbridge and Kildare town. The Curragh, with an estimated population of 7,000, was the largest urban area in the county.[4] The camp was substantial, with accommodation for 4,488 army personnel or 72 per cent of the entire military population in the county.[5] With a population of 3,842, Naas was the county town and the principal market town in the county.[6] The local barracks was the main recruiting centre for the Royal Dublin Fusiliers. Newbridge, with a population of 3,400, had a cavalry barracks on one side of Main Street and shops and dwellings on the other. Almost the entire workforce of the town was employed either directly or indirectly by the army.[7] At nearby Kildare town, where a substantial artillery barracks was sited, the population was 2,639. The railway station in the town was the transport hub for the military in both the Curragh camp and other local military barracks.[8]

Of the non-garrison urban centres, Athy was the main town in south Kildare with a population of 3,535. It was an important market town situated in a noted tillage area with several industries including mills and brickworks. Flour was produced at Ardreigh Mill; M.J. Minch and Son, one of the largest producers of malt in the country, also operated from the town.[9] In north Kildare, Maynooth, with a population of 886, was the largest town. Its two biggest employers were St Patrick's College, and the duke of Leinster's estate at Carton. There was also a medium-sized mill in the town.[10] Nearby, Celbridge, with a population of 842, had all the trappings of a deserted industrial town.[11] Across the centre of the county, Monasterevin (population 732) and Rathangan (population 547) were market towns. Industries such as Cassidy's Distillery in Monasterevin and Hank's Mill in Rathangan provided additional employment.[12] Kilcullen's proximity to the Curragh meant that it gained significant trade from the British army. Other market towns of note included Kilcock, Castledermot and Ballymore Eustace. Clane was an important village in north Kildare in which residents benefitted in terms of employment and trade from the proximity of Clongowes Wood College, the Jesuit secondary boarding school. Leixlip, with a population of 585, was the closest County Kildare settlement to the capital. As a result, many of its residents worked in west Dublin.

At almost eighteen per cent, the Protestant population in Kildare in 1911 was sizeable.[13] By comparison, Dublin city had a Protestant population of seventeen per cent, while Wicklow, with twenty per cent, had the highest Protestant population outside Ulster.[14] Unsurprisingly, within Kildare the highest concentration of Protestants was recorded in the Curragh camp (62 per cent).[15]

In 1846 the Church of Ireland diocese of Kildare was united with the archdiocese of Dublin and Glendalough. Thereafter, the archbishop of Dublin had direct ecclesiastical authority over the entire county of Kildare. In 1912 there were twelve Church of Ireland parishes in the county served by twelve rectors and two curates.[16] Joseph Peacocke, a native of Abbeyleix, County Laois, served as archbishop from his consecration in 1897 until his retirement on the grounds of ill-health in 1915. He showed a willingness to work with his

Catholic counterpart and in 1908, the two combined to act as mediators to resolve the carters' strike in Dublin. The home rule crisis in 1912 compelled Peacocke to engage in political matters.[17]

County Kildare was divided between two Roman Catholic dioceses. The archdiocese of Dublin encompassed much of the east and south, while the remaining area (about sixty per cent) belonged to the diocese of Kildare and Leighlin.[18] In 1912 twenty-one Catholic parishes in County Kildare were served by twenty-one parish priests and thirty-one curates. This did not include clergy in Catholic colleges such as Maynooth, Clongowes Wood and Newbridge or the Curragh camp which was served by a chaplain and his assistant.[19] In 1912 William J. Walsh was Catholic archbishop of Dublin. A former president of Maynooth College, he was a declared nationalist.[20] Patrick Foley, a native of Carlow and a former president of Carlow College, was bishop of Kildare and Leighlin from 1896 until 1926. He was particularly interested in educational matters and served for a time as a commissioner for national education.[21] A supporter of the Irish Parliamentary Party (IPP), Foley was on occasion consulted about parliamentary nominations within his diocese. For instance, in 1904 he approved the offer of North Kildare to Tom Kettle, who, in the event, declined and the nomination went to John O'Connor who was elected.[22]

In 1912 County Kildare was served by a force of 176 members of the Royal Irish Constabulary (RIC) in twenty-seven barracks.[23] The CI was based in Naas, and for administrative purposes Kildare was divided into three districts: Naas, Kildare and Athy – with a district inspector in charge of each.[24] The number of barracks and policemen was smaller than in other counties with a similar population. In Sligo, for instance, there were 34 barracks and 216 policemen, a ratio of 365 persons to one policeman.[25] In Kildare, the ratio was 378 persons to one policeman. Dundalk-born Kerry Supple was appointed CI in 1910 and remained in post until his retirement in 1921.[26] Supple was popular with his men, partly because he was generous with leave.[27] His policing role was not onerous as he presided over one of the most peaceful counties in Ireland.

Agriculture was Kildare's dominant economic activity and was responsible for the direct employment of 11,656 or 17.5 per cent of the working age population in 1911.[28] This was similar to Wicklow, but lower than the adjoining counties of Meath, Offaly, and Laois where agricultural employment engaged twenty-five per cent of the population.[29] The most important livestock category in economic terms was cattle, followed by sheep and horses. Regarded as one of the leading equine counties in Ireland, there were 14,200 horses in Kildare.[30] Although many neighbouring counties had a larger number of horses, the quality of the stock in Kildare was higher, with 2,300 animals used primarily for recreation purposes. Only County Cork, with 3,300 animals, recorded more horses of this type.[31] The area of land under crops was 105,600 acres. Not surprisingly, hay at 59,000 acres was the most common crop, followed by corn crops at 27,700 acres.[32] Total farming land was divided among 9,810 holdings in 1912. Just over 35 per cent of this number were very small farms of between 1 and 15 acres; 20 per cent were between 15 and 50 acres. By Kildare standards, a holding of between 50 and 100 acres was regarded as the farm of a strong farmer. This category accounted for ten per cent of all holdings, while those of 100 to 200 acres accounted for 7.2 per cent. The proportion of very extensive farms of over 100 acres was larger in Kildare than in the neighbouring counties of Meath (5 per cent) and Offaly (4 per cent).[33]

The fact that approximately two-thirds of farmers in Kildare had purchased their holdings by 1912 suggests the successful implementation of both the Wyndham Act of 1903 and the Birrell Land Act of 1909. The Wyndham Land Act ushered in a social revolution that saw substantial numbers of tenants obtain freehold status and, in due course, they became a numerous, prosperous and powerful landowning class. In 1912, 65.5 per cent of occupiers were freeholders, while 34.5 per cent remained as tenants. Kildare was 12 per cent above the Leinster average of 53.55 per cent of freeholders.[34] The Wyndham Act provided generous terms for landlords to sell their estates and for tenants to purchase. This benefitted richer tenants in the wealthier eastern parts of Ireland such as County Kildare.[35] One of the earliest and largest estates sold under the Wyndham Act was that of the duke of Leinster – Ireland's leading peer and head of the FitzGerald family. The estate comprised approximately 45,000 acres and was mainly centred around Carton in Maynooth in the north of the county and Athy in south Kildare.[36] The sale in 1903 was not without considerable controversy. Many tenants in the Castledermot area of south Kildare complained first, that the terms favoured the landlord over the tenant, and, second, that they were set by north Kildare men, who were generally graziers with convenient access to the Dublin market.[37] The protests fell on deaf ears. The sale set a precedent for the price of land under the act which was imitated not only in Kildare but nationally.[38] Many leading landowners in Kildare followed the example of the Leinster estate and negotiated terms with their tenants under the Wyndham Act. By 1906 many of the great estates in County Kildare were reduced to the core demesne land surrounding their residences.

In 1912 Kildare was a prosperous county. The quality of housing stock was comparatively good. There were 12,697 inhabited houses, occupied by an average of 4.7 persons per household and 46.4 per cent of the population lived in larger dwellings of three and four rooms.[39] At 13,023, the number of individual families was only marginally higher than the total number of dwellings. Fortunately, the numbers in overcrowded conditions were relatively small: 4.6 per cent of families occupied one room and 25 per cent occupied two rooms. The numbers receiving poor relief were not excessive, with 1,648

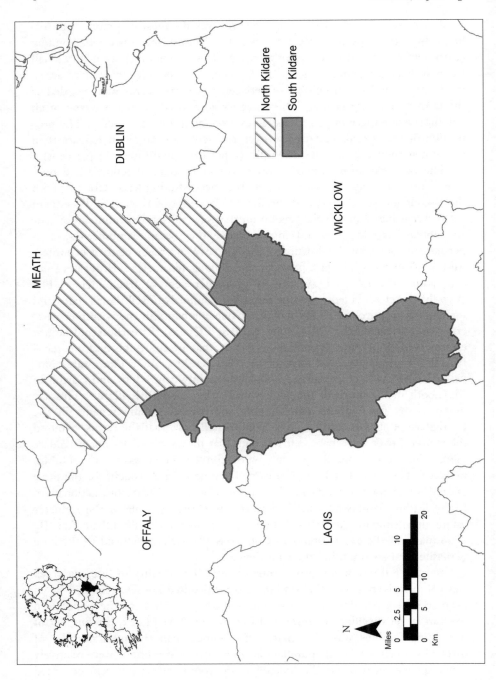

**2** Parliamentary constituencies in 1910 and 1918

(1:40) availing of assistance. Significantly, there was a high literacy rate of 93.8 per cent in Kildare; indeed, illiteracy had reduced by 4.7 per cent over a twenty-year period since 1891.

In 1912 there were 25,887 army personnel of all ranks in Ireland of which more than one-fifth (5,993 including 230 commissioned officers) were stationed in County Kildare. The vast majority of 4,472 were in the Curragh camp, the largest military camp in Ireland. The remainder were stationed at Newbridge (810), Kildare town (566), and Naas (145). As the most militarized county in the country, army numbers in Kildare exceeded the Dublin figure of 5,346 by almost 650.[40]

Not surprisingly, the British army was the largest employer in the county and a substantial percentage of the population in central Kildare was directly dependent on the British army for their livelihood. Virtually every class and several occupations benefitted – graziers, dairy farmers, market gardeners, carters, drivers and labourers. Provision for army horses alone (which numbered 2,124 in 1912) had significant economic ramifications in terms of stabling, handling and forage.[41] At full capacity, 2,830 army horses could be stabled.[42] Sales of horses held in the camp each summer were a particularly lucrative event for merchants, huntsmen, hotel owners, jarveys and dealers. In 1911, for example, 150 horses were offered for sale, of which approximately 100 were sold without reserve.[43]

The economic impact of the British army was significant. Newbridge prospered on its military contracts. Few townspeople were directly employed in the barracks. Only carters who delivered supplies, farmers who removed manure, or washerwomen who worked in the laundry were regularly admitted within its confines. However, on occasions other work such as cleaning chimneys, lighting lamps or washing bed linen was carried out by locals.[44] Newbridge was also the retail hub for the military. The variety of businesses reflected the wide-ranging requirements of the garrison with several high-class grocers, confectioners, drapers, laundries, pawn-brokers and a forage contractor located in the vicinity. Another means of measuring the impact of the army on local trade is to examine the number of pages of advertisements in *Porter's directory*. Newbridge accounted for seventeen pages, Kildare town nine, and Kilcullen six. This compares to fifteen pages for Naas, the county town.[45]

Shops within the Curragh camp itself also provided significant employment. Branches of Eason newsagents, Todd Burns' drapers and McCabes' fishmongers, as well as those of Llewellyn coal merchants, Richard O'Mahony, builder, and H.W. Church, cycle agent, were all located within the barracks. There was also a photographer, jeweller and motor engineer, and the Army and Navy Co-operative Stores. The military presence explains the prevalence of the large number of hotels in the Curragh area. These included the Prince of Wales and the Crown Hotels in Newbridge; the Railway and the

Leinster Arms Hotels in Kildare town; the King's Arms in Kilcullen; Stand House Hotel at the Curragh racecourse; and John Mallick's Hotel in Athgarvan on the perimeter of the Curragh camp.[46] The spending (and drinking) power of the army was reflected by the fact that there were more than fifty public houses within a three-mile radius of the Curragh camp. Surviving trade ledgers in the Guinness archives reveal an extensive porter trade with the garrison towns in Kildare.[47] Towns not adjacent to the military camps were indirectly dependent on the army for business. Beef production, for instance, which was the most important agricultural activity in the country, was heavily dependent on buyers purchasing for the army and other British markets.[48] Kildare was economically more reliant on the War Office than any other Irish county.

As indicated in map 2, the county was divided into two single-seat parliamentary constituencies, North Kildare (with 4,740 electors) and South Kildare (4,955 electors).[49] In 1912 the sitting MP for South Kildare was Denis Kilbride who occupied the seat from 1903 until 1918. He had a colourful career as an agrarian campaigner during the Land War and was later jailed for his part in the Plan of Campaign.[50] In North Kildare, John O'Connor, a barrister, was MP from 1905 until 1918. He, too, had an interesting career. A Fenian and arms importer during his youth, O'Connor was jailed at least five times.[51] In March 1905 John Redmond became aware of divorce proceedings in London involving O'Connor and his estranged wife. Fearing a damaging divorce scandal comparable to the Parnell episode, the IPP leader urged O'Connor to settle the case by a deed of separation or else his resignation would be demanded.[52] O'Connor took Redmond's advice and no details of the affair came to light. Indeed his last will and testament in 1928 made no reference to his marital status.[53] In 1908 he survived allegations of corruption following acceptance of judicial office in England and Wales.[54]

The Local Government Act of 1898 transferred the administrative powers and duties of the grand juries to democratically elected local councils. In Kildare, the measure established Kildare County Council, two urban district councils (UDCs) at Naas and Athy, and a town commission at Newbridge. Five rural district councils (RDCs) – Athy No. 1, Baltinglass No. 3, Celbridge No. 1, Edenderry No. 2, and Naas No. 1 – were also formed.[55] Kildare County Council, the upper tier of the new system, was responsible for road maintenance, water supply, sanitation, housing, courthouses, coroners, agricultural and technical instruction committees, asylum committees and raising funds for the subsidiary RDCs.[56] The UDCs came into operation in 1900 with responsibility for housing, water and sewage, markets and fairs, lanes and lighting within the town bounds. Newbridge Town Commission had few functions, although its role in housing was significant. The various poor law unions, which had been established in 1838 and administered by a Board of

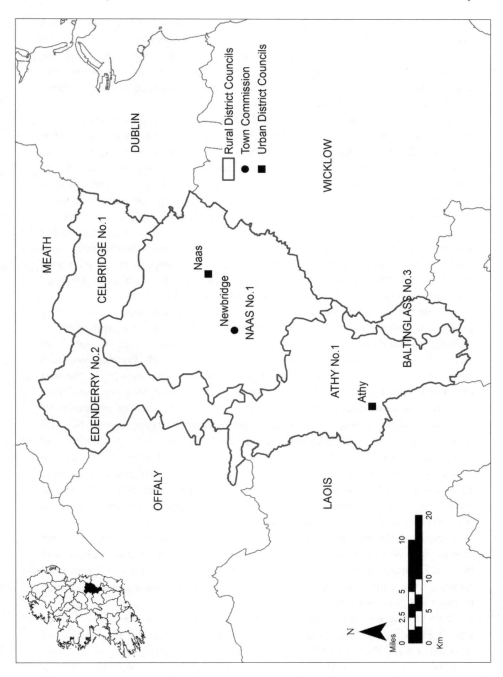

**3** Local government divisions

Guardians, were not affected and continued to oversee welfare assistance, orphans' and children's welfare and workhouses which, by the turn of the century, were increasingly functioning as hospitals. As map 3 indicates, the functional responsibilities of local government traversed county boundaries and in this way, for example, Celbridge Union embraced part of County Dublin and also part of County Meath.

The Local Government Act removed the property qualifications that had existed for elections to the poor law unions throughout the nineteenth century. Boards of Guardians also became more democratic with RDC and UDC members eligible to serve as members. However, the county council and UDC vote was not a perfect franchise. Women could not vote unless they were heads of households and were over thirty years of age. County council elections were held every three years and decided by simple majorities in single-seat constituencies. The majority of those elected were nationalist which resulted in a substantial loss of power for unionists. Nationalist councillors were strong supporters of the IPP and were mainly returned unopposed. When elections were held, however, they could be vigorously contested even by opposing candidates claiming allegiance to the IPP.[57]

During its first two decades, Kildare County Council was dominated by prominent nationalists such as Stephen Brown, a Naas solicitor, and Matthew Minch, a prosperous maltster from Athy and MP from 1892 to 1903.[58] In 1912 Minch was chairman of the county council, with George Wolfe, a Protestant and member of the landed gentry, as vice chairman.[59] At the first election in 1899, three of the twenty-one county councillors returned were unionist; the remainder were allied to the IPP. The success of the unionists was due to their widespread appeal to the electorate irrespective of political stance. The successful unionist councillors were popular landowners and employers. Generally, three unionists were returned until the death of Ambrose More O'Ferrall in 1911.[60] In 1912 the unionist councillors were Lord Frederick FitzGerald, uncle of the duke of Leinster, and W.G. Dease, a land agent.[61] Of the twenty-eight members of the county council, five members were *ex-officio* and two were co-opted.

Despite Kildare's proximity to Dublin there were no organized trade unions, or 'combinations' to use CI Supple's term, in 1912, although, as will be seen in the next chapter, this changed in 1913.[62] Labour had no representation on the county council or UDCs. This was not unusual and pertained in the rural counties adjacent to Kildare.[63]

The largest political organization in the county in 1912 was the United Irish League (UIL), the local arm of the IPP. It was formed in 1898 by the nationalist MP, William O'Brien, for the purpose of reallocating ranch land. The position of the UIL in Kildare was weaker than counties such as Longford where it remained involved in agrarian activity between 1906 and

1911.[64] In March 1912 only eight branches were recorded in Kildare with a combined membership of 411 – the second lowest in Ireland. County Dublin had the same number of branches but a smaller membership of 344. A reduction in UIL strength occurred in many counties in the immediate pre-war years because without serious land agitation or elections to fight, there was little for branches to do.[65] Nevertheless, the organization in midland counties was far from insignificant. The weakness of the UIL in Kildare was the product of the Wyndham Land Act, which had gone a long way towards settling the land issue, and the absence of serious agrarian agitation.

Home rule was the dominant political issue in Ireland and in Kildare in 1912. The power of the House of Lords' veto was long seen as a barrier against home rule. At a UIL meeting in Naas in December 1910, John O'Connor MP claimed that home rule would follow abolition of the veto.[66] The budgetary crisis of 1909 led the Liberal government, backed by the IPP, to implement the Parliament Act (1911) which effectively removed the right of the House of Lords to veto money bills completely, and replaced a right of veto over other public bills with a maximum delay of two years.[67] This transformed the prospects for home rule. The price of the IPP's support was the introduction of a home rule bill in the House of Commons in April 1912. Reaction in Kildare was predictable. Nationalists gave unquestioning support to the IPP while unionists vigorously opposed the bill. In June 1912 Kildare County Council approved the measure 'so dear to the heart of every Irish nationalist' as 'an honest attempt to settle the longstanding quarrel between this country and Great Britain'.[68] By contrast, two months later, the unionists of Kildare declared their 'unabated attachment to the legislated union between Great Britain and Ireland' and stressed their 'fixed determination … to resist home rule in whatever shape it may be presented'.[69] Unionist opposition in Ulster culminated in the signing of the Solemn League and Covenant on 28 September 1912. At least two women living in the Curragh signed the declaration, the version of the Covenant for women.[70]

While CI Supple's reports curiously claimed there was little interest in home rule in County Kildare,[71] local newspapers gave a different picture, reporting lively home rule debates at county council and UDC level, and at UIL meetings.[72] Bizarrely, Supple also failed to mention the attendance of practically the entire elected membership of Kildare County Council and several chairmen of UDCs at a massive home rule demonstration in Dublin on 31 March 1912.[73] At a local level support was demonstrated by subscription to a home rule fund. In one parish in Kildare, 150 named individuals contributed an impressive £77 4s. 6d.[74] Supple's personal anti-home rule stance explains the selectivity of his monthly reports. Similarly, the CI omitted to report on the largest meeting of advanced nationalists in the county in 1912 at Bodenstown in June. It was attended by Countess Markievicz, John

MacBride, Cathal Brugha and Thomas Clarke who presided, with the key-note speech delivered by Bulmer Hobson.[75]

Supple monitored the extension into Kildare in 1912 of the Ancient Order of Hibernians (AOH). Between March and October six branches had been formed in the county.[76] The AOH in Ireland, which was closely aligned with the IPP, qualified for administering benefits under the National Insurance Act of 1911 and, as a result of its participation, the movement spread throughout Ireland.[77] Although the Hibernians were overtly sectarian nationally, in Kildare they were controlled by the UIL which maintained good relations with Protestants and were not normally involved in sectarian activity. The largely unionist *Kildare Observer* was not impressed by the new movement and maintained that it merely linked bigotry with insurance.[78] Although concerns about civil and religious liberties were not as prevalent in the south as in Ulster, there was, notwithstanding the AOH, genuine concern among unionists in Kildare. This may have been heightened by the substantial number of Catholic clergy who openly supported local branches of the UIL and the IPP in Kildare. Two of the eleven nomination papers proposing the outgoing MP John O'Connor for re-election in December 1910 were signed by parish priests.[79] Although not actively engaged in politics, Bishop Foley supported the nationalist cause and in February 1912 contributed five guineas to the home rule fund.[80] John O'Connor vigorously refuted accusations that home rule would be Rome rule and he also denied claims that home rule did not enjoy widespread support.[81]

Although numerically small, unionists in Kildare were determined to organize resistance to home rule lest it lead to a complete severance of the links with England, papal domination, or force the mass migration of the Anglo-Irish.[82] Home rule deepened the pre-existing political division between the landowning class, which was firmly unionist, and the overwhelmingly nationalist majority. Political sensitivities were exposed in 1908 when a reception for the duke of Leinster on his coming of age was abandoned by the people of Maynooth after it became known that he had donated £300 to the Unionist Association of Ireland.[83] Opposition to home rule in Kildare was led by Lord Mayo (Dermot Bourke) of Palmerstown House, Kill, a prominent unionist in the House of Lords and a future Irish Free State senator whose unionist activities made him unpopular in the county.[84]

In early 1912, two branches of the Women's Unionist Association (WUA) were established in Kildare, one in each parliamentary constituency. The South Kildare branch, presided over by Lady Alice Borrowes, met in Barretstown Castle close to Ballymore Eustace on 2 February 1912, where speeches opposing home rule were given by a number of unionists including Lord Mayo.[85] Lady Mayo was president of the North Kildare branch, which held its first (drawing-room) meeting later in February in Killadoon House, close to Celbridge. A letter from Lady Londonderry, the wife of a former lord lieutenant and president of the Ulster Women's Unionist Council, was read which urged loyalist women all over Ireland to oppose home rule.[86] The meeting generated controversy when Revd Lionel Fletcher, rector of Straffan, engaged in a personal attack on the pope. This rankled with local nationalists. Two weeks later a UIL meeting in Staplestown passed a resolution criticizing Fletcher's remarks and accusing him of 'stirring up religious animosity in the country'.[87] The impressive Kildare turnout at the home rule rally in Dublin at the end of March might also have been a riposte.

This may have influenced other Church of Ireland clergymen in Kildare to maintain a discrete silence on the home rule issue with no public statements appearing in local newspapers. The Church of Ireland bishops were less circumspect, however. At a special Church of Ireland synod in Dublin on 16 April 1912, Archbishop Peacocke condemned home rule. He maintained that 'there are occasions when the church ought not shrink from making a pronouncement of a political character when it concerns the welfare of the whole community of which she is part'.[88] He adopted a cautious approach towards more militant anti-home rule opposition and in September 1912 was wary of associating the Church of Ireland with the signing of the Ulster covenant in case the AOH and UIL might raise hostilities against the Church outside Ulster.[89] Nonetheless, within days, he devised a special form of prayer against home rule which was read at Sunday services in all parishes of the Southern Province of the Church of Ireland.[90] The following year, during the Dublin Diocesan Synod, he went further and spoke with unusual passion, calling the home rule bill a menace to religion and civil liberties.[91]

By autumn 1912, practically all of the landed gentry in Kildare actively supported organized opposition to home rule. This was illustrated by the attendance at an anti-home rule meeting organized by Lord Mayo at his residence on 24 August 1912. The local press reported the presence of the Conollys of Castletown, the Bartons of Straffan, the Aylmers of Kerdiffstown, the Clements from Killadoon, the Wogan-Brownes from Keredern and Baron de Robeck of Gowran Grange. According to Mayo, the purpose of the meeting was to protest against the home rule bill and to show solidarity with unionists in other counties.[92]

Home rule overshadowed all other political campaigns of the era, including the suffrage question. In April 1913 the Irish Women's Franchise League (IWFL) held a public meeting in Naas town hall that was attended by 250 people, one third of whom were women. It was addressed by founder members Hanna Sheehy-Skeffington and Marguerite Palmer who were among the Dublin suffragettes imprisoned the previous year. Sheehy-Skeffington asserted that women were discriminated against in the way that Catholics had been under the penal laws, and she pointed out that the same arguments were used against Catholic emancipation as were now being used against the emancipation of women. The *Kildare Observer* suggested that the speakers impressed many with their intellect and moderate language.[93] Overall, the meeting was a success. It highlighted the campaign for women's political rights and countered the negative publicity directed at the movement by the press. It should also be mentioned that the Ulster Women's Unionist Council supported female suffrage.

As a garrison county it was not surprising that advanced nationalism made little headway in Kildare. The memory of Theobald Wolfe Tone and Lord Edward FitzGerald, who had Kildare connections, was a source of inspiration to advanced nationalists in Kildare in the early twentieth century.[94] According to Christopher Woods, Tone's grave at Bodenstown had become a place of pilgrimage for nationalists of every viewpoint and eventually commemoration of Irish independence.[95] In June 1913, Patrick Pearse described the site as the holiest place in Ireland.[96] John Devoy, leader of Clan na Gael in the US, was born at Kill and was another source of inspiration. Maynooth man, Patrick Colgan, recalled his surprise when reading the Irish Republican Brotherhood (IRB) newspaper *Irish Freedom* in 1911 to discover that Devoy was a native of Kildare. That year, Colgan was part of a group which opposed the visit of King George V to Maynooth College; he subsequently took part in the 1916 Rising and War of Independence.[97]

Advanced nationalist activity increased in north Kildare in 1912 when Seán O'Connor, a Gaelic League organizer in the county, began to develop the IRB.[98] Michael O'Kelly, who also arrived in Kildare in 1912 as editor of the *Leinster Leader* newspaper, was another member of the IRB. O'Kelly had previously met O'Connor in nationalist circles in Limerick. His surprise at O'Connor's efforts to promote the IRB was captured in his claim that 'he might as well attempt such organizing work in Yorkshire or any other English county'.[99] Kildare was not a happy hunting ground for Sinn Féin (SF) in the early years of its existence, and the organization, despite not having a republican agenda, made no impact in the county. The first branch did not emerge until early 1917.[100]

Interest in cultural nationalism was evident in Kildare from the beginning of the twentieth century. Father Eugene O'Growney, professor of Irish at Maynooth, was involved in the formation of the Gaelic League, but it made slow progress in the county. It was not until 1902 that the Irish language was first used in the *Leinster Leader*. The first branches of the League were formed in Naas, Maynooth and Newbridge in 1901, and by 1913, eighteen branches had been established. In all but three branches, the local parish priest or curate served as president.[101] During winter, language and dancing classes were usually held twice weekly while festivals in the summer promoted Irish dancing, singing and recitation.[102] Two controversies involving the

League had Kildare links. In 1906 Domhnall Ua Buachalla, to the fore in establishing the Maynooth branch, became embroiled in legal proceedings in the High Court over the use of Irish on his cart. The case was defended by Patrick Pearse, but the conviction was upheld.[103] A close friendship subsequently developed between Pearse and Ua Buachalla.[104] Traders such as Ua Buachalla suffered commercially for their stance on the Irish language. Some of his customers objected to Irish signage and billheads. The objectors were mainly retired army residents, and many of the strong unionist community in the Maynooth area withdrew their custom from his business.[105] Another to gain notoriety was Revd Michael O'Hickey, professor of Irish at Maynooth College from 1896 to 1909.[106] He served as vice president of the Gaelic League from 1899 to 1903, but is best remembered for his involvement in the agitation in 1908–9 to make Irish compulsory in the National University of Ireland matriculation examination. During the controversy, he publicly attacked Cardinal Logue and other members of the hierarchy, and was dismissed by Daniel Mannix, president of Maynooth College in 1909. O'Hickey appealed his dismissal to the Vatican, but was unsuccessful.[107]

Kildare embraced the revival of Gaelic games following the establishment of the Gaelic Athletic Association (GAA) in 1884. It enjoyed a golden age on the field during the first decade of the twentieth century, reaching the All-Ireland football final of 1903 (played in 1905). The connection between the GAA and nationalism received a massive boost in 1907 when Kildare won its first All-Ireland (the 1905 event, which was played in 1907). The victory was celebrated in every town and village in the county. However, sport and politics were never too far apart. Jack Fitzgerald, one of the players from the All-Ireland winning team, got into difficulties with the authorities when he asserted that 'GAA members ... would possibly do more for Ireland than kick a football or shake a hurley should the opportunity offer'.[108] By 1913 he was serving as president of Kildare County Board.[109] Mike Cronin has observed that early in the first decade of the twentieth century the GAA had fulfilled its mission to revive the native games of Ireland and to awaken national spirit.[110] This also applied to Kildare, where the movement created an awareness of native Irish games and a sense of Irishness among a substantial portion of the population. It adopted the same method of branch organization as the Irish National League, and linked local parochialism to a new nationalism in the county. A large section of the public from all social backgrounds, and particularly the youth, became involved.

The local press played a key role in shaping public opinion in Kildare. The largely unionist *Kildare Observer* was established in 1879, and the nationalist *Leinster Leader* in 1880. In 1912 Seumas O'Kelly was succeeded as editor of the *Leinster Leader* by his brother, Michael, who was a more militant nationalist.[111] Although the *Kildare Observer* was a unionist newspaper, nation-

alist opinion was extensively covered. Editorials were usually of establishment
tone. With two other local nationalist newspapers in circulation in the county
– the *Meath Chronicle* in the north and the *Carlow Nationalist* in the south –
Kildare readers had an ample choice of local newspapers.

In many respects, Kildare in 1912 was unrepresentative of the country at
large. It was one of the best-known and travelled counties. From the perspective of the RIC, it was a model county with a largely law-abiding population.
The agricultural community prospered due to the military presence which in
effect constituted a large consumer population in the centre of the county. The
towns in this area, particularly in the Curragh region, were also different to
most towns in other counties due to the trade and employment generated by
the army. The predominant political opinion in the county was moderate
nationalism. However, by 1912 more advanced nationalist impulses were
beginning to surface, assisted by the influence of cultural nationalism. Clearly,
among nationalists there was a high level of support for the third home rule
bill. The measure began to polarize politics in the county from early 1912,
with the dominant IPP and their supporters on one side, and the local unionist community, which was predominantly but not completely Protestant, on
the other. Kildare's garrison status and the general approval of and support for
the British military presence made the county something of an outlier, often
deemed less nationalist than other counties in the south of Ireland.

# 2 Redmondism and home rule, 1913–14

The home rule crisis of 1912–14 was one of the most intense and polarizing political conflicts in Ireland in modern times. Although 1913 saw continued low key support for home rule among Kildare nationalists and largely refined opposition from local unionists, the following year was characterized by a succession of dramatic developments as Ireland moved towards civil war. Kildare was central to one of the most serious episodes when, in March 1914, the Curragh incident brought the loyalty of the army into question. It resulted in the summer of 1914 becoming one of the most politicized periods in the history of the county due to the development of paramilitary politics. This was belatedly embraced by nationalists of all ages and genders in Kildare. However, home rule was not the only major issue in this period and the industrial unrest in Dublin in 1913 spilled over into north-east Kildare.

By the summer of 1913 political tensions in Ireland had risen considerably due to strident unionist opposition to home rule, and the prominence of the Ulster Volunteer Force (UVF). The AOH in Kildare began to take a leading role in defending home rule.[1] On 8 June a well-attended general meeting in support of home rule was held in Newbridge, chaired by Monsignor Thomas Tynan, the local parish priest. The meeting criticized the opposition to home rule exhibited by the two principal Protestant Churches on the island. The keynote speaker, Professor Thomas Kettle, was critical of the Presbyterian general assembly for imposing a ban on any members who supported home rule. He also described as blasphemous a prayer against home rule introduced by the Church of Ireland.[2]

While meetings of the AOH in the county were well supported, the UIL was not as fortunate, with Denis Kilbride, the local MP, expressing his disappointment at the apathy of Kildare people towards nationalist matters, and at the small number of UIL branches in the county. He dismissed the UVF as a 'mock-volunteer force'.[3] Such a remark was typical. At this time, nationalist politicians regarded the UVF not as a military threat but as part of a political and propaganda campaign, 'a bluff' to undermine British support for home rule. For this reason nationalists remained confident that Ulster's political challenge could be defeated.[4] By the end of 1913, however, unionist opposition had weakened the resolve of the Liberals and made the exclusion of some part of Ulster a serious prospect. Only then was the extent of the crisis properly appreciated by nationalist Ireland; it transformed local politics. The realization that active support for home rule needed to be encouraged saw fundraising by the UIL in Naas and the AOH in Newbridge.[5]

On 6 March 1914, at the second reading of the third home rule bill, Prime Minister Herbert H. Asquith proposed the concept of 'county option' that would allow the temporary exclusion for six years of Ulster counties that rejected home rule.[6] To the disquiet of supporters, the IPP eventually agreed to the temporary exclusion clause as the price of peace. Crucially, the 'county option', which provided for a local plebiscite in each county, was rejected by the unionists.[7] Many Nationalist MPs were unhappy with the government's concessions, but they refrained from making any public comments on the measure and it was not debated by any local councils.[8] In late March a Dublin Corporation resolution protesting against the division of Ireland was sent by Alderman Thomas Kelly (SF) to a meeting of Naas No. 1 RDC. Although Éamon Ó Modhráin proposed its adoption, no one would second it as that would be tantamount to criticism of Redmond. In addition, SF was most unpopular among the IPP in Kildare and one councillor suggested that the resolution should be burned![9]

Although Redmond's acceptance of the concessions was not a cause for concern among politicians in Kildare, the *Leinster Leader*, under the influence of its editor, Michael O'Kelly, highlighted negative aspects of the concession. Partition was mentioned, and comparisons were made with the medieval Pale boundary.[10] While O'Kelly was a lone voice among nationalists in Kildare in publicly criticizing Redmond's policy at this time, the concessions caused no great concern among the readership of the *Leinster Leader*. The unionist *Kildare Observer* described the exclusion proposals as 'a national mutilation' and blamed religious indifference for the prevailing political situation.[11] This was the first indication in Kildare that southern unionists were unhappy with the mooted partition. It had become clear that for Carson, Ulster exclusion was no longer a tactical measure to defeat home rule but a solution in its own right.[12]

In the aftermath of the IPP concession on the home rule amendment, the run-up to the local elections in May 1914 produced a lacklustre election campaign with very few electoral divisions contested. Celbridge was an exception. W.G. Dease, an outgoing unionist member of the county council, was defeated by James O'Connor, a nationalist.[13]

While the vast majority of seats on the county boards were unopposed, the elections returned several Protestants in the county who supported home rule. As a result, there was an unusually high number of Protestants serving in positions of importance on various county committees. The vice chairmen of Kildare County Council, Athy No. 1 Council, Celbridge No. 1 Council and Celbridge Board of Guardians were all Protestant. The *Kildare Observer* proclaimed that this was proof of religious tolerance in the county.[14] During the first parliamentary circuit of the home rule bill, a number of Protestants were appointed to positions by several councils and boards of guardians in nationalist counties. It led to accusations of contriving to demonstrate religious tolerance. So-called tolerance proving was less applicable in Kildare as many Protestant councillors were elected prior to the home rule crisis.[15]

While local elections were taking place at home, in late May 1914 the third reading of the home rule bill was passed in the House of Commons. This was celebrated with torch-light processions and bonfires in all main towns in Kildare. At a meeting of Kildare County Council on 25 May, a motion welcoming the development, proposed by George Wolfe, was adopted unanimously despite the presence of unionist councillors, Lord Frederick FitzGerald and W.G. Dease.[16]

As the home rule bill continued its passage through parliament, the rift between nationalists and unionists widened and suspicions increased.[17] In July Lord Mayo, leader of the Kildare unionists, suggested that a clause be inserted in the home rule bill that would exclude the home rule parliament from having powers relating to compensation for criminal injuries or malicious injuries. Mayo was motivated by fears that unionists and the landlord class might be vulnerable to acts of malicious damage to their property in a post-home rule Ireland in which compensation would be denied.[18] Unionists in the south also voiced their fears of a loss of status and cultural identity. According to Mayo, 'home rule would mean the degradation of their country in status by cutting her off from the stream of Imperial life'.[19]

The emergence of labour troubles in Dublin in August 1913 drew attention away from the all-consuming home rule bill for a period of five months. Little progress had been made in Kildare on improving the conditions of labourers. As a consequence, the lockout in Dublin spilled over into north-eastern Kildare. The expansion of an organized labour movement in the capital inevitably influenced workers in that area of Kildare, and would ultimately contribute to the growing militancy in the county.

The first sign of labour difficulties in Kildare was recorded by CI Supple when he discovered that meetings of the Irish Transport and General Workers' Union (ITGWU) were held in August 1913.[20] In fact, membership of the union had already spread to north-east Kildare. On the first day of the strike in Dublin, William Shackleton, one of the proprietors of the Anna Liffey flour mills in Lucan, demanded that his employees choose either their jobs or the ITGWU. The men refused to resign their union membership and by evening the mill was closed and picketed.[21] Some of the workforce were from Leixlip in Kildare, less than two miles away.[22]

Eventually, strike-breakers, mainly from Dublin, were taken on and this resulted in the strikers becoming more militant, organizing demonstrations in which local music bands participated. On 16 October a demonstration turned nasty with some windows of the mill broken and a policeman injured.[23] The following evening demonstrators were baton-charged by police when they refused to turn back as they crossed the Liffey Bridge in Lucan. About two dozen men were injured, one seriously.[24] The heavy-handed action by the police and the successful use of strike-breakers began to take a toll on the strikers, and the strike ended in late October when the majority of the men applied for reinstatement to their jobs and agreed to the terms imposed by management.[25]

Leixlip suffered on the double due to a strike at Wookey's flock-mill, the village's largest employer with forty-eight employees. On 1 September, following an ultimatum by the owner, Frederick W. Wookey, to his employees to remove union badges or get off his premises, thirty-six men walked out. The strike escalated when Wookey told twelve women employees, who had remained and were not in any union, that he had no work for them until they could persuade the men to abandon their membership of the union.[26] As a result, some of the produce from Wookey's was blacklisted on the docks by men working in Dublin port who refused to handle the weekly consignment of mattresses.[27] Unlike the management at Shackletons' Mill, Wookey did not take on strike-breakers. A week after the strike began, several of the strikers, who were not members of the ITGWU, returned, together with the female employees.[28] From November to January, the strike continued and the RIC in both Leixlip and Celbridge escorted the employees to and from work. The strike ended in early February 1914, when eighteen of the strikers returned to work on Wookey's terms having resigned from the ITGWU.[29]

As the strike progressed, a greater level of labour militancy was evident in the Leixlip–Lucan district. Some of those who had been dispersed by heavy-handed police methods joined the newly-formed Irish Citizen Army. This body of trained trade union volunteers from the ITGWU in Dublin was formed to protect demonstrating strikers against the police.[30] One month after the Lucan Bridge 'riot', Leixlip and Lucan strikers marched to a Citizen Army meeting in Croydon Park, Fairview in Dublin. Led by Leixlip man, James O'Neill, they were followed to Fairview by the RIC from Lucan, a distance of eleven miles. On the homeward journey the police sergeant approached O'Neill at O'Connell Bridge and offered to pay the strikers' tram fare home. The constabulary, who were heavily-built, middle-aged men, were exhausted and unable to continue on foot. The offer was accepted and the strikers and RIC returned to Lucan together.[31] This was something of a moral victory for the strikers. Though not a major act of militancy, it was important in marking the emergence of a Citizen Army corps in Leixlip.

As a result of the labour disputes in Wookey's and Shackletons' Mills, their produce was 'blacked'. In early September staff at Dawson's general traders in Maynooth refused to handle a load of meal-stuffs from Shackletons. The following week two employees of Domhnall Ua Buachalla, who refused to handle a wagon load of flour from Shackletons, were paid off and not replaced.[32] Ua Buachalla and the Shackletons were acquainted in nationalist circles. In his youth William Shackleton had been a member of SF, and his brother, George, contributed to the Maynooth Gaelic League fund during the lockout.[33] Ua Buachalla himself was anti-Larkin, and his stance on the issue caused a rift between himself and Patrick Colgan, another prominent nationalist in Maynooth, who supported the strikers.[34]

The impact of the lockout was also felt in Naas, causing difficulties for the Carpet Factory, which employed eighty.[35] In mid-October an order from Philadelphia for drawing-room carpets was delayed at the North Wall depot. Instead of being transported directly to America, the merchandise had to be shipped to Britain and then onwards to the US.[36] Ultimately, the lockout strike caused serious financial difficulties for the firm and jeopardized its plans to expand.[37]

The strikers found an unlikely champion in Mary Lawless, a member of the Kildare aristocracy and daughter of Valentine F. Lawless, 5th Baron Cloncurry, who resided at Lyons House, near Ardclough. Lawless first came to public attention as an active member of the Irish Reform League (IRL), a non-militant suffragette organization.[38] She was particularly concerned about undernourished children as a result of the strike. On one occasion she obtained a cow from her father's estate to supply milk for the children of strikers and drove the animal along the Grand Canal tow-path to Liberty Hall.[39]

Lawless also supported the 'Kiddies' Scheme' by which children of strikers would be sent on a temporary basis to families of British trade unionists.[40] The scheme was vigorously opposed by the Catholic Church and also by the AOH, which claimed that Catholic children would be subject to Protestant influences when in Britain. In an effort to prevent the implementation of the scheme, the AOH formed vigilante committees, supported by the Catholic Church, that were active at ports and railway stations. The children were not only prevented from moving to temporary foster homes in England, but also to rural areas in Ireland.[41] In late October Lawless arranged for two sons of a striker to be fostered temporarily by an agricultural labourer employed by her father at Lyons estate. However, it resulted in an ugly incident at Kingsbridge station when the children were prevented from travelling to Hazelhatch by the AOH and prompted the *Manchester Guardian* to describe the events as 'Mob Law in Dublin'.[42] During the episode one of the boys was abducted from his father, Mary Lawless was jostled, and Francis Sheehy-Skeffington, an observer at the station, was assaulted as he protested to a policeman.[43] A number of individuals involved were later questioned, including two priests, but a subsequent court case collapsed.[44]

The strike also affected services to Celbridge Union in late November when supplies of coal could not be delivered in the usual way. Alternative arrangements, however, resulted in a price increase of two shillings per ton.[45] Although the military was not used to any great extent to quell demonstrations, troops escorted essential supplies such as coal to military barracks, hospitals, prisons and government offices in Dublin. For example, in early October a military escort was provided to guard a delivery of coal from 'Wallace Brothers' depot at Ringsend to Kingsbridge station from where the coal was delivered by train to the Curragh camp.[46]

Overall, the lockout and strike had a significant impact on north-east Kildare. The worst effects were the inconvenience and disruption caused, particularly to transportation. The IPP, whose members were mostly middle class and drew their support from the farming community, were hostile to the strike. Even those who felt sympathy for the plight of the striking workers feared that the strike would distract attention from what they regarded as the more serious struggle with Carson's Ulster unionists. By February 1914 the strike had virtually ended, but within four weeks a much more significant incident, which would have widespread consequences, was about to unfold in Kildare.

Prior to 1914 there had been no serious incident involving the British army during peacetime in Kildare. But in spring 1914 the eyes of the world were focused on an incident at the Curragh camp that came about as a result of a combination of personal politics and lack of military discipline. In March 1914, Lieutenant General Sir Arthur Paget, general officer commanding-in-chief, was based at army headquarters at Parkgate Street in Dublin.[47] The Irish Command consisted of two infantry divisions and two cavalry brigades. A line extending from Sligo to Wexford divided the country in two, with one infantry division and one cavalry brigade located north and south of this line. The 5th Division was located north of the line and the 6th Division to the south. From 1913 Major General Sir Charles Fergusson, in the Curragh, commanded the 5th Division. The 3rd Cavalry Brigade was commanded by Brigadier General Hubert Gough, also based in the Curragh. It was not part of the 5th Division and came under the direct jurisdiction of Paget.[48] Although the brigade was largely stationed in the Curragh, one regiment, the 5th Royal Irish Lancers, was quartered in Marlborough barracks in Dublin.[49] Gough was born in London to Irish parents and was raised in County Waterford. He came from a decorated military family and was a veteran of the Boer War.[50]

In March 1914 only 2,773 members of the British army, or 11.5 per cent of the total of 24,032 in Ireland, were stationed in the nine counties of Ulster. This was less than half of the 5,806 stationed in Kildare.[51] The biggest threat to the authority of the government came from Ulster, where an estimated 84,000 UVF threatened to establish a provisional government should home rule be implemented.[52] For this reason, the government considered redeploying troops to Ulster. However, army officers, mainly of unionist and conservative background, were known to be concerned with the political circumstances.[53]

Any redeployment of the army in Ireland would have to involve movement of the military from Kildare and, in particular, from the Curragh camp where 4,067 men were stationed. The 14th Infantry Brigade in the Curragh comprised the 1st Battalion Duke of Cornwall's Light Infantry in Beresford barracks, 2nd Battalion Suffolk Regiment in Gough barracks, and 2nd Battalion Manchester Regiment in Keane barracks.[54] Troops in Newbridge included the 3rd Brigade Royal Horse Artillery and the 27th Brigade Royal Field Artillery, while the 7th Brigade was stationed in Kildare town. The 3rd Cavalry Brigade, commanded by General Gough, was also in the Curragh camp. The 4th Hussars, a large portion of which was southern Irish, were in Stewart barracks, and the 16th Lancers were in Ponsonby barracks.[55] Also attached to the 3rd Cavalry Brigade were D and E Batteries, Royal Horse Artillery, which were stationed in Newbridge.

During the early months of 1914 rumours were rife that the UVF were planning to import arms, or that the government was about to curtail the force.[56] On 11 March the cabinet received disturbing police reports of possible UVF raids on arms depots in Ulster. The movement had, by this time, already acquired 17,000 weapons.[57] Equally alarming was the growth of the Irish Volunteers in the early months of 1914, particularly in Ulster, and by late March it numbered 14,000, spread over twenty-five counties.[58] Irish civil war seemed a distinct possibility.

A cabinet sub-committee, established on 11 March, summoned Paget to London for consultations regarding planned movements of army personnel to Ulster on 18 and 19 March.[59] Given the high-ranking personnel involved in talks lasting two days, there can be little doubt that larger military operations were discussed. Having raised the possibility that some of his officers might be unwilling to participate in action against Ulster, Paget was given an option (later known as the 'ultimatum') to exempt officers domiciled in Ulster. They were allowed temporarily 'to disappear'. Any other officer unwilling to serve would be dismissed from the service.[60] Orders from Winston Churchill, First Lord of the Admiralty, to move warships to northern Irish waters to coincide with the troop movements greatly added to the suspicion that something bigger than redeployment was planned.[61] One of the Royal Navy officers who received the order was Kildare-born Admiral Sir John de Robeck, who commanded four flotillas of destroyers.[62]

Paget's meeting with senior generals on his return to Ireland exacerbated the situation. He implied that active operations were to commence against Ulster, and rashly suggested that 'the whole place would be in a blaze tomorrow'.[63] The effect of this sudden outburst was to increase the anxieties of officers, particularly Gough. The generals were also informed of the 'ultimatum', the concession obtained from the War Office relating to officers who lived in Ulster.[64] Paget was most unprofessional in managing this sensitive issue and was tactless, especially in dealing with Gough who came from an Anglo-Irish background and who was sympathetic to the Ulster unionist cause.[65]

The first sign of significant dissent surfaced when an incensed Gough, following his meeting with Paget, addressed the officers under his command at nearby Marlborough barracks, Dublin and offered them the 'ultimatum'. Seventeen of the twenty officers present decided that dismissal would be preferable to active service in Ulster.[66] Later that day, Gough put the 'ultimatum' to the officers of his brigade in the Curragh and a total of sixty-one officers resigned.[67] The Curragh camp was now at the centre stage of a crisis usually referred to as the Curragh incident, but sometimes termed a mutiny or proto-mutiny. Although the dissenting officers had indicated that they would disobey orders, technically they had not actually disobeyed because no orders had been issued. Nevertheless, it was a serious rebellion of officers who objected to carrying out their duties as soldiers. Two senior officers attempted to contain the crisis. First, Fergusson followed Gough to the Curragh and undertook an extensive round of visits to his troops in order to nullify the impact of the resignations among the cavalrymen.[68] He brought officers under his command around to his point of view, whereas those under Gough followed the example of their immediate commander. Paget also addressed officers in the Curragh on 21 March, but this intensified the dissension.[69]

On obtaining details of the revolt, John Seely, secretary of state for war, summoned Gough and four of his officers to the War Office. While in London, Gough was counselled and briefed on unfolding developments by his brother, General John Gough, chief of staff to General Douglas Haig, commander-in-chief at Aldershot, and Major General Henry Wilson, director of military operations at the War Office since 1910 who was strongly unionist.[70] Wilson gave considerable support to Gough, with the two endeavouring to obtain concessions from the government.[71]

Following two days of meetings at the War Office, Gough, who steadfastly refused to withdraw his resignation unless he obtained assurances in writing, was eventually granted his demands.[72] Two paragraphs, not sanctioned by Asquith, were also inserted by Seely, indicating that the government had 'no intention whatever of taking advantage of this right to crush political opposition to the policy or principles of the home rule bill'.[73] He also received a written guarantee from Sir John French, chief of the imperial general staff, that troops would not be called on to enforce the home rule bill in Ulster.[74] To receive a guarantee in writing from the secretary of state, and the head of the army was a remarkable achievement, particularly for a junior brigadier.

During the crisis details of the events were passed on to some unionists in Kildare who immediately made contact with the leadership of the Conservative party. Sir William Goulding in Millicent House wrote to Bonar Law, the Conservative leader, giving him the exact number of resignations in the Curragh area.[75] Captain Henry Greer, a retired officer who resided close to the Curragh, was sent to London on behalf of the protesting officers to lay their case before Law and Lord Lansdowne. Apart from the political aspect of the affair, another issue of contention was the threat made by Paget in the Curragh that any officer who resigned due to the ultimatum was regarded as dismissed, thus forfeiting the right to a pension. However, due to the resolution of the affair Greer's mission was unnecessary.[76]

By the time Gough returned to Ireland on 24 March, he had become a hero among the officers in the Curragh.[77] An anonymous non-commissioned officer's wife described how 'all the cavalry turned out in review order and escorted him home in his carriage as if he was a king'.[78] According to the *Kildare Observer*, his speech to a welcoming party thanked all ranks for backing him and his fellow officers in their fight with the War Office.[79] When Asquith became aware that Seely had added two unsanctioned paragraphs, he publicly repudiated the guarantee.[80] In the Commons he condemned the assurances sought by Gough and his fellow army officers as putting 'the government and the House of Commons, upon whose confidence the government depend, at the mercy of the military and navy'.[81] The three individuals most closely connected with the guarantee – Seely, Spencer Ewart and French – resigned.

Depending on their political affiliation, the various news organs such as *Freeman's Journal*, *Irish Times*, *Leinster Leader* and *Kildare Observer* gave opposing interpretations of the incident. All detailed political plots of some sort. The nationalist *Freeman's Journal* claimed that Gough was guilty of indiscipline in demanding assurances relating to his duties as a soldier and suggested the incident was 'a Tory conspiracy to secure a general election'.[82] According to the *Leinster Leader*, the objective was to prevent the government proceeding with home rule and to destroy the Parliament Act.[83] The unionist *Irish Times* was closer to the truth. It attacked the government for its initiation and handling of the affair. It suggested that a deliberate attempt was made by at least three cabinet members to provoke 'civil war in Ulster, and that it could have succeeded but for the resignations at the Curragh'.[84] Generally, editorials from newspapers of a pro-government and pro-home rule viewpoint denounced the stance taken by the Curragh officers, while newspapers from a mainly unionist perspective gave a positive account.

In terms of the parliamentary battle between government and opposition over the home rule bill, the Curragh incident represented an own goal conceded by the cabinet. In London, the resignations of the secretary of state for war and the head of the army greatly damaged the credibility of the government. It lost any military initiative to quell growing militarization in Ireland and its freedom of movement to implement home rule in Ulster was now limited. Ulster unionists must have taken heart from the fact that an attempt to force them to accept home rule had been thwarted by the army. By contrast, the Curragh incident severely dented nationalist confidence in the government. The events merely confirmed their increasing doubts about Asquith's real commitment to granting Irish self-government and about his willingness to ever grapple with unionist militancy. The idea of the army being above politics was undermined and the most significant consequence of the episode in County Kildare was increased support for the Irish Volunteers. Prior to the Curragh incident, there had been no Volunteer presence in the county.

The Volunteer movement had a major impact on society and politics in Kildare by uniting nationalists from every strata of society, both male and female. Founded in November 1913, its inaugural meeting in Dublin was described by Michael O'Kelly of the *Leinster Leader* and the IRB as 'the emergence of a great nationalist movement'.[85] The RIC inspector general reported that at the end of March there were an estimated 14,171 Irish Volunteers in eighty-three branches across the country.[86] However, Kildare was an outlier. A survey of CI monthly reports and of the *Irish Volunteer* indicates that no Volunteer corps had been established in Kildare before May 1914; the same was true for County Wicklow.[87] The Volunteers were led by advanced nationalists, and in Kildare, a county dominated by Redmondites, there was little support for the movement. A number of events between early March and late April 1914 stimulated the growth of the Volunteers in Kildare. The Curragh incident greatly dented trust in the army in a county where it enjoyed a respect not evident in other counties outside Ulster. The landing of arms by the UVF on 24–5 April 1914 further alarmed nationalists in Kildare.[88] This accelerated calls for more militant action by nationalists to counter unconstitutional activities aimed at preventing the passage of the home rule bill. After Larne, Irish Volunteer numbers jumped from 123 branches with 19,306 members to 191 branches with 25,000 members by 1 May.[89]

In Kildare, which had no Volunteer presence, the *Leinster Leader* was the sole voice in condemning the Larne gun-running and was strongly critical of both the government and unionists.[90] By 1 May Kildare and Wicklow were still the only remaining counties without any Volunteer corps. That position changed radically during May, by which point the IPP was forced to reassess the role of paramilitarism within its political strategy. In early April Joseph Devlin, grandmaster of the AOH, instructed the movement in Ulster to associate with the Volunteers.[91] After the third reading of the home rule bill at the end of May, MPs made a spectacular effort all over the country to claim the movement as their own.[92]

While the Volunteer movement continued to expand, it received extensive coverage in the Kildare press. Behind the scenes Seán O'Connor, an Irish-language teacher in Celbridge, had been secretly organizing for the IRB in the northern part of the county, laying the groundwork for the Volunteer movement in his area.[93] The official launch of the Athy Volunteers on 14 May was attended by The O'Rahilly, on behalf of the provisional committee, who called for donations to obtain weapons.[94] Naas was the first garrison town to form a branch of the Volunteers and Michael O'Kelly was to the fore in this development. The first meeting attracted substantial numbers, with the result that the gathering withdrew to the outer yard of the town hall. When that became too small, the meeting was moved to the disused jail nearby.[95] The movement included two prominent county councillors, George Wolfe and Michael Fitzsimons, as well as members of the local UDC. Wolfe was one of a small number of Protestants prominent in the Volunteers and became the recognized head in Naas and eventually in the county.[96]

The formation of the various corps in Kildare continued apace. RIC reports indicate that by the end of May, there were seven branches within the county. Two branches had been established during the month at Athy and Castledermot, and branches were in the process of formation at Naas, Celbridge, Maynooth, Monasterevin and Kildare town. The movement had the support of all sections of nationalists, and those joining included shopkeepers and their assistants, farmers, labourers and tradesmen.[97] Local MPs who had been slow to give approval now began to cash in on the popularity of the new movement. When John O'Connor attended a Volunteer meeting in Naas, he addressed members as 'fellow soldiers of Ireland'.[98]

Members of the provisional committee in Dublin were frequent visitors to Kildare. For example, Thomas MacDonagh was present when a Volunteer company was established in the garrison town of Kildare on 31 May and on 7 June. The O'Rahilly, Laurence Kettle and Patrick Pearse gave rousing speeches at meetings throughout Kildare.[99] Pearse inspected a new company in Kilcock and instructed them to get ready to do their duty for Ireland.[100] Undoubtedly, local Redmondite supporters would have felt uncomfortable with some of the language used.

The official launch of the county Volunteer movement was held at Gibbet Rath on the Curragh on 7 June. The location was chosen as it was an ancient site adjacent to the Curragh camp and the scene of a massacre of rebels by Crown forces in 1798.[101] It sent a strong message to the establishment and especially to General Gough and the army. Owing to fears of attempts to prevent a meeting taking place so close to the biggest military camp in the country, the location was kept secret until forty-eight hours before. Even so, an estimated 7,000 people, representing branches from all over Kildare and some adjoining counties, attended. Volunteer contingents from the two garrison towns of Kildare and Newbridge marched in military formation to the site. The gathering represented a strong show of unity among nationalists, and the meeting was addressed by the two MPs for the county as well as The O'Rahilly. O'Connor's speech reflected the general theme of the day – that the army had failed to defend their liberties and that it was 'the army of one political party not the army of the nation'. That the Volunteers were launched with the assistance of the two local MPs, and practically the entire local nationalist leadership, gave an appearance of nationalist unity in response to recent political developments.[102]

By early summer 1914 Redmondite supporters constituted the bulk of the membership, but the IPP did not have a prominent role in the leadership of the Volunteers. Negotiations that had been taking place for several weeks between Eoin MacNeill and Redmond stalled, and on 9 June the IPP leader issued an ultimatum demanding that the provisional committee co-opt twenty-five of his nominees.[103] There was general support among the nationalist population in Kildare for Redmond's demand for a majority on the provisional committee, and a resolution calling on the Volunteer leadership to agree to this was unanimously passed by Kildare County Council. A reluctant provisional committee acceded to Redmond's demand, the only apparent criticism in Kildare coming from Michael O'Kelly in the *Leinster Leader*.[104] Despite the conflict concerning the leadership, members of the provisional committee continued to be in demand at Volunteer public meetings. MacDonagh addressed a meeting in Athy, with an estimated attendance of 5,000, which was the biggest local parade to date of Volunteers in the southern section of the county.[105] By late July the Volunteers in Kildare had increased to an estimated membership of 3,000 members or about 9 per cent of the male population which totalled 32,194 (excluding army personnel).[106] The figures were similar in neighbouring Offaly (3,100/10.4%) and Laois (2,290/8%).[107]

The meeting in Athy witnessed the emergence of a Cumann na mBan branch in Kildare with Elizabeth Bloxham from headquarters in Dublin addressing the crowd.[108] Cumann na mBan also extended to the three garrison towns of Naas, Newbridge and Kildare. Bloxham attended all the inaugural meetings to set out the purpose of the movement, which included first aid, involvement in the Defence of Ireland Fund and collecting money to buy rifles to arm the men.[109] One of the most unusual aspects of the first meeting in Naas was the attendance of representatives of the two religious traditions. Bloxham and Maud Wolfe, daughter of George Wolfe, were members of the Church of Ireland. There was also Catholic clerical involvement in the form of the local parish priest, Fr Michael Norris.[110]

On 26 July 1914 the Volunteers took delivery of some 900 Mauser rifles from a private yacht at Howth and this injected new enthusiasm into the movement. There was a small but significant participation by Kildare Volunteers in the gun-running. A detachment of Volunteers from Celbridge, assisted by Art O'Connor, president of the local company, travelled by car to Howth and collected twenty-five rifles and ammunition. The guns were then hidden in an outhouse on the O'Connor farm.[111] Jim O'Keeffe, a member of the Kilcock Volunteers, also participated and smuggled some of the rifles to Kilcock on an evening train.[112] That evening the army fired on civilians at Bachelor's Walk, which resulted in the death of three people while thirty-eight others were injured. The incident was widely condemned in Kildare in the press and at public meetings and marches. For example, John Shiel O'Grady, chairman of No. 1 Naas RDC, claimed 'there was one law for the Ulster Volunteers and another law for the Nationalist Volunteers'.[113] Volunteer recruiting increased significantly with the formation of new branches, while existing branches reported a surge in membership.[114] With a sense of anger and revulsion directed towards the army, there were even threats of trouble from local nationalists if the King's Own Scottish Borderers, the regiment responsible, were moved to the Curragh.[115] The events at Howth and Bachelor's Walk were overtaken, however, by news of a much greater magnitude – the outbreak of the First World War.

The initial stages of the passage of the home rule bill through parliament caused little excitement or interest among the ordinary people of Kildare. This was in contrast to local politicians who strongly supported the measure. However, forceful and aggressive opposition by Ulster Unionists generated additional interest in the bill in Kildare and eventually activated strong backing for the measure. Throughout the period, support for Redmond remained dominant in Kildare. Michael O'Kelly was one of the few to promote more advanced nationalism. The Dublin labour conflict spilled over into Kildare, but only affected areas adjoining Dublin and it did not seriously diminish the dominance of the home rule issue.

As one might expect given its economic importance, the British army was popular in Kildare. The Curragh incident altered this. The breach of trust with the army never healed. Within weeks, Kildare became a politically reawakened county with companies of Irish Volunteers formed in every locality, determined to uphold a role they believed had been relinquished by the army. Kildare was one of the very last counties to adopt the Volunteers. Volunteer headquarters placed considerable emphasis on Kildare as indicated by the number of meetings addressed by Pearse, MacDonagh and The O'Rahilly. Nationalists in Kildare watched the unfolding of double standards by the army, which in March refused to engage the unionists for political reasons, and yet had no difficulty in engaging militarily with nationalists in late

July, resulting in loss of life at Bachelor's Walk. Given the large army presence in the county, the ensuing backlash was more evident in Kildare than elsewhere. But the outbreak of war soon became the focus of attention across the country, and passions generated by the Bachelor's Walk incident were suddenly cooled.

# 3 The impact of the First World War, August 1914–March 1916

The First World War had a profound impact on Ireland, politically, socially, economically and in terms of casualties. In Kildare, given the sheer extent and size of the British army garrison, and the fact that large numbers from the county had a tradition of army service, the impact would be more pronounced than in most other counties with the exception of the Ulster counties. To add to the complexity of the period, the initial support for the war that existed between August 1914 and March 1916 evolved into an increasing opposition and even hostility from some elements in society. The home rule question remained the central political issue, but as the war progressed, the uncertainty of its implementation added to increased political pressures. The issue of conscription also emerged, and vigorous recruitment methods both contributed to the tension and had an important effect on the political mood of the nationalist population.

The chain of events that began on 28 July 1914, when Austria–Hungary declared war on Serbia, was closely monitored in Ireland. There was much support for the British government's policy relating to the impending war.[1] In the House of Commons on 3 August Redmond proposed that the Irish Volunteers should join with the Ulster Volunteers and take the place of the army in guarding the country against a German invasion.[2] This was welcomed by both nationalists and unionists in Kildare and the county council pledged that staff who took up arms would have a job to which they could return. Another sign of the changed atmosphere was the granting of permission by the army for the Volunteers of Naas and district to drill in the barrack square three times a week from 11 August.[3] George Wolfe, Volunteer chief inspecting officer for Kildare, euphorically declared that he would provide the British army with seven battalions if home rule was passed. Support for the war effort in Kildare was confirmed by CI Supple's observation of a 'spirit of loyalty ... among the masses'.[4]

This spirit of loyalty in Kildare was aided by Bishop Patrick Foley's pastoral letter on 17 August. Redmond deliberately attended Mass in the diocese at Baltinglass and was so impressed with the wording that he sent the pastoral to Asquith on 22 August as well as the sermon given by the officiating priest in which he defended the justice of England's cause.[5] Foley's pro-war stance contrasted sharply with that of Archbishop William Walsh of Dublin who forbade the placing of recruiting posters on the railings of churches and did not aid the recruiting campaign in any way.[6] In Kildare, Catholic clergy were

more publicly vocal in supporting the war than their Church of Ireland coun-
terparts who left it to the House of Bishops to comment. When hostilities
began, Archbishop Peacocke offered prayers that God would 'bless our efforts
and defend our right'.[7] His successor, John H. Bernard, who lost a son during
the Gallipoli campaign, justified the war as a fight for 'civilization against a
sudden revival of barbarism'.[8]

The outbreak of war jeopardized the implementation of home rule. On 30
July the prime minister, with Redmond's consent, announced that the amend-
ing bill would be postponed in the interests of national unity.[9] The *Leinster
Leader* questioned Redmond's judgement and suggested that 'a one-sided deal
had been made regarding postponement of the amendment bill'. It also proposed that nationalists should take advantage of the war to gain political concessions.[10] The largely unionist *Kildare Observer* accepted the inevitability of
home rule, 'not total separation but the utilitarian home rule which preserves
and increases loyalty to the British constitution'.[11] Redmond's efforts to have
the home rule bill signed into law met with limited success. On 15 September
Asquith announced that the bill would be put on the statute book, but along
with a measure that suspended its operation for the duration of the war.[12]
This was celebrated as a victory by nationalist Ireland, and in Naas the local
Volunteers marked the event with bonfires while in other Kildare towns similar celebrations were held.[13]

With strong support for Redmond's home defence policy, and the threat
of civil war receding, large numbers continued to join the Irish Volunteers
throughout August and early September when 4,492 members in thirty-two
branches were recorded. However, only 162 were armed.[14] The IPP
attempted to redress the deficiency of Volunteer arms. As early as mid-June
1914 Redmond had secured 4,000 rifles with ammunition from Belgium.
Tom Kettle, together with three MPs – Willie Redmond, Richard McGhee
and John O'Connor – were involved in the transportation of the rifles from
the Continent. O'Connor had past experience of gun-running for the Fenians
in the 1870s. He delivered some weapons to Kildare, leaving Broadstone station in Dublin with a consignment of rifles for the Kilcock Volunteers in late
September.[15] More of the weapons were delayed on the Continent and various attempts by O'Connor to acquire rifles over the following twelve months
proved unsuccessful, despite contacts with Asquith, Sir Edward Grey, the
foreign secretary, and General H.H. Kitchener, secretary of state for war.[16]

Having obtained the concession that placed the home rule bill on the
statute book, Redmond was obliged to respond with a substantial nationalist
initiative towards the war effort. This came on 20 September at
Woodenbridge, County Wicklow when he urged Irish Volunteers to engage
'where the firing line extends'.[17] This call to join the British army for foreign
service caused much disquiet among nationalists and split the Volunteers. The

original members of the pre-Redmondite provisional committee denounced Redmond's exhortation to enlist and expelled his nominees from the committee. They broke away, retaining the name Irish Volunteers with the Redmondite majority becoming the National Volunteers.[18] Following Woodenbridge, the decline in Volunteer membership was as dramatic as the increase had been in the early summer. In late September a membership of 181,722 was recorded but by December the figure was 147,050. The number of Irish Volunteers at the end of 1914 was an estimated 9,700.[19]

The split within the ranks of the Volunteers did not become evident in Kildare until the first week of October. The Kildare county committee met at Naas town hall on 6 October and condemned the action of the MacNeillite provisional committee. Yet, almost half expressed reservations about Redmond's call to action; this was carried by nine votes to five with four members abstaining. Art O'Connor and Éamon Ó Modhráin[20] who led the opposition to the motion departed.[21] This was a great loss to the organization as O'Connor had been to the forefront in promoting the Volunteers, especially in north Kildare. The dissention that surfaced at the county committee was replicated in branches throughout the county, but in particular those near Dublin where advanced nationalists occupied leading positions. In north Kildare, the Volunteers in most towns split into two factions, but in all cases Redmond's supporters were overwhelmingly in the majority.[22] The Celbridge committee initially declared its allegiance to the Irish Volunteers, but at a meeting on 4 October, with twenty members present, a majority including Hubert O'Connor declared for Redmond and formed a new corps of National Volunteers.[23] In Maynooth 135 of the 157 present backed Redmond.[24] In Kill the majority were in favour of Redmond's policy, while in Staplestown there was only one dissenter.[25] The scale of the division was similar to other counties with Redmond winning the support of every branch of the movement. In late November 1914 CI Supple believed there were only 344 Irish Volunteers in the county and that they did not pose a threat.[26]

The most blistering attack on Redmond's policy came from Michael O'Kelly in the *Leinster Leader* on 10 October. He accused the IPP leader of engaging in propaganda for recruitment while Edward Carson used every opportunity to undermine home rule.[27] It was unwise for the editor of a newspaper with a Redmondite readership to criticize Redmond's policy in such a manner. The pronounced anti-English tone of the article, as well as the editor's penchant for publishing articles from advanced nationalist newspapers in Dublin, were noted by the CI who described the article as seditious.[28] Under pressure from the directors of the newspaper, who repudiated the editorial, O'Kelly was forced to adhere to a pro-Redmondite line in future editorials. Nevertheless, he published advanced nationalist views and articles that were negatively disposed towards war whenever the opportunity arose.[29]

Redmond's Woodenbridge speech was well received by unionists in Kildare, many of whom offered support to the Volunteers. Lord Mayo donated £15 and his near neighbour, Colonel T.J. de Burgh, £25.[30] The *Kildare Observer* commended Redmond and suggested that it was the duty of Irish and Ulster Volunteers to unite in defending the country.[31] Colonel Francis Wogan-Browne, a prominent Catholic unionist and magistrate, motivated by Redmond's speech of 3 August, established a mounted volunteer corps, drawn from the gentry and farming class. It was named the 'Kildare Horse' but did not progress as anticipated. When the corps assembled in Naas barracks for its first drill on 13 August, its leadership, including Wogan-Browne, refused to sign a Volunteer enrolment form because it would have suggested support for home rule.[32] The mounted corps was an example of the somewhat unreal atmosphere in August and September 1914 which led to some unionist-nationalist military collaboration. The corps continued to drill afterwards, with newspapers reporting their activity until early November.[33] Although unionists and nationalists supported the war, their motivations differed considerably. Unionist support emanated from a loyalty to king and country while nationalists were motivated by nationalist objectives such as support for the IPP and the implementation of home rule. This spirit of unusual cooperation in Kildare, however, did not last, and by September had dissipated, just as it had in other counties.

On the outbreak of war, the RIC in Kildare detained and subsequently released a handful of foreign visitors suspected of being German or Austrian nationals,[34] while support for the army throughout Kildare revived overnight, particularly for the Royal Dublin Fusiliers (RDF) based in Naas. Many of the non-officer rank in the RDF were nationalist in politics and supporters of home rule. A considerable number of the Volunteer drill instructors were ex-British army, and most were army reservists. When over 300 RDF in Naas left for Flanders on 6 August, they were given a spectacular send-off. The band of the Naas Volunteers led a procession, followed by the regimental band which played 'A nation once again', 'Who fears to speak of 98', and 'The wearing of the green' as the men marched to the train station at Sallins. The soldiers joined in the singing and even cheered for home rule![35] Similar scenes occurred in Dublin when the Royal Field Artillery from Kildare left for the front on 15 August 1914.[36] Meanwhile, at the Curragh camp, with large numbers of new recruits arriving to avail of training facilities, existing quarters soon filled to capacity and tented accommodation had to be provided. By early October an estimated 14,000 soldiers were camped at the Curragh, in addition to those in Kildare and Newbridge. Training areas became inadequate and additional shooting ranges had to be constructed.[37] This resident army fuelled an economic bonanza for shopkeepers and publicans in the towns surrounding the Curragh. Reports suggest that in the nearest licensed premises to the Curragh, at Maddenstown, up to fifty soldiers socialized during the daytime. In an effort to prevent drunkenness, the authorities issued an order restricting opening hours.[38]

In Kildare Redmond's supporters did not flock to enlist after Woodenbridge. The CI reported that many preferred to stay at home and leave the fighting to others.[39] Nonetheless, over 400 men from Athy had enlisted by the end of 1914. Active members of the National Volunteers were prepared to fight and defend Ireland as a home defence force, but not to carry the fight abroad as members of the British army.[40] Throughout October drill practice among the National Volunteers declined quickly with the CI predicting that interest would soon disappear completely.[41] The position of the National Volunteers was not helped by the War Office, which refused to recognize them in the same way as the Ulster Volunteers. One of Kitchener's many snubs to the Irish war effort included the return of proposed colours for the Irish brigade produced by the Countess of Mayo's School of Art.[42] Although Lord Mayo had supported the National Volunteers in August 1914, his clumsy public statements in the House of Lords in January 1915 alleging cowardice on the part of the Irish Volunteers hindered enlistment.[43] This related to a demonstration in Dublin on 7 December at which Irish Volunteers in uniform distributed anti-recruiting leaflets. Mayo alleged that if the Germans came to Ireland, the Irish Volunteers would 'most likely run away'.[44] Nationalists in Kildare denounced the statement, arguing that it might be misinterpreted as referring to the Redmondite National Volunteers.[45] In an attempt to limit the damage, Mayo made the situation worse by suggesting that if Irish nationalists had supported the Irish National Volunteers with money and arms to the same degree that Ulstermen had supported their Volunteers, the force would have been efficient and capable of resisting invasion.[46] This seemed to imply that the Ulster Volunteers were superior to the National Volunteers. On 13 January 1915, Naas Board of Guardians passed a resolution urging the government to intern Mayo as the speech impeded recruitment. Kildare County Council condemned Mayo's behaviour as 'scandalous and murderous'.[47] Mayo's credibility was damaged and he made no further public comments about the Volunteers for the remainder of the war.

As elsewhere, the agricultural sector in Kildare received a substantial boost due to an extraordinary price increase in almost every farm-related product. Similarly, the price of imported foodstuffs and other essential goods such as sugar, bread and tea rose sharply in the first week of August. Sugar increased from $1\frac{3}{4}d$. to $4\frac{1}{2}d$. per pound almost overnight on 5 August.[48] Commodities in the shops in Newbridge and the Curragh camp, where members of the military largely did their shopping, also increased in price.[49] By mid-August increased prices even outpaced those in Britain as it was reported that bacon was selling in Athy at 1s. 6d. per pound while it was fetching 1s. 2d. in Manchester. By late August it was reported that householders in Naas had to pay 1d. per pound more for their meat since the war began.[50]

In terms of farm produce the price of cattle, the largest sector in Kildare, rose significantly. Between 1910 and 1913 the average price for 3-year-old cattle was £12 18s. 9d. By the end of 1915 it was £18 2s. 9d., a staggering increase. There were similar sizeable increases in the prices of lamb, mutton, pork, butter, eggs, and particularly wool which rose by over fifty-five per cent in the twelve-month period between December 1914 and December 1915.[51] The price of crops also increased dramatically; wheat was fifty-one per cent more expensive at the end of 1915 than twelve months previously.[52] The equine industry benefitted handsomely too. On the outbreak of the war, the cavalry divisions at the Curragh requisitioned horses, beginning with those in the Kildare hunt stable at Jigginstown.[53] While temporary arrangements were made to requisition the horses, unusually there was no formal remount depot in the Curragh. On 30 March 1916 Denis Kilbride raised both points in the House of Commons and proposed that a remount depot be opened in the Curragh so that Kildare farmers could offer their horses to help the war effort.[54] His intervention was successful as a remount depot was opened two weeks later and eventually provided employment for 200 men for the duration of the war, with a solid weekly wage of £1 5s.[55]

As consumers suffered inflated prices, the families of servicemen received generous financial benefits known as separation allowances. The allowance to the wife of a soldier at the front amounted to 1s. 1d. per day with an extra 2d. a day for each dependent child and 3s. 6d. from compulsory allotment out of her husband's pay. From 1 March 1915 the allowance was increased. Wives of privates and corporals were paid 12s. 6d. per week with further allowances for children, ranging from 5s. per week for the first child to 3s. 6d. for a second child and an additional 2s. for each child thereafter. A sergeant's wife got an extra 2s. 6d. over and above these rates.[56] In October 1915 the weekly payment of separation allowances from Naas post office alone amounted to £155.[57] The separation allowances far exceeded most wages earned at the time. Labourers earned between 15s. and 18s. a week, although agricultural wages could be as low as 13s.[58] By contrast, Mary Reilly, the wife of a soldier from Naas in the RDF with three children, received an allowance of 23s.[59] While the overwhelming majority of women in receipt of allowance behaved uprightly, the conduct of a minority gave cause for concern. Unable to manage their money, some were convicted of various charges of anti-social behaviour, mainly drunkenness. In Kildare, it was considered a prevalent problem in all the garrison towns of the county. Holly Dunbar has argued that the First World War exacerbated concerns about women's drunkenness, even though the problem had not, in real terms, become worse.[60] The increased focus on this behaviour, which was not likely to encourage enlistment, certainly caused unease in Kildare.[61]

The welfare of troops was another concern and various fund-raising activities for the RDF took place from the beginning of the war. A stream of wealthy and well-connected people in the county, mainly of unionist background, volunteered to assist on relief committees. Many ladies were to the forefront of this relief work. Numerous fund-raising events such as collections, dances, fêtes, sales of produce and raffles were held all over the county. Regular supplies of comforts were sent to the troops at the front.[62] Comforts were also provided to prisoners of war in Germany.[63] By mid-1916 it was reported that forty-one men from the county were in German prison camps.[64] County Kildare RDF sent out fortnightly food parcels to all the RDF prisoners of war who were confined in over twenty different camps in Germany.[65]

Kildare hosted a small number of Belgian refugees who were accommodated for a short time in Celbridge workhouse.[66] The first group of refugees recounted graphic stories of German atrocities on their arrival on 17 October 1914.[67] The refugees were treated as guests and care was taken to avoid linking them with the stigma of pauperism.[68] Collections for the refugees were taken up in local Catholic parishes and were well supported.[69] Some of the Belgians from a well-to-do background were provided with dwellings more in keeping with their socio-economic status. Madam de Monck was accommodated in Straffan Lodge, a two-story over basement residence, and provided with maintenance for herself and her household, which included wages for servants.[70] The sojourn in Celbridge workhouse was relatively brief and gradually the refugees were transferred between mid-December and late March 1915 when the last eleven left Celbridge for Dunshaughlin.[71] The plight of the Belgians was used for pro-war propaganda and recruitment purposes. At a dance in Naas town hall for the local Belgian refugees fund, the premises was decorated with Union Jacks and Irish, Belgian and French flags.[72] Similarly, at a subsequent concert, the Union Jack and Belgian flag provided the backdrop while children danced jigs and three-hand reels.[73] However, the special treatment of Madam de Monck, who remained in Straffan Lodge until November 1915, was hardly an incentive to support the war effort.[74]

Reporting of the war in the press was curtailed by censorship. The Defence of the Realm Act (DORA), enacted four days after hostilities began, gave the authorities power to suppress criticism of the war effort.[75] The Kildare local press reflected the viewpoints of their respective readership in reporting the war. The *Kildare Observer* published selected accounts of bravery and heroism, whereas the *Leinster Leader* was more impartial in its coverage of military engagements. When conscription became an issue in 1915, the divergent stances of the two newspapers became more noticeable with the *Observer* generally supportive.[76] Although publishing recruitment advertisements and enlistment figures, the *Leader* was strongly opposed to conscription.[77] Both newspapers generally supported the Liberal government. However, this consensus ended when the new coalition administration, which included Tory and Unionist ministers, was formed in May 1915. While the *Observer* supported the inclusion of new cabinet ministers, the *Leader* was vocal in its opposition.[78] The tone of two other nationalist newspapers with a circulation in Kildare, the *Meath Chronicle* and Carlow's *Nationalist and Leinster Times*, reflected the somewhat more radical viewpoint in neighbouring counties. This may have encouraged Michael O'Kelly's constant promotion of an advanced nationalist agenda in the *Leader*, despite Kildare's status as a moderate nationalist county. Although press censorship seemed to work effectively, the weekly reports of mounting casualties had a negative effect in Kildare.

The Gallipoli campaign had a particularly significant impact. Reports from the first week of May 1915 indicated that large numbers of officers and men from the county had been killed.[79] A list of casualties, including a number of officers connected to Kildare and the RDF depot in Naas, was also published.[80] Despite strict censorship, the horror of the Dardanelles campaign became evident by 7 July when casualties arrived in the RDF depot military hospital in Naas and were allowed visitors.[81] Letters from the front highlighting the bravery of Irish soldiers were published occasionally with many including graphic details of loss of life. For instance, an account detailing an ill-conceived military manoeuvre was published in the *Leinster Leader* in which William Harris from Athy described how there were only four survivors in his platoon.[82] Letters from servicemen at the front published in the *Kildare Observer* had a more jingoistic tone with detail not likely to damage morale. Nonetheless, many letters captured the excessive losses, with W.J. Clery, a bank official from Naas, writing on 19 September that his brother, who was an officer in the 6th RDF, had been killed and that his own company had been 'practically cut up, and about four officers left in the battalion out of about twenty-five'.[83] Although the full particulars of the war were censored, the local populace was in no doubt about the scale of the carnage. This did not entice further enlistment.[84]

Between the outbreak of the war in August 1914 and October 1916, some 1,644 recruits from County Kildare out of 2,581 available for military service enlisted. This represents an enlistment rate of about sixty-four per cent. Neighbouring counties ranged from a high of seventy-one per cent in Carlow to thirty-one per cent in Meath.[85] In this light, the figures for Kildare, a garrison county, appear to be disappointing. In the twelve-month period from 15 December 1914, 689 Kildare men enlisted, which was the second highest in Leinster. Of these, 611 were Catholic and 78 Protestant.[86] It was estimated that 390 or sixty per cent of these were National Volunteers. Contemporaneous press reports suggested that a staggering 800 men from Athy were at the front in mid-1915. Celbridge, a smaller town, provided as many as 200 recruits by the same date, of which fifty-four per cent had been National Volunteers.[87]

Inevitably, as casualties mounted, enthusiasm for the war waned. This was apparent by the summer of 1915. During the first five months of the war, sixty-four Kildare men had died in the conflict, with another 220 fatalities during 1915.[88] The first sign of disenchantment was noticed when the number of recruits began to fall. Nationally, 95,152 men enlisted between August 1914 and February 1916. A total of 75,342 enlisted during the first year of the war but only 19,323 joined the army between August 1915 and February 1916.[89] Heavy losses prompted calls for a more intense recruitment drive to fill depleted ranks. Conscription began to be discussed and was used as a threat to entice enlistment.[90] The formation of a coalition government in May 1915 generated considerable anxiety in Kildare about the fate of home rule and the possibility of conscription. At a county council meeting on 31 May 1915 several councillors claimed that Carson's appointment to government would undermine support for the war and enlistment in Ireland.[91] The *Observer* linked the formation of the new ministry with the inevitability of conscription, amid general fears that this would come to pass.[92]

In an effort to stave off conscription, several IPP MPs, aided by local politicians at constituency level, assisted in a new recruitment drive across the country.[93] While John O'Connor wholeheartedly supported the war, Denis Kilbride was not as active. In August 1915, when the two shared a platform at a UIL meeting in Athy, Kilbride gave one of his only speeches on conscription, pointing out that the measure would never become law so long as Redmond, Devlin and the IPP sat in parliament.[94] Many of the most prominent county councillors such as George Wolfe, Michael Fitzsimons, John Healy and Patrick Phelan, all stood side by side on platforms at recruiting meetings with MPs, army officers and local unionists such as Lord Frederick FitzGerald.[95]

Despite Archbishop Walsh's lack of support for the war effort, many of his diocesan clergy assisted at recruiting meetings. Canon Edward Mackey, parish priest of Athy, was one of the most vocal. Justifying the war effort at a meeting in Athy in August 1915, he declared that 'our soldiers are defending a cause both sacred and just.'[96] In November 1915 a letter from Bishop Foley was read at a recruiting meeting in Carlow, acknowledging his support for recruitment. He believed that Ireland had contributed more proportionately than England or Scotland.[97] At the Church of Ireland Dublin diocesan synod on 15 November 1915, Archbishop Bernard expressed the view that 'we continue to give freely of our best ... and every able-bodied man that we could spare' because 'the cause of the Allies is the cause of Ireland no less than of Britain'.[98]

By early winter the public mood at recruitment meetings had become increasingly hostile with heckling and jeering a common occurrence. When

John O'Connor denounced Bishop Edward O'Dwyer of Limerick at a meeting in Maynooth on 22 November, a voice from the crowd called for a cheer for the bishop and a cheer was given.[99] The prelate had taken issue with the pro-British policy of the IPP and incurred the wrath of the party when he publicly criticized Redmond's description of attempts by Irish emigrants in Liverpool at avoiding conscription as cowardly.[100] When Lieutenant Delaney urged recruits to come forward and fill the gaps in the Irish regiments, a voice from the crowd suggested he fill them with the King's Own Scottish Borderers and that he should remember Bachelor's Walk. Unsurprisingly, despite the attendance of high-profile speakers, no recruits came forward.[101] The army was now so desperate for recruits that offenders on minor charges had their summons withdrawn if they undertook to enlist. At the conclusion of Robertstown petty sessions in early December, the sergeant produced a number of warrants against men who had joined the army since the summonses had been issued, and, as a result, charges were cancelled.[102] Attempts to compel some to enlist also occurred at this time. Michael Cosgrove from Timahoe near Robertstown, who had found work in County Kilkenny, was dismissed from his employment so he would have to enlist. Instead, he secured employment in Dublin and joined the Irish Volunteers.[103]

Conscription was introduced in Britain in January 1916, but not in Ireland. Although Ireland's exclusion was greeted with relief in Kildare, a fresh recruiting scheme caused disquiet. Canvassers called to almost every house in the county with householders having to explain why eligible family members had not joined the army.[104] The diary of Barbara Synnott, a member of the Kildare gentry who undertook a recruitment drive near Naas in early 1916 at the request of the Central Council for the Organization of Recruiting in Ireland, captures how unpopular the war and recruitment had become.[105] One man whose son was of military age indicated that he would rather see his son shot by the Germans at his own door than let him go to the front where so many went to be killed. Another informed her that he was not going to fight and if the authorities brought in conscription, 'they can shoot me or put me in prison'.[106] The war had become very unpopular, with politicians, whose word was previously unquestioned, now facing mounting criticism. As a member of the Athy Board of Guardians put it: 'the people could not understand the attitudes of the MPs going about as recruiting sergeants and at the same time saying they were opposed to conscription [then] telling the people if enforced they would take to the hillsides with them'.[107] Notwithstanding such sentiment, within Leinster, excluding Dublin city, County Kildare had the second highest enlistment rate up to 1916, and in two towns, Athy and Celbridge, recruitment was above average. Beyond Ulster, the only other county with the same level of enlistment was Waterford.[108]

The outbreak of war, which brought to an end the political tensions caused by the home rule crisis, was felt in a more immediate and visible way in Kildare than in most other parts of Ireland due to the army presence in the county. From the beginning, there was widespread support in Kildare for the war. The local economy benefitted greatly, both through an increased need for materials and animals, and as a result of the financial assistance that was made available to soldiers and their dependants. With John Redmond enjoying unqualified support among nationalists, his offer to provide volunteers for home defence unified all strands of nationalist and unionist opinion in the county, albeit for a short time. However, the impact of his Woodenbridge speech split the Volunteers and the Redmondite National Volunteers soon faded away. Although the rank-and-file unionists were not visibly active in politics, they were to the forefront in assisting in the war effort. Unionist women dominated comfort committees that provided war-related relief to soldiers at the front. Despite initial enthusiasm for the war, numbers enlisting in Kildare began to decline after the summer of 1915, with more noticeable reductions outside the garrison towns. The extent to which the war had become unpopular and the reluctance of young men to enlist in many areas of Kildare proved a challenge for the authorities who began to consider conscription. In addition to waning enthusiasm for the war effort, political tensions that emerged following the appointment of Carson to the cabinet during the summer of 1915, had a further negative effect on enlistment, as well as evoking criticism from nationalist bodies in Kildare. Despite an initial outcry, local politicians continued to support the government's policy on war and enlistment. By the winter of 1915, signs of a breach between local MPs and constituents had emerged. John O'Connor's criticism of Bishop O'Dwyer of Limerick was indicative of a collapse in support for the war, but also an early sign of waning support for Redmondism and the IPP.[109]

# 4 Rebellion and its aftermath: Kildare in 1916

The 1916 Rising and the response of the British government to it was a watershed in Irish history. The small Kildare rebel participation in the Rising has been well documented.[1] By contrast, the central role played by the British army based in the Curragh camp in suppressing the insurgency has not been adequately explored. Augustine Birrell, Irish chief secretary, told the Royal Commission on the Rebellion in Ireland that the outbreak was a failure from the beginning because reinforcements arrived quickly and in number from the Curragh before the end of the first day of the Rising.[2] This study utilizes accounts from army field journals to shed greater light on how the British army stationed in Kildare responded to the Rising. The unpopularity of the rebel leaders' executions and an emerging political prisoner issue, which had a profound impact nationally, influenced the political mood in Kildare. Public disquiet saw the beginning of a changing political landscape with prisoner support groups emerging and forming a base for an advanced nationalist movement that challenged IPP dominance.

Advanced nationalists, who were small in number in Kildare, vigorously opposed the war. Following the Volunteer spilt, only two Irish Volunteer companies – Maynooth and Celbridge – remained active. Both were influenced by well-known individuals in their respective areas, notably Domhnall Ua Buachalla in Maynooth and Art O'Connor in Celbridge.[3] Other prominent advanced nationalists such as Michael O'Kelly, Éamon Ó Mordháin and Jack Fitzgerald either fronted depleted companies or served as individual Irish Volunteers.[4] During 1915 a number of events gave the local organization an impetus that led to a revival. In July the annual Wolfe Tone Bodenstown commemoration attracted an attendance in excess of 2,000.[5] Some of the Irish Volunteers and Citizen Army who were accompanied by their leader, James Connolly, were armed with rifles and bayonets.[6] They were joined by local contingents of Irish Volunteers and National Volunteers from Newbridge, Naas and Kill.[7] Addressing the gathering, Thomas Clarke presciently indicated that 'the time for words is past ... it is now action and action alone'.[8] Clarke, who fronted an IRB military council along with Seán Mac Diarmada, gave the clearest signal yet to militant activists that they would soon be called into action. In his opening remarks he addressed both Irishmen and Irishwomen, indicating that both would be expected to serve. Unambiguously, he declared that 'the rifle is talking the world over to-day and is going to talk in Ireland too.'[9] Although the event was monitored by the RIC, no alarm bells were sounded. The CI simply detailed the size of the attendance and the different groups present.[10]

The second event was the funeral of Jeremiah O'Donovan Rossa on 1 August 1915, which saw an involvement by the Kilcock branch of the National Volunteers.[11] A former member, Jim O'Keeffe, who was living in Dublin, acted as a pall bearer and one of the firing squad who discharged a volley over the grave.[12] The second half of 1915 saw a re-alignment of Volunteer companies in Kildare as many National Volunteers switched allegiance to the Irish Volunteers. The Kill National Volunteers was one example.[13] Similarly, a split in the Athgarvan Volunteers in the autumn of 1915 caused the majority to go over to the Irish Volunteers.[14] A section of National Volunteers in Kilcock did likewise in November 1915.[15] The re-emergence of Irish Volunteer companies signalled the beginning of a period in which an even greater level of militancy developed.

Ted O'Kelly, a medical student from Maynooth and a member of the IRB, was appointed Irish Volunteer organizer for Kildare, Carlow and Kilkenny. His brief in Kildare was to reorganize local Volunteers so as to hamper troop movements from the county to the capital during the planned Rising.[16] From September 1915, O'Kelly based himself in the Prince of Wales Hotel, Newbridge, almost opposite the Dublin entrance into Newbridge military barracks. His presence soon came to the attention of the local RIC, which was aware that he held meetings with Jack Fitzgerald, the chairman of the GAA Kildare board, and William Jones, a demobilized army reservist and drill instructor of the Athgarvan Irish Volunteers.[17] O'Kelly made rapid progress in promoting and reorganizing the Irish Volunteers and gained the support of Ua Buachalla, Michael O'Kelly, Ó Modhráin and Art O'Connor.[18] By October O'Kelly had formed an organizing committee for north Kildare where at least five companies were now active with Michael Smyth, captain of the Athgarvan company, appointed secretary.

Due to its strategic position on the edge of the Curragh, the Athgarvan company was selected by O'Kelly for special activities, and, as a result, it became one of the most active units in the county. The activities included rifle and revolver practice. Ironically, these sessions took place in trenches on the Curragh created by the British army.[19] In November Smyth was given about £300 mandated by Volunteer headquarters in Dublin to purchase Martini Enfield rifles and 10,000 rounds of ammunition from the British army. This material was then passed to Dublin Volunteers.[20] Within six months of his arrival in Kildare, O'Kelly had reorganized a handful of companies working to a plan dictated by Volunteer headquarters.

As the military council's plans progressed, help was received from the United States. The most significant figure was Kildare-born John Devoy, president of Clan na Gael. He bankrolled the Rising and was reputedly responsible for the inclusion of the phrase – 'Ireland … supported by her exiled children in America' – in the 1916 proclamation.[21] He was held in high-esteem in his native Kildare, even hero-worshiped by some advanced nationalists such as Patrick Colgan.[22] Devoy was at the centre of the three-way transatlantic negotiations between Germany, the IRB and Clan na Gael from 1914 to 1916. Immediately before Easter Week several couriers working for Devoy delivered some $25,000 to the Volunteers.[23] One of those who also acted as his personal envoy to Germany was fellow Kildare-man John Kenny, president of the New York branch of Clan na Gael.[24] Some of the funds couriered by Kenny were used in Kildare by Michael Smyth to purchase arms.[25]

In the weeks before Easter 1916 there were rumours among the Kildare Irish Volunteers that a rising was imminent. According to the CI, three Volunteer companies with a total of fifty-three members were active. There was a similar level of activity in the neighbouring counties.[26] Two weeks before Easter 1916, Tom Byrne, a captain in the Dublin Volunteers and a Boer War veteran, was appointed by Pearse to take charge of Kildare, with O'Kelly as second-in-command. Pearse wanted someone who had knowledge of explosives and military experience to carry out the military council's two-pronged plan for Kildare.[27] First, the various companies were to mobilize and march to Bodenstown churchyard. A railway bridge on the Great Southern line near Sallins was to be blown up to cut off rail transport and delay British army re-enforcements from reaching Dublin. Second, the Kildare units were to reconnoitre the area between the Curragh and Dublin and hamper communications by destroying telegraph and telephone lines as well as railway tracks and roads.[28] If the railway line in Kildare was closed, then British army reinforcements – those in Kildare, numbering a quarter of the total number in Ireland, as well as troops from Cork, Limerick, Waterford – would be forced to route march from the Curragh to Dublin.

On 19 April, Byrne and O'Kelly travelled to Kildare and made contact with the active Volunteer companies. The following day Byrne received a dispatch from Pearse indicating that the Rising was definitely fixed for Easter Sunday with orders to mobilize all companies and assemble in Bodenstown. These instructions were conveyed to all companies. On Saturday evening explosives for the Sallins bridge operation were delivered by Miss Sheehan from Phibsboro, who travelled from Kingsbridge to Newbridge with sixty sticks of gelignite. At Newbridge station some soldiers helped her carry the bag containing the explosives.[29] The gelignite was hidden overnight near the Dominican College.[30]

On Easter Sunday Eoin MacNeill's countermanding order, published in the *Sunday Independent*, virtually cancelled all mobilization activities. In Kildare some of the companies, unaware of the cancellation, were already heavily engaged in preparations. Michael Smyth had the Athgarvan company mobilized for 11 a.m. Confusion then reigned when they became aware of

MacNeill's countermand, which was also sent around the country by courier. Ó Modhráin passed MacNeill's dispatch to other companies without consulting Ted O'Kelly. Smyth proceeded to Newbridge where O'Kelly instructed him to keep his unit mobilized.[31] Similarly, the Maynooth Volunteers mobilized. No sooner had they received MacNeill's order than a second arrived from Pearse with the instruction that they 'were not to leave their district but to await further orders'.[32] The Kildare leadership in Newbridge refused to believe the countermanding order.[33] Despite a dispatch from Pearse informing O'Kelly that activities were postponed until noon on Easter Monday, MacNeill's countermand had thrown everything into confusion.[34] Byrne and O'Kelly, assisted by Thomas Harris of the Prosperous company, had a busy afternoon on Sunday as they contacted companies to inform them of the postponement.[35] Overall, the response in many of the areas visited was poor.

The first incident of the Rising in Kildare involved Laois Volunteers, under Éamon Fleming, who blocked a section of the Kilkenny to Kildare railway line at Maganey just outside Athy. The aim was to disrupt troop movements from Rosslare. Telegraph wires were also cut.[36] Little went right for the Kildare Volunteers tasked with blowing up the railway bridge at Sallins. First, the expected support did not turn up at Bodenstown. Second, the bridge at Sallins was deemed too risky as the local RIC barracks was only fifty yards away. Sherlockstown bridge, one mile from Bodenstown graveyard, was targeted instead.[37] It was expected that trains would cease operating from Kingsbridge when the Rising commenced and Byrne was puzzled when trains continued to use the line.[38] These were probably special military trains sent from Kingsbridge to the Curragh siding when the Rising began. The first of these passed under Sherlockstown bridge at approximately 1.30 p.m.[39] Prioritizing the safety of rail passengers, Byrne aborted the demolition and curiously did not consider alternatives such as cutting the railway line. The explosives were disposed of in rabbit-holes close to the railway line in Sherlockstown. Byrne and his two companions went to Maynooth and from there to Dublin.[40] A handful of other Volunteers such as Michael O'Kelly proceeded to Bodenstown, but suspecting that something was amiss, returned home.[41]

The countermand only partially explains the failure of the Volunteer operation in Kildare. Another contributory factor was the caution of Byrne and the IRB who did not share the plans with local company leaders. The failure to blow up the bridge or cut the railway line had a major bearing on the course of the Rising. A successful operation would have prevented troop movement by rail to Dublin possibly for several days and this could have prolonged the Rising. In Maynooth, the local company had received no word from Byrne or O'Kelly. On Easter Monday, Ua Buachalla cycled to Dublin in an unsuccessful attempt to obtain instructions.[42] Meanwhile, Colgan mobilized twelve members of the Maynooth company. This included Patrick

Weafer, captain of the local National Volunteer branch.[43] Byrne took command on his arrival and fifteen men proceeded to Maynooth College to solicit clerical support for their actions. The only armed incident involving a Volunteer and the RIC in Kildare during Easter Week was when Ted O'Kelly threatened two RIC constables with his revolver to prevent them from following. Monsignor Patrick Hogan, president of Maynooth College, appealed to the Volunteers to return home, stating 'they were poor fools who were going to be slaughtered' and blessed them.[44] The contingent followed the Royal Canal tow-path to Dublin and spent the night in Glasnevin cemetery before reaching the GPO on Easter Tuesday morning where they were welcomed by Pearse and Connolly.[45] This contingent was the only sizeable number of Volunteers to reach Dublin after the Rising had begun. It had been an exhausting journey, especially for the Newbridge based trio who covered thirty miles, twice the distance of the Maynooth company.

At least twenty-six Kildare-born men and women took part on the rebel side during the Rising in Dublin. In addition to the contingent that arrived from Kildare, five others based in Dublin were members of the GPO garrison. These included James O'Neill, a senior Citizen Army officer, and the Burke siblings from Carbury.[46] Frank Burke was a former student of Pearse and a member of the Scoil Éanna company.[47] His sister, Eve, was a nurse who offered her services to Pearse when the Rising broke out. She later assisted in dressing James Connolly's wounds. At the evacuation she accompanied the wounded to Jervis Street Hospital and avoided capture.[48] Two other Kildare men were members of Boland's Mills garrison and three were members of the Four Courts garrison.[49] Katie Daly, a 27-year-old Cumann na mBan activist from Kildare town, was attached to the Four Courts garrison. She delivered dispatches to the garrisons on the north side of the city and ammunition to the GPO. Her statement to the Military Service Pensions Board conveyed the danger involved: 'if you were in the GPO or in the Four Courts you would have been safer, but we [Cumann na mBan] were out under fire, out in the streets looking at the dead men on the street, the whole time'.[50]

George Geoghegan was the only rebel born in Kildare who was killed in the fighting. A member of a Citizen Army unit that captured City Hall, he was shot through the head during heavy crossfire in the early hours of Wednesday 26 April.[51] Although he was of Dublin background, he was born in the Curragh camp in 1880 where his father, a member of the RDF, was stationed.[52] Of the Kildare rebel participants, twenty-two were detained, including three who returned to Kildare. Among them was Thomas Harris who was wounded in the evacuation of the GPO and taken to Dublin Castle hospital where all the patients were closely guarded.[53] Ted O'Kelly received a foot wound in the evacuation of the GPO and was removed to Jervis Street Hospital, but on admission was recognized by medical staff who placed him among civilian casualties in the hospital.[54] Katie Daly avoided arrest.[55] Astonishingly, Tom Byrne, the highest-ranking Kildare Volunteer, also escaped arrest.[56]

Four of the dead civilians were originally from Kildare. Among them was Michael Kavanagh. He was born in Ballinafagh, Prosperous, in 1880 and moved to Dublin in his youth. A carter by occupation, on Easter Monday he was delivering theatrical equipment to the Shelbourne Hotel when his cart was commandeered for barricading purposes by the Citizen Army. He was shot in the head while remonstrating. Kavanagh lingered on until 17 May and was interred in Ballinafagh, his native area in Kildare.[57] Peter Connolly, a 39-year-old shopkeeper and native of Celbridge, was one of several civilians killed by the British military in the North King Street area on 29 April.[58] Edward Murphy, a 42-year-old from Kilcullen, and Francis Salmon, a teenager from Straffan, were accidentally shot dead.[59]

British troops stationed in Kildare played a leading role in suppressing the rebellion in Dublin. Prior to Easter Week the military authorities were mindful of the threat posed by the Irish Volunteers, and were aware that a rising was contemplated.[60] A report in March 1916 indicated that 'young men of the [Irish] Volunteers were very anxious to start business at once, and were backed up strongly by Connolly of the Citizen Army, but the heads of the Volunteers were against the rising at once'.[61] General Lovick Friend, General Officer Commanding (GOC), concerned at the deteriorating situation, wrote to Kitchener in March to request extra troops. Arrangements were made to have a reserve brigade sent at once to Ireland if required by the Irish authorities.[62] Two weeks before the Rising, Major Ivor Price, intelligence officer at military headquarters, reported that the Sinn Féiners 'were working up for a rebellion in Ireland if they got the chance'.[63] This intelligence prompted Friend to request that an expert be appointed to command the special reserve in the Curragh. Colonel Bertram Portal, who was engaged in active service in France, was transferred to the Curragh in this capacity.[64] No stranger to Ireland, having lived in Kildare with his wife for long periods,[65] Portal recalled being warned by Friend two weeks before Easter that an outbreak was possible.[66] Nonetheless, Friend spent Easter in London and appointed General William Lowe of the Curragh Command as acting GOC in his absence. When informed of the Rising on Easter Monday, he immediately returned to Ireland.[67]

At 12.30 p.m. on Easter Monday Lowe received a telephone message notifying him of the serious disturbance in Dublin. Captain Henry de Courcy-Wheeler, the administrator in the Curragh in charge of the service side of the barracks and a native of Robertstown, County Kildare, was informed that 'the Sinn Féiners are out, they are trying to take over Dublin'.[68] Lowe mobilized the special column and dispatched it to Dublin, under Portal's command, on trains which first had to be requested from Kingsbridge. Service timetables for Kingsbridge confirm that four empty trains left the station for the Curragh siding between 1:10 p.m. and 2:10 p.m. on Easter Monday. By 5:20 p.m. the entire column comprising 1,600 officers and other ranks from the 3rd Reserved Cavalry Brigade had reached Dublin. The records also show an additional order later that evening for two trains to convey 1,000 troops from the Curragh siding that left at 8:25 p.m. and 8:50 p.m. respectively.[69] In addition, military reinforcements from Athlone, Templemore and Belfast were ordered to Dublin. Portal served as the operational commander throughout Easter Week, making on-the-spot decisions, but working in close consultation with General Lowe who assumed direct command of the forces in Dublin on Easter Tuesday.[70] The fact that large numbers of troops could be deployed from the Curragh within five hours of the beginning of the Rising demonstrated the significance of the rail link. Arguably, in military terms the failure of the Volunteers to destroy the rail link doomed the Rising to failure.

Throughout the remainder of the week, troops garrisoned in Kildare continued to spearhead the push against the insurgents. By Thursday evening, the military had formed a cordon around the O'Connell Street area.[71] All the leading officers involved in Pearse's surrender were from the Curragh[72] but Portal's prominent role in suppressing the Rising has largely been overlooked by historians.[73]

De Courcy-Wheeler was ordered to report to Lowe's staff in Dublin on Easter Friday. He was initially instructed to keep guard over Pearse. Later he was sent to Dublin Castle where James Connolly was a prisoner to obtain his signature on a surrender document. Another duty was to transport and accompany Nurse Elizabeth O'Farrell to the various rebel commands around the city with surrender orders. One of the most difficult duties for de Courcy-Wheeler was the arrest of Countess Markievicz who was his wife's first cousin.[74] He later gave evidence at her court-martial as well as those of Pearse, Connolly, MacDonagh and Mallin.[75] His respect for Markievicz was not just an empty gesture. His daughter Kathleen, born in the Curragh shortly before the Rising, was given the additional names Constance Gore after the countess.[76]

De Courcy-Wheeler was one of many Kildare men serving in British army regiments in Dublin during Easter Week. Three men from the county, Captain Alfred E. Warmington, Private James Duffy and Private William Mulraney, were among the fatalities. Warmington from the 3rd Royal Irish Regiment, a veteran of the Boer War, was from Naas where his father was a local bank manager.[77] He was killed on Easter Monday while leading a charge on the Volunteer position at the South Dublin Union as was Private Duffy, who was originally from Kilteel.[78] A veteran of the Boer War, Mulraney from Timahoe re-enlisted when war broke out in 1914 in the King's Royal Irish

Hussars. He had been gassed on the Western Front and was recuperating in the military hospital in the Curragh when ordered to Dublin on Tuesday. The following day he died in an exchange on the north side of the city.[79]

The inevitable arrests began as early as Easter Thursday when Michael O'Kelly, his 15-year-old nephew, Alphonsus Sweeney, and five others from Naas were detained by the RIC.[80] In swoops, both guilty and innocent were arrested over the following days, including Volunteers such as Michael Smyth, Éamon Ó Modhráin and Jack Fitzgerald.[81] Five of the Rathangan National Volunteers, who had been in contact with Ted O'Kelly during Holy Week, were also arrested. Although CI Supple emphasized that the National Volunteers did not support the Rising, he was suspicious of their loyalty and pointed out that 239 members were not in sympathy with Redmond or the IPP.[82] The Maynooth participants in the Rising, Patrick Weafer, Seán Graves and Joseph Ledwith, were picked up on their return to Maynooth, court-martialled and sentenced to two years imprisonment.[83] Michael Smyth was given a similar sentence.[84] All the Kildare prisoners were initially confined in the Curragh camp.

A total of fifty-two Kildare men were arrested, including twenty-one who had actually participated in the Rising in Dublin. Eighteen were detained at the surrender in Dublin and three in Kildare.[85] A further five non-participants were also detained in Dublin.[86] Twenty-six were arrested in Kildare.[87] A number of prominent Volunteers who were not suspected of involvement, such as Art O'Connor, remained free. Many of those arrested were innocent and some were released within a week of arrest; Thomas J. Williams was detained for only a day. In late May, John O'Connor MP visited many of the prisoners in British prisons and suggested the release of a number of influential prisoners.[88] The following week some men were freed, including Michael O'Kelly and Jack Fitzgerald.[89] Ted O'Kelly recuperated in Jervis Street Hospital. With the assistance of his fiancée, Maisy Stallard, her sister Josephine and Fr Conlon, a Dominican priest from Kilkenny, O'Kelly sensationally escaped, disguised in clerical garb.[90]

The widespread arrests and, in particular, the executions of the leaders of the Rising alienated even moderates. According to Michael Laffan, the arrests provoked nationwide resentment and may have been as important in transforming public opinion as were the firing squads in Kilmainham.[91] This was certainly the case in Maynooth College. On 21 May, General Sir John Maxwell discussed the rebels' visit to the college on the first day of the Rising with Monsignor Hogan. The clerical students had prior knowledge of the visit and were confined to their quarters after expressing their negative feelings towards the general. Over dinner, Hogan insisted that interference with the spiritual authority of the Catholic Church would not be tolerated.[92]

The three bishops with ecclesiastical jurisdiction over Kildare reacted differently to the events of Easter Week. Archbishop Walsh, who showed an understanding of the rebel position, had put his name to a petition urging clemency for Casement. He had long been sceptical of the IPP strategy and in one of his first statements in the aftermath of the Rising, he wrote disapprovingly about the party's policy.[93] By contrast, Bishop Patrick Foley of Kildare and Leighlin was a vocal opponent of the outbreak. At a confirmation ceremony in Allen church on 10 May 1916 he told his congregation that any grievence that would justify the rebellion had been removed during the previous twenty years and that they were living under one of the most democratic governments in the world. He warned that Catholics who took up arms to resist the civil authorty, or who aided and abetted those resisting, were liable to excommunication.[94] Archbishop Bernard was also vocal in his condemnation, emphasizing that 'the guilty must be punished for the sake of the innocent and of the generations to come'.[95] The events of Easter Week seemed to rekindle fears among unionists. Prominent Kildare unionist, Sir William Goulding, chair of W. & H.M. Goulding Limited, and of the Great Southern & Western Railway, had been marooned at Kingsbridge during Easter Week, and under fire for two days. In a letter to Bonar Law in early May, he alleged that 'In my own county Kildare three-fourths of the people were waiting for news of success of the rebels to at once join in, so-called National Volunteers and others – and I have met every train from the country and friends from all parts of the south and west have told me that it was exactly the same in every county'.[96] Although this was an exaggeration, Goulding had every reason to feel aggrieved as the outbreak had not only resulted in personal financial losses, but rekindled memories of atrocities from 1798.[97] Furthermore, Goulding was acutely aware of advanced nationalist activity, which was openly displayed each year at Bodenstown, half a mile from his residence, Millicent House, Sallins.

The gradually changing popular mood become more evident as the summer progressed. During May the insurrection was condemned by the various councils in Kildare, including the county council, but the executions were also condemned.[98] In late May Asquith proposed an initiative to bring about a permanent home rule settlement in Ireland and appointed David Lloyd George, then minister for munitions, to implement the scheme. This was doomed from the start as Carson was given a written guarantee that Ulster would not be forced into home rule. The IPP, sensing a slippage in support in the aftermath of the Rising, was prepared to concede the temporary exclusion of six Ulster counties from the initial implementation of the Home Rule Act.[99] Its supporters on Kildare County Council loyally followed the party line and endorsed the policy of temporary exclusion in July.[100] However, the scheme collapsed in late July when amendments, insisted on by unionists, proposing permanent exclusion and a reduction of Ireland's representation in the House of Commons, were tabled. This was unacceptable to both Redmond and southern unionists and inflicted considerable damage on the IPP.[101] By early August, with the political initiative in tatters, the changing mood was illustrated by Athy Union, which unanimously carried a resolution sympathizing with Roger Casement's relatives, though the chairman's description of Casement as a patriot and great Irishman 'done to death by tyrannical rulers' did not receive general acclaim.[102]

The Casement affair was soon eclipsed by news from the western front where the Somme offensive began on 1 July 1916. The first day of the battle was the bloodiest day of the entire war with 19,240 British troops losing their lives, among them at least nine Kildare men.[103] Thirty-three of the 3,500 Irish soldiers who died in the Somme were from Kildare but press censorship meant that this was not immediately disclosed. During 1916, a total of 183 Kildare fatalities were recorded.[104]

Meanwhile, recruitment in Kildare collapsed. The RDF recruiting depot in Naas recorded a decrease of fifty-two per cent in the six months from February to August of 1916.[105] In the House of Commons, John O'Connor MP, a strong supporter of the war and recruitment, blamed the mishandling by the authorities of their response to the Rising and its aftermath:

> Before these events happened, I could go down to that constituency [North Kildare] and stand upon platforms side by side with high sheriffs, landlords, with people of the class who had regarded me as their enemy from the past 40 or 50 years – I could go on the platform with them and call ... for recruits and my appeal was never made to my constituents in vain. Since these events have taken place I dare not address my constituents and ask them for recruits to the army.[106]

O'Connor succinctly captured the reasons for the changed mood in Kildare and why enlistment drives in a garrison county no longer obtained support. The fall-off was also noted in CI Supple's monthly reports: for example, in May enlistment was at a standstill and the following month was 'practically a dead letter'.[107]

The declining popularity of the army and the war led to a row in Naas that involved the *Leinster Leader* and the local UDC. Michael O'Kelly criticized Naas UDC's decision to provide a tea recreation room in the town hall for the Sherwood Foresters who were quartered in the town.[108] Differences between O'Kelly as editor and directors of the newspaper had been festering for a long time and his employment was terminated. However, this backfired when the directors were pressured to rescind their action by a deputation from the UDC. O'Kelly was duly reinstated and his reputation restored.[109] Before the Rising the importance of the British army to the local economy ensured that criticism of it was not tolerated; that no longer obtained in the second half of 1916.

Mounting public disquiet due to arrests and internments soon found an organizational outlet when in May 1916 the Irish Volunteer Dependents' Fund (IVDF) and Irish National Aid Association (INAA) emerged to assist the families of imprisoned and dead Volunteers.[110] According to Townshend, these groups provided a link to the deported prisoners, whose incarceration became a key aspect to the rebellion's ultimate impact.[111] As long as the prisoners were detained, they became the objects of widespread sympathy and agitation.[112] The IVDF was made up primarily of female relatives of the executed men with Kathleen Clarke, Áine Ceannt and Sorcha McMahon the most prominent.[113] The INAA was founded by influential women, men and clerics and was much more widespread than the IVDF. Significantly, it had the support of the Catholic clergy with Archbishop Walsh agreeing to act as president.[114] After a tedious series of negotiations, the two groups amalgamated to become the Irish National Aid and Volunteer Dependants' Fund (INAAVDF).[115]

Initially, many areas in Kildare were slow to assist the INAAVDF. The first donation of £60 came from Maynooth College where practically the entire teaching staff contributed. This may have been a means of expressing displeasure with General Maxwell's attempted interference with the spiritual authority of their president. The first organized collection in the county took place in Kildare town in mid-July and yielded £8.[116] Two individuals from the area had been imprisoned: Laurence Rowan, a popular local doctor who was not a member of the Irish Volunteers, was incarcerated for a short time as was Michael Smyth from nearby Athgarvan.[117] Collections in various parishes followed in July and August. In Kill parish, Fr Matthew O'Brien, the curate, organized the collection that raised £23 14s. 6d. He had been closely connected with the Kill Volunteers during Easter Week. Even though large numbers from Athy were serving at the front, £37 14s. was raised.[118] Fund-raising in Naas was not straightforward. After many difficulties, such as opposition to the INAA from the parish priest, the first recorded contribution to the INAAVDF was £45 on 20 January 1917.[119] Many local nationalists in Kildare suspected that the organization was in the hands of advanced nationalists and that this would adversely affect support for Redmond and the war effort. The RIC also disliked the INAAVDF, with the inspector general alleging that the joint secretaries were 'extremists' and that the movement was 'controlled by advanced nationalists'.[120] The INAAVDF kept the separatist spirit alive in Kildare.

The first batch of Kildare internees were released in late July 1916 when many of the lesser-known participants in the Rising were freed.[121] By the end of October only six Kildare men were still incarcerated: Domhnall Ua Buachalla, Patrick Colgan, Thomas Mangan and John Maguire, all from Maynooth; Frank Burke, Carbury and Michael Smyth, Athgarvan. Smyth was a sentenced prisoner, whereas the others were internees.[122] A campaign to obtain their release was initiated with local councils passing motions to this effect. When Lloyd George dislodged Asquith as prime minister, he released all remaining internees in December 1916.[123] On Christmas Day the six men returned to a rousing reception in Kildare. Ua Buachalla and his fellow Maynooth men returned home as heroes and, in Athgarvan, Smyth was given an ovation when he attended a concert shortly afterwards.[124] They provided the impetus for and leadership of the SF movement in 1917. Although the war continued to influence opinion in Kildare throughout 1916, it was the traumatic events of Easter Week that had catastrophic consequences, leading to a collapse in enlistment and a shift in political affiliations. In contrast with many other counties where the decline in IPP support was quite immediate, the change happened slowly in Kildare.

# 5 The emergence of a new political order, 1917–18

The period between the 1916 Rising and the 1918 general election saw a radical realignment of political opinion in Ireland that had a significant impact on Kildare. The emergence of a strong SF and Volunteer movement, dominated by released prisoners, initially eroded support for Redmond and eventually caused the collapse of the IPP. The internees had plenty of time to consider their future strategy with the key to this being the linkage of the reorganized Volunteers to a revamped SF party that could supply a broad political platform and strategy. According to Laffan, many people, and especially young men, were waiting for a lead and once it was given, they followed it with enthusiasm.[1] Early in 1917 the released men began to reorganize the Volunteers. But they also reactivated the political wing of the separatist movement that had been dormant for many years. In Clare, for instance, it was noted that 'in each place where an interned prisoner has returned, the Sinn Féiners have begun to meet, use seditious expressions and up to a certain point defy law and authority'.[2] The same applied in Kildare. Redmondite nationalists, however, did not regard the Easter Week participants with admiration. Although Frank Burke received a joyous welcome at Enfield train station before his return to Carbury, he was aware that there were not many supporters of revolutionary action among the strong farmers and professional class in that parish.[3] The decline of the IPP in Kildare during the period had a number of causes. These included the 1917 by-elections, the failure of the Irish Convention to salvage home rule and the continuing war in Europe in which Kildare participants suffered heavy casualties. As conscription loomed large in early 1918, Kildare played a critical part in the anti-conscription campaign, with all sections of nationalism uniting in common cause to defeat the measure. During the crisis, memories of the Curragh incident were revived when General Gough was dismissed as head of the 5th Division.[4] As elsewhere in Ireland, the conscription crisis prepared the ground for SF's landslide victory at the December 1918 general election. The contest in Kildare demonstrated the extent to which dissatisfaction with the IPP led voters to transfer their allegiance to SF between the 1916 Rising and the end of the First World War.

The first attempt at reorganization of the Volunteers was made by Michael Collins, then an unknown activist, who was secretary of the National Aid Committee. In Frongoch internment camp he shared a hut with Patrick Colgan and swore him into the IRB on 16 December 1916.[5] In February 1917 Colgan was invited to a meeting in Dublin attended by Collins and other activists, including Richard Mulcahy. Collins instructed Colgan to reorganize the Volunteers in north Kildare. Using his GAA and Volunteer connections, Colgan set about the task. Prominent pre-Easter Week Volunteers contacted by him such as Art O'Connor in Celbridge, Thomas Patterson in Naas, Patrick Dunne in Kill and Jack Fitzgerald in Newbridge all re-formed companies in their respective districts.[6] In Maynooth, Ua Buachalla, then aged 50 and one of the oldest participants in the Rising, surprisingly took a back seat in the leadership of the company.[7] The RIC seemed unaware of this Volunteer activity.[8] The reorganization even took place in Athgarvan, within one mile of the Curragh camp, and at Naas and Newbridge, both garrison towns. Three months later there were companies in sixteen locations and Colgan was instructed by Collins to appoint battalion staff. Following a meeting in Prosperous on 17 May 1917 Colgan was appointed battalion commandant, Thomas Harris vice commandant, Art O'Connor quartermaster, and Michael Smyth adjutant.[9] This was an extraordinary success for Colgan within five months of his release. In Meath the expansion did not occur until late 1917 and early 1918 when Seán Boylan organized new companies in every town and parish.[10] The Volunteers in south Kildare were organized from Carlow by Gearóid O'Sullivan, a cousin of Collins and fellow west Cork man who was a teacher in Knockbeg College, just outside Carlow town. O'Sullivan became officer commanding (O/C) of a battalion based in Carlow that initially included south Kildare.[11] Throughout 1917 he laid the groundwork for a future brigade that included all County Carlow, south Kildare and parts of Laois and Wicklow.[12] In south Kildare Éamon Ó Modhráin and Éamon Malone were prominent. Malone was largely responsible for establishing the Volunteers in Athy in 1917. With the formation of a Volunteer company in Kildare town that same year, all garrison towns in the county had a Volunteer presence.[13] The first activity by the re-formed Volunteers occurred during the anniversary of Easter Week when rebel flags were erected in several locations throughout the county, including a number of hotspots noted for dissident activity during the previous year such as Maynooth and Athgarvan.[14] Clearly, the intention to commemorate Easter Week and the executed leaders succeeded in a very visual way, particularly in the two districts that participated in the Rising.

As first anniversary commemorations of Easter 1916 were taking place, the Volunteers had already moved to an involvement in constitutional political activity by assisting in the promotion and formation of SF. Count Plunkett's victory in North Roscommon in February had opened up the possibility of a dramatic reinvention of the separatist movement.[15] According to Laffan, it was through the informal process of working together in Roscommon that they initiated the formal and deliberate policy of reviving the movement.[16] The victory had consequences for Kildare, generating debate in many of the local district councils. Plunkett's aim was to inaugurate a national policy whereby

Ireland would take control of its affairs. A circular, inviting delegates to a conference in the Mansion House, Dublin, was sent to various organizations, every county and district council in the country.[17] The Plunkett circular was not well received in Kildare. At Athy Guardians, John Conlon, a prominent Redmondite county councillor, claimed that the new policy was misguiding the young and leading them on to revolution and socialistic paths. At a meeting of Naas No. 1 RDC on 4 April George Wolfe denounced Plunkett's abstentionist policy.[18] Although the motion was defeated, it was supported by three district councillors, including Éamon Ó Modhráin.[19] James Corrigan, who lived close to Athgarvan, voted against the initiative and on 15 April a meeting of Athgarvan SF called for his resignation from the RDC. This marked the arrival of SF politics in Kildare and a new form of constitutional opposition to Redmondism in the county.[20]

By the late spring and early summer 1917 the Volunteer companies in north Kildare had established SF clubs as the legal political wing of the more secretive Volunteer branch. With the existing organization structure already in place, this new constitutional movement, consisting mainly of young activists, quickly extended throughout the county. This followed a general pattern taking place elsewhere.[21] The by-elections were watched with great interest by the Kildare public. Michael Smyth and Éamon Ó Modhráin assisted with the campaign of Joe McGuinness in South Longford in early May, and the SF success was celebrated in Naas.[22] Archbishop Walsh's criticism of the IPP policy on partition on the eve of the South Longford by-election in a letter to the *Evening Herald* is regarded as contributing to SF's success.[23] The archbishop's opposition to the IPP and partition was a message that would not go unheeded in Kildare where SF continued to flourish.

Michael O'Kelly from Naas was central to the emergence of the SF organization in the county. Not only was he instrumental in publicizing the movement locally in the *Leinster Leader*, but he was influential in the formation of the Naas SF club that eventually became the hub of the organization in Kildare. O'Kelly was also actively involved in forming a County Kildare SF organizing committee.[24] Delegates from Athgarvan, Naas, Straffan and Carbury attended a meeting on 3 June 1917 with Ó Modhráin presiding and Smyth serving as secretary.[25] Art O'Connor and Jack Fitzgerald also emerged as promoters of the local SF organization. Within four weeks the movement had spread in a more general way throughout the county. Many of the newly formed branches were established in a blaze of local publicity with large numbers joining, such as in Clane and Rathcoffey where reports suggested sixty-four new members.[26] James O'Connor of Celbridge and William Burke of Carbury were now representing the party on the county council and an increasing number of district councillors also switched to SF.[27] At the end of July the RIC recorded four SF clubs in Kildare compared to twelve in Offaly and six in Laois; and 336 in the country overall.[28] This may have underestimated the strength of SF in the county, but it lagged behind neighbouring counties. By that time Redmond and the two Kildare MPs were rarely mentioned in the local press. With the IPP in disarray, the government proposed an Irish Convention aimed at producing agreement on the home rule issue, and in the hope that it might reverse the decline in constitutional politics.[29] The announcement was welcomed at a meeting of Kildare County Council on 14 June 1917, although there were differences of opinion with James O'Connor pointing out that a large section of the people did not favour the convention.[30] Throughout the summer, more open support for SF surfaced at local authority meetings, particularly following the election of Éamon de Valera in East Clare, which was celebrated with bonfires in Naas and Timahoe.[31] A proposed vote of congratulations to de Valera caused unease at Naas Board of Guardians on 8 August. Michael Gogarty described SF as 'rainbow chasers' who wanted 'to do away with the flag and set up this miserable tri-colour rag and call it a republic'. He proposed a counter motion welcoming the convention and supporting the IPP, which was carried by twenty votes to four against.[32] The fact that four members elected as Redmondites were opposed to IPP policy was another sign that the old order was crumbling. The decline in IPP support was also recognized by CI Supple, who noted in June 1917 that 'SF ideas are spreading'.[33] The following month he suggested that a SF candidate could be elected in Kildare if there was a by-election.[34] Although the mood had changed radically in the county, it was still not fertile territory for advanced nationalism and it was unlikely that either of the Kildare constituencies was ready to elect a SF MP.

The sitting MPs, as one might expect, sharply criticized SF. Denis Kilbride deemed an Irish republic an impossible dream, and John O'Connor described the policy as 'the greatest humbug put before the Irish people.'[35] By the late autumn, however, in an attempt to staunch the flow of support from the IPP, O'Connor adopted a conciliatory tone. At a committee meeting in the Commons in October 1917, he complained of biased treatment of nationalists. He reminded the committee that in suppressing the recent rebellion, Irish rebels who were already wounded were put into a chair and shot, while at the same time the arch rebel, Edward Carson, was not only elevated to a government position but into the War Ministry. 'These things', he stressed, 'irritate the people of Ireland and they object to this differential treatment'.[36] Two months later he swung back towards the IPP by denouncing SF in the Commons as 'irresponsible advocates of wildcat schemes of government'.[37]

Bishop Foley also attacked SF. While not condemning the party by name, he warned in September 1917 that 'rebellion … was absolutely unjustifiable from the point of view of Divine Law' and that if 'any man of influence, lay or cleric, asserted the contrary there or elsewhere in the diocese, it would be his duty to warn the people against him'.[38] This was a warning not only to the laity but also to priests in the diocese who openly associated with SF – such as Fr Matthew O'Brien, curate in Kill, who chaired several public SF meetings in north Kildare.[39] Although many of the clergy were in agreement with Foley's politics, others disagreed. When a new SF branch was established at Suncroft three weeks after the bishop's sermon, it was presided over by the local curate, Fr A. Farrell.[40] As SF continued to gain momentum, clerical support became more explicit. When a branch was established in Ballymore Eustace in the Dublin archdiocese, Fr Patrick J. Bryan wrote: 'As the archbishop said a few months ago that the IPP had sold the country, I believe that the SF party are the only real national party in Ireland'.[41] SF's support continued to increase and the IPP's to decline. Much now depended on the success of the Irish Convention.

Kildare unionists had a strong voice in the Convention with the participation of Lord Mayo, a representative of the Irish peers; William Goulding, a government nominee; and John Bernard, Church of Ireland archbishop of Dublin. Representing Kildare County Council, Matthew Minch was the sole nationalist representative from the county. Goulding was the most active of the three and was a supporter of the Midleton initiative.[42] So too was Bernard. Lord Midleton, leader of the southern unionists, promoted a home rule settlement without partition subject to certain financial restrictions.[43] It provided for certain safeguards for unionists in an all-Ireland assembly with powers to levy internal taxes but with customs duty remaining under the jurisdiction of Westminster.[44] The prelates with ecclesiastical authority over Kildare were clearly divided in their political viewpoints, with Bernard and Foley sharing a distrust of SF, while Walsh proved more receptive. On the issue of partition, Walsh and Bernard shared common ground and both actively campaigned against the measure.

While the principal news topic of 1917 both nationally and in Kildare was politics and the growth of SF, the war on the Western Front continued relentlessly. The year also saw a higher number of causalities than the previous year, with 187 from Kildare dying on the battlefield, four more than in 1916.[45] Enlistment nationally continued to decline with 11,400 joining between February 1917 and January 1918. The only figures available for Naas RDF depot are from the period February to August 1917 which indicated that 1,238 recruits joined, 429 fewer than the previous six-month period.[46] In March the CI described recruitment as bad; by May he indicated that it was practically nil.[47]

In the second half of 1917, as support for enlistment and the war continued to decline, SF became more audacious. The first outdoor public meeting of the party in the county, planned for 5 August on the Main Street in Naas, was banned under the DORA. But the organizers outmanoeuvred the authorities by changing the venue at short notice to the local football ground. The meeting marked the first occasion of a public address in Kildare by Arthur Griffith.[48] The following month SF headquarters appointed Éamon Fleming, who had participated in Easter Week in the Athy area, as the party organizer for Kildare. He quickly established several new branches in areas such as Carbury and Prosperous.[49]

Meanwhile, many of the Easter Week participants had resumed political activity and were re-arrested under the DORA. Thomas Ashe and Austin Stack had gone on hunger strike. On 23 September a large public meeting in Naas, addressed by Fr O'Brien, Jack Fitzgerald and Éamon Fleming, protested against the arrests.[50] Two days later Ashe died as a result of force feeding, and a wave of anger swept across the county. Large numbers from Kildare attended the funeral in Dublin, with many of the local SF branches represented. The following week resolutions condemning his death and the treatment of political prisoners by the government were passed by both Naas and Athy UDCs.[51] Every action involving SF generated immense publicity and sympathy, with supporters of the IPP in local councils being placed in the difficult position of passing resolutions condemning the authorities for various acts committed against their rivals.

A number of Kildare delegates attended the SF ard fheis in the Mansion House on 25 October at which de Valera replaced Griffith as leader of the party. Also at this time local SF officers organized two large outdoor meetings at Newbridge and Athy on the weekend following the ard fheis. The two principal SF leaders, de Valera and Griffith, agreed to speak at both meetings. However, the choice of Newbridge was contentious as it was the most garrisoned town in the country with the civilian population totally dependent on the garrison for their livelihood. The authorities, fearing general disorder and violence in the town, banned the meeting, but allowed the event to proceed in Athy.[52] Strong preventative measures were put in place around Newbridge to stop the meeting taking place. Mounted detachments of military guarded the different roadways bordering the Curragh while the railway was strongly protected by RIC and military guards. Some 300 RIC were on standby in Newbridge and the surrounding district.[53]

By contrast, security was not as intensive in Athy, with only thirty members of the RIC on duty. Almost 2,000 attended the meeting, with contingents travelling from all parts of south Kildare and adjoining districts. De Valera used the opportunity to deliver a major policy speech in which he defended the right of priests to participate in politics.[54] This may have been in response to Bishop Foley's intervention five weeks previously. The meeting passed off largely without incident, although there were some interruptions by relatives of soldiers with a number of women waving Union Jacks and shouting 'for king and country'. De Valera responded that he 'felt very sorry and sympathetic for the poor ignorant people who did not know any better when they followed the advice of their leader [Redmond] and went out [to the front]'.[55] Bizarrely, Supple did not mention de Valera's speech in his monthly report. Instead, he stated that no clergy or people of note attended which, he concluded, 'put a damper on Sinn Féinism in the county'.[56] Although several elected boards in the Athy area passed resolutions welcoming the visit, support was far from unanimous. The vote by Athy UDC was carried by only one.[57]

By November Michael Smyth claimed thirty branches of SF had affiliated. The following month a reorganization of the SF county committee took place. An executive organization was formed for each of the two parliamentary divisions.[58] In North Kildare, Fr Matthew O'Brien became president, with Fr John James of Balyna and Art O'Connor as vice presidents. In South Kildare, Éamon Ó Modhráin was elected president. Michael Smyth was appointed secretary and also served as joint secretary of the northern executive.[59]

Although the political side of the movement was active in a more public way, a vigorous militant side continued to progress in the second half of 1917. By the late autumn they became more daring. On 21 October an estimated 150 Volunteers took part in a mobilization in Maynooth that blatantly contravened DORA.[60] The RIC took no action, a sign of the force's weakness in the face of increasing militancy. Volunteer activity also increased in south Kildare. In September 1917, Éamon Price, an Easter Week veteran, came to Carlow as a Gaelic League organizer and joined the Carlow Brigade staff.[61] When Gearóid O'Sullivan was recalled to Dublin, Price served as vice commandant with Seán O'Farrell as new O/C. Price remained in position until he joined general headquarters (GHQ) staff as director of training in autumn 1919.[62] As in north Kildare, the Volunteers grew bolder. When de Valera and Griffith addressed a meeting in Athy on 4 November the local Volunteers wore uniforms and carried arms.[63] Later that month 170 Castledermot Volunteers commemorated the fiftieth anniversary of the Manchester Martyrs with some wearing uniform and bandoliers.[64]

By late 1917 the Volunteers and SF had gained sufficient support to enable them to engage in issues of a more socio-economic nature. SF's involvement in land agitation capitalized on the widespread disenchantment of small farmers and the landless.[65] The land issue in Kildare was not as overt as in constituencies such as North Roscommon where SF called for agitation to 'secure the ranches for the landless people of Ireland'.[66] Nonetheless, Kildare was still a county of large estates, where substantial divisions were let to graziers on the eleven months system. The graziers and substantial landowners tended to be moderate nationalists while the smallholders and farm labourers were more likely to be shifting their political allegiance to SF.

The most effective weapon used in land protest was 'cattle-driving', and in the Kill area in early 1918 a number of holdings were targeted, including land owned by the earl of Mayo and N.J. Synnott. The cattle were discovered wandering the roads with placards tied around their necks which read: 'the land for the people and the road for the bullocks'.[67] Thirty extra police were reportedly drafted into Kill and, according to the CI, Fr O'Brien, president of the North Kildare SF executive, and Patrick Dunne, captain of Kill Volunteers, were the ringleaders.[68] In Kildare the agitation was supported by leading SF figures and Laurence Ginnell, the maverick MP, who attended a function in Naas in January 1918 to encourage the protests.[69] The land agitation quickly spread to other localities, including Clane, Donadea and Kilcock.[70] Although many local politicians stayed out of the row, two councillors, John Healy and Patrick Phelan, shared a platform with Art O'Connor and supported the land agitation.[71] John O'Connor was noticeably silent. Cattle-driving was also prevalent in Laois and Offaly.[72]

The agitation achieved one notable success, which related to the O'Kelly estate of Barrettstown, outside Newbridge, where notorious evictions had taken place during the Land War.[73] The local SF branch objected to the letting of a small portion of land and demanded that it be divided among uneconomic holders. A protest meeting attended by over 1,000 people included large numbers of Volunteers in uniform. The trustees of the Barrettstown land immediately settled with the protestors and the land was acquired by the adjoining tenants.[74] This was a classic example of SF championing a local issue for its political advantage. Protests of this nature were not always successful. Forewarned of a cattle drive in Donadea, the RIC under CI Supple baton-charged the drivers and arrested six men.[75] By March agitation had eased in Kill following negotiations between the protesters and Lord Mayo.[76] But in other areas such as Kilcock an inflammatory speech by Ginnell on 2 March appeared to advise the landless to take possession of land by force.[77] However, before his advice could be carried out, the conscription crisis had gripped Ireland.

In early April 1918 nationalist Ireland was stunned when it was revealed that the government intended to apply conscription to Ireland. This was prompted by the success of the German spring offensive in which Allied lines were breached in several sectors of the Western Front. The main thrust of the German offensive on 21 March was in the area defended by the 5th Army that included the 16th Division with large numbers from Kildare who mainly belonged to RDF.[78] The 5th Army was commanded by Lieutenant General Sir Hubert Gough, whose role in the Curragh incident did not hinder his promotion in the army. The casualties suffered by the Irish Divisions were exceedingly heavy.[79] Gough lost his command. He had never been forgiven by certain elements of the government for his part in the Curragh incident and became the scapegoat for the March disaster.[80] Under public pressure following the reversals in the war, Lloyd George sought to extend conscription to Ireland and also to older men and further groups of workers in Britain under a Military Service bill.[81] That the government linked the implementation of home rule to the enactment of conscription not only added to the anger of nationalists, but also alienated unionists.

In addition, the conscription crisis made irrelevant the Irish Convention which in any case had failed to find agreement between nationalists and unionists on home rule.[82] This had significant implications for southern unionism a few months later. At a meeting of the Irish Unionist Alliance (IUA) in Dublin on 24 January 1919, Lord Midleton, leader of the southern unionists, proposed that the political destiny of southern unionists, who were opposed to partition, should be decided by southern unionists alone.[83] This position was supported by Lord Mayo and Sir William Goulding, the leading Kildare unionist figures. The motion was defeated and this caused an open split among unionists with Midleton leading a break-away Unionist Anti-Partition League (UAPL) drawn from the southern provinces.[84] There was a strong Kildare representation on the executive of the two opposing unionist camps. Lord Cloncurry remained one of the joint vice presidents of the IUA along with other executive members from Kildare, including Percy Le Touche, John A. Aylmer and William J.H. Tyrrell.[85] Some IUA figures from the county such as H.J.B. Clements and William T. Kirkpatrick switched to the UAPL.[86]

Opposition to conscription united all shades of nationalist opinion, including SF and the Catholic Church. In Kildare the CI reported that 'the priests and all nationalists have taken up the anti-conscription agitation'.[87] Within a week of the news breaking, local councils and boards had passed protest resolutions. Naas Union deemed the measure a betrayal of the liberties and rights of small nations which was one of the Allies' objectives in the war.[88] The attendance at public protest meetings throughout the county on Sunday 14 April exceeded all expectations. The extent of nationalist unity was demonstrated in Newbridge when an anti-conscription motion was proposed by P.J. Doyle, an IPP supporter, and seconded by Jack Fitzgerald of SF. The *Kildare Observer* predicted that the unrest had the potential to be comparable to proportions not seen since 1798.[89]

The history of the conscription crisis at a national level is well known with a conference of all shades of nationalist opinion at the Mansion House on 18 April leading to an anti-conscription pledge modelled on the Ulster Covenant and successful overtures being made to the Catholic hierarchy. Although Cardinal Logue favoured passive resistance, Archbishop Walsh's advocacy of practical action and clear instructions for those prepared to oppose conscription won out.[90] The bishops issued a statement declaring the conscription decree unjust and calling on Catholics to resist 'by all means that are consonant with the law of God'.[91] An anti-conscription pledge was taken after Mass on 21 April, 'Pledge Sunday'. The active involvement of the Church was critical. As Fergus Quinn, assistant commissioner of the DMP, observed 'that ends conscription in Ireland'.[92] By contrast, the main Protestant Churches supported conscription. Archbishop Bernard told a service in Dublin that young men should join at once without waiting for conscription.[93]

County Kildare played its part on Pledge Sunday, with thousands attending meetings throughout the county and taking the anti-conscription pledge. At Mass in Carlow Bishop Foley informed his congregation that they could safely take the pledge.[94] At a meeting in Naas John O'Connor MP urged the gathering to obey the instructions emanating from the Mansion House conference. The meeting in Athy drew in people from adjoining districts in Laois and a local anti-conscription committee of twenty-four members was formed which included six Catholic clergymen.[95] At Kill some 3,000 people were reported to have taken the pledge, which was administered by the curate Fr Matthew O'Brien. The signatories included the parish priest Fr J.J. Donovan and N.J. Synnott, chairman of the Bank of Ireland, who had also addressed the meeting.[96] In Rathangan a reported 2,000 people congregated at the meeting which was presided over by Fr Michael Rice.[97] Meetings in small villages also attracted substantial numbers. In Staplestown the signing of the pledge was carried out over several days to facilitate non-Catholics and reports suggest a sizeable number signed. In Ballymore Eustace two local men assisted Nelly O'Brien, an anti-conscription activist, who aimed to obtain signed pledges from non-Catholics. Their canvass yielded twenty signatures.[98] In Kildare all the garrison towns and every parish participated in what was the largest and most united demonstration the county had seen to date. Catholic clergymen in Kildare acted in a leadership role throughout the anti-conscription campaign as was the case in other counties.[99]

Within two days of Pledge Sunday there was another successful national demonstration – an anti-conscription strike by the Trades Union Congress. In early 1918 labourers had begun to organize in different areas of Kildare. The first branch of the ITGWU was in Naas.[100] The organization soon spread to Newbridge, Athy and even the Curragh camp, where in mid-March 200 men employed at the remount depot were informed by the military authorities that they would be liable to dismissal if they remained in the union. The men were also informed that they would be required to wear khaki or face dismissal. The majority of the men who belonged to the union refused, although seven complied. The workers feared that if they agreed they would be drafted into a labour battalion. However, within days there was a U-turn by the military that lifted objections to union membership.[101] This defused the situation and prevented a strike during one of the most serious set-backs suffered by the army during the war. The anti-conscription strike was effective throughout the country, with the exception of Belfast and the northeast.[102] A complete suspension of work in Dublin resulted in the absence of railway transport in Kildare. There was no service on the Midland Great Western or the Great Southern & Western railways. The strike had a severe effect on the Punchestown races. Owners of horses were unable to get their animals to the racecourse in time, and the programme had to undergo various alterations and curtailments.[103] In Athy business was suspended with all shops and workshops closed.[104] The strike was also well-supported in small towns such as Ballitore where work on the land stopped and education even ceased in the local schools.

On 29 April Kildare County Council strongly opposed conscription at its quarterly meeting.[105] The most important contribution was made by Joseph O'Connor, a councillor who was not well-known:

> When Redmond offered Volunteer support the offer was sneered at, and they were practically told they could win the war without them … Carson had set an example to them of preaching rebellion. The people could now claim a distinguished example of rebelling against this act. Carson was promoted to the highest position whilst for the same thing other men were put with their backs to a wall and shot. It was a cruel thing to see there was one law for one section of the people and another law for the rest.[106]

This was a viewpoint not only shared by the councillors present but also by a substantial section of the general public. There was some support for conscription at a meeting of Celbridge Union with J.W. Shackleton describing opposition to it as cowardly.[107] Nationalists now focused on financing the anti-conscription campaign, and the National Defence Fund which was collected after Mass on Sunday 12 May was well supported throughout the county. Surprisingly, the biggest collection was in the garrison town of Newbridge where £400 was raised. Accounts from less than half of the parishes in the county which were published in the two local newspapers recorded a sum in excess of £2,300.[108] Coming from a garrison county, this sent a strong message to the government.

In the event, the conscription measure was deferred by the government, but a new round of arrests of nationalist leaders who had frustrated its plans was implemented under the bogus cover of a 'German plot'.[109] Art O'Connor was the only Kildare SF activist on the wanted list. However, details of his impending arrest were leaked by RIC Sergeant Jeremiah Maher, a clerk in the CI's office with nationalist sympathies. This intelligence was conveyed to O'Connor by Alphonsus Sweeney and also to Volunteer headquarters by

Seumas O'Kelly.[110] O'Connor went into hiding. Kildare County Council condemned the arrests and deportations on 27 May.[111] A SF protest meeting the previous day resulted in a public relations coup when O'Connor came out of hiding to address the meeting. Following his speech, guarded by Volunteers, he made an even more dramatic escape amid scuffles between police who attempted to arrest him and Volunteers who resisted.[112] O'Connor was eventually arrested in Galway in August.[113] At a meeting of Kildare County Council on 27 May the leading councillors, while emphasizing that they did not support or have any connection with SF, expressed the opinion that the government's action was inspired 'solely to misrepresent the Irish people in the eyes of the allied nations'.[114]

Kildare remained in an unsettled state into June. On 18 June at a confirmation ceremony in Derrinturn church in Carbury, Bishop Foley waived the requirement to attend weekly Mass should young men have 'to fly to the bogs and hillsides in resisting conscription'.[115] Such a statement from Foley was particularly uncharacteristic as he had been sympathetic to the war effort for the previous three-and-a-half years. Undoubtedly, large numbers of Catholics either serving in the army or dependent for their livelihood on the army would have been dismayed by the bishop's comments. Nevertheless, there was no criticism of the Church by lay Catholics connected to the army.

The conscription crisis boosted Cumann na mBan.[116] In mid-June members organized an anti-conscription meeting in Naas town hall with women signing the pledge and giving an undertaking not to take the place of any man who lost his position to conscription.[117] In this way conscription would prove a double-edged sword. Recruits might be obtained, but if women refused to work male jobs, the economy in Kildare would come to a standstill.

The Volunteers experienced a surge in new members during the conscription crisis and the government extended the powers of the DORA to regain authority and curb the growing power of SF. A military proclamation on 4 July proscribed the holding of meetings, assemblies, or processions in public places, without a permit.[118] The nationalist organizations affected included SF, the Irish Volunteers, Cumann na mBan, the Gaelic League and the GAA.[119] The new legislation was immediately put to the test in Kildare town where a protest rally had been organized for Sunday 7 July along with a football match. Both the meeting and match were banned by the authorities, but the organizers pressed ahead. RIC reinforcements poured into Kildare. The field where the football match was to take place was occupied by the military and the goal posts were removed. However, the GAA secretly rearranged the game for the following Sunday in a different field close by and the banned meeting and game were held at the same venue.[120] In protest at the requirement for permits, the GAA organized a series of matches throughout the country for Sunday 4 August, which became known as Gaelic Sunday. In Kildare, football matches

were played without a permit in almost every parish.[121] No attempt was made
to prevent games taking place, even in garrison towns such as Newbridge or
Naas.[122] SF now followed the example of the GAA by holding meetings without permits all over the country on 15 August at which a statement supplied
by headquarters was read.[123] Three meetings were held in Kildare and led to
the arrests of Michael Stapleton at Kilcock, Michael Sammon, a member of the
county football team, at Kilcullen, and at Athy J.J. (James) O'Byrne, a local
schoolteacher.[124] All were court-martialled for taking part in a meeting without
a permit and making statements likely to cause disaffection.[125] O'Byrne and
Stapleton were convicted on both charges and sentenced to one year, while
Sammon was convicted of the first charge only and given a sentence of one
month's imprisonment.[126] The arrests continued to enhance the status and popularity of the party in the county during the autumn of 1918 at a time when
IPP supporters appeared to be inactive.

The end of the First World War on Armistice Day, 11 November 1918,
was cause for celebration throughout Ireland, and especially in military centres.
But due to the altered political climate, celebrations were restrained in many
areas. The Spanish influenza may also have been a factor as regular reports of
the epidemic were given on the week prior to the armistice when the death rate
was at its highest.[127] Kildare suffered the highest rate of death per head of the
population of any county in the country.[128] It has been suggested that Kildare's
associations with the army, through the Curragh barracks, combined with inadequate sanitary conditions in Naas, were contributory factors.[129] Joy at the end
of the war was tinged by sorrow for the families and friends of the more than
800 Kildare people who died; in 1918 alone there were 151 fatalities. Athy suffered in excess of 118 fatalities, twenty more than Naas, the next highest.[130]
Three days after the war ended it was announced that the long-awaited general
election would be held on 14 December.[131] There had been no election since
1910. The extended franchise due to the Representation of the People Act,
1918 had more than doubled the electorate nationally. Voting rights for women
over thirty had been granted for the first time, and men over twenty-one and
military servicemen over nineteen could vote in parliamentary elections without property qualifications.[132]

The election was a straight contest between the IPP and SF as Labour had
agreed not to participate. In October, delegates from trade unions in north
Kildare met in Newbridge and unanimously decided not to contest the election
in the constituency.[133] A well-prepared SF had selected its candidates for the
two Kildare constituencies two months earlier. However, at the North Kildare
convention, held in Prosperous on 12 September, a split arose due to the emergence of two distinct points of view within the party. One was a militant
stance, supported by the original Volunteer wing, while the second was a more
pragmatic and constitutional position, espoused by new SF members. Patrick

Colgan, O/C North Kildare Battalion, supported by his colleagues, proposed Ted O'Kelly. Significant backing also emerged for the imprisoned Art O'Connor from delegates favouring a more constitutional agenda, including Seumas O'Kelly.[134] They strongly advocated adopting the example of South Longford the previous year by putting O'Connor in to get him out. The split was resolved when Colgan proposed Domhnall Ua Buachalla who reluctantly agreed.[135] The South Kildare SF convention was held two days later and O'Connor, the only candidate, was unanimously selected.[136]

John O'Connor was selected as the IPP candidate for North Kildare at a convention in Naas on 25 November. Although the speakers denounced SF policy, with one referring to it as political suicide, there seemed to be a grudging admiration for Ua Buachalla.[137] Doubts about whether 70-year-old Denis Kilbride would stand for re-election were dispelled when he was chosen at a well-attended convention in Athy on 22 November.[138] Kilbride was noted for raising concerns in parliament on behalf of unionists in his constituency and his nomination was supported by Thomas Plewman, a prominent local unionist.[139] During the second week of the campaign three of the four bishops in the ecclesiastical province of Dublin, Brownrigg, bishop of Ossory, Codd of Ferns and Foley of Kildare and Leighlin, published letters in support of the IPP. Foley had 'no faith in Sinn Féinism as a policy nor in abstention from parliament as a means of political salvation'.[140] Archbishop Walsh, who was sympathetic to SF, differed from his suffragan bishops.[141] On 27 November he explained that he had lost confidence in the IPP as early as 1904 and that his views were 'altogether different from those expressed in the letters of those three venerated prelates'.[142] For the first time the Catholic clergy in Kildare were on opposite sides in an election. It was common practice for clerics to sign nomination papers. John O'Connor was proposed by Fr Norris, parish priest of Naas, and his nomination papers were signed by Monsignor Thomas Tynan, parish priest of Newbridge, and Fr Joseph Seaver, a curate in Maynooth. Kilbride was proposed by Canon Mackey, parish priest of Athy. SF also had clerical support with Fr Matthew O'Brien seconding Ua Buachalla whose nomination papers were signed by Fr John James and Fr J.J. Doyle from Celbridge.[143] A generational divide among the clergy in the election was evident with senior parish priests supporting the IPP and younger priests more inclined to support SF. In terms of female involvement in the campaign, SF was the more progressive. Hanna Sheehy-Skeffington urged the women in Monasterevin to vote for independence while in Straffan Miss Ryan urged support for Ua Buachalla.[144] The IPP, damaged by conscription and the lack of progress on home rule, was pitted against the rising political party. Even before the campaign began, the signs pointed to a triumph for SF with its superior party machine. Nationally, twenty-five constituencies were uncontested by the IPP but Kildare experienced the novelty of contested elections for the first time in decades.[145] North Kildare was last contested in 1900 and South Kildare in 1892.[146] John O'Connor's campaign was plagued with difficulties. On 20 November he attended the Naas fair. Although the town was thronged with farmers who usually supported the IPP, no interest was taken in the proceedings and a planned public meeting was abandoned. The following Sunday he was unable to hold an after-Mass meeting in Two-Mile-House due to constant heckling.[147] On 1 December the most serious disruption to O'Connor's campaign occurred in Kilcock, where, due to a noisy SF procession, twenty armed soldiers intervened to allow a meeting to continue without interruption.[148] The support of the military was not likely to enhance O'Connor's chances of re-election. On the same day Ua Buachalla encountered some hostilities in Naas where he was accompanied by Fr Michael O'Flanagan, SF vice president, who was on a speaking tour in the constituency.[149] Soldiers erected a Union Jack, which was pulled down by younger SF adherents and a minor scuffle ensued.[150] It was hardly surprising that anti-SF sentiment surfaced in Naas, a garrison town with large numbers of service men, ex-service men and relatives of casualties. As it happened, Kilbride was also heckled at a meeting in Athy on 1 December. Tactlessly, given the imprisonment of Stapleton, O'Byrne and Art O'Connor, he raised the treatment of political prisoners in inflammatory terms:

> one would think that for the first time in Ireland men went to jail in 1916. The first thing done in 1916 was to show the sore leg. In the old days they took their punishments and their plank beds without showing the sore leg. Today, no political prisoners had to lie on plank beds. All they wanted was cigarettes, chickens etc.[151]

Kilbride also denounced SF: 'As for establishing a republic of Ireland they might as well ask for a piece of the moon.'[152] The claims did little to enhance his campaign. Art O'Connor's imprisonment in England gave him a significant advantage.

National issues such as the viability of SF's policy of abstention from parliament and attendance at the Peace Conference dominated the election campaign. But local matters, notably IPP support for the war and the political prisoner issue caused the most heated exchanges. SF capitalized on concern about the war, with Ua Buachalla accusing John O'Connor of attempting to 'send the manhood of Ireland to leave their bones bleaching in France or Gallipoli'.[153] In Kilcock, veteran Volunteer Jim O'Keeffe described O'Connor as a recruiting sergeant for the British army. In addition, he reminded the audience that O'Connor had served as Crown prosecutor in Bristol in 1909.[154] Apart from a handful of incidents, the campaign passed off without any significant disturbance.[155] This was in contrast to other counties such as

Waterford where the rough and tumble of elections was very evident.[156] The Kildare Volunteers guarded the polling booths and the ballot boxes until the counting began; this was also the case in other counties.[157]

In North Kildare, as expected, Ua Buachalla had a resounding victory by 5,979 votes to 2,772 for O'Connor. However, with an electorate of 13,275 eligible voters, the turnout was just 66 per cent.[158] It was obvious that a sizeable number, mainly farmers, did not vote. They were disenchanted IPP supporters who were unwilling to support SF. The size of Ua Buachalla's majority was a surprise given that the constituency included a large number of strong farmers and two major barracks at Naas and Newbridge. In South Kildare, Art O'Connor received 7,140 votes to Kilbride's 1,545.[159] Although apathy in the southern constituency was similar to the northern constituency, the votes cast for SF represented a clear majority of the total on the register. It is obvious that the result was not influenced to any great extent by commercial advantages relating to the Curragh camp and the garrison at Kildare town. The Kildare result surprised SF headquarters, which had predicted that the party would be disadvantaged by the large military vote.[160] Although the army presence in Kildare was a factor, it did not have a significant effect on the election result. The decisive margin of victory for the two Kildare SF TDs confirmed the extent to which public support had shifted from the IPP.

The new political order that emerged during 1917 was slow to gain ground in Kildare, unlike other counties where by-elections led to the defeat of nationalists. It was not until the conscription crisis that SF could claim superiority. The experience of Kildare exemplifies how revolutionary movements succeed in mobilizing popular support against a perceived threat or injustice rather than in favour of a vision or an ideology.[161] The decisive victory margin for the two SF candidates in the 1918 election confirmed the extent to which public support for the IPP had faded. However, although SF held an electoral mandate from Kildare, supporters of the old order who controlled the local councils and boards would clearly present challenges in the months ahead. During 1917–18, when Volunteer activity such as raiding for arms signalled an escalation of violence early in the next phase of the struggle nationally, the absence of such activity in Kildare intimated the low level of violence that was to follow.[162]

# 6 War of Independence, 1919–21

The War of Independence between January 1919 and July 1921 was a conflict in which both political activists represented by SF and IRA militants (as the Volunteers were styled from 1919) combined to make British rule impossible and advance the objective of an Irish republic. At the beginning of 1919 local government bodies in Kildare were in the hands of the IPP and, over the next eighteen months, SF engaged in a political struggle for local dominance. Peter Hart, Tom Garvin and Michael Hopkinson have all pointed to Kildare's low level participation in advanced nationalist militancy. In his study of the geography of the revolution from 1917 to 1923, Hart found that only Counties Dublin, Wicklow and Antrim had similar or lesser levels of IRA violence per 10,000 people than Kildare from January 1920 to December 1922.[1] Garvin concluded that in east Leinster, only Wicklow and Kilkenny were less active, whereas Hopkinson maintains that Kildare and four neighbouring counties 'adopted an almost apologetic air as excuses are sought for their minimal involvement'.[2] Kildare was not suited to an overt military campaign due to the overwhelming concentration of Crown forces in the county. Caution marked the approach of the IRA in Kildare who, to some extent, lacked the leadership of their Munster colleagues and were inhibited by a lack of arms. Militant activity took different forms such as acts of civil disobedience. Labour played a decisive role in this regard by supporting republican hunger strikes with a countrywide work stoppage in April 1920 and also through the munitions strike. Many Labour activists in Kildare were also members of the IRA. As will become apparent, the Kildare IRA played a pivotal role in supplying intelligence to IRA GHQ, which arguably changed the course of the War of Independence during which efforts were made to enforce the Belfast boycott, establish Dáil courts and progressively make the county ungovernable by undermining the RIC.

Following the general election, SF activists in Kildare concentrated on securing the release of the German Plot prisoners at a series of public meetings on 5 January 1919. In Naas, Ua Buachalla claimed the arrests were futile because if the authorities 'put a thousand SF leaders in jail there would be a thousand more to take their place'.[3] Art O'Connor was in jail when Dáil Éireann met for the first time on 21 January 1919, but Ua Buachalla was present. The Dáil met for two days in January, but there was no further session until April. During the intervening period, Ua Buachalla, while attending a meeting in Staplestown, emphasized that SF politicians and the Dáil were not inactive, giving assurances that their work 'would bear fruit'.[4] At a local level the focus remained on political prisoners and the tactic of obstructing fox-hunting, already used in other counties, was adopted.[5] This was the principal sporting pastime of the landed gentry, the magistrates and the British army in Kildare. In late January the master of the Kildare Fox Hunt was informed by the secretary of Kilcock SF that he would not be permitted to hunt until the prisoners were released.[6] The threat to the hunt was not supported by RDCs in the county. At a meeting of Naas No. 1 RDC on 5 February, George Wolfe suggested that SF 'may as well stop golfing'.[7] Protests at hunt meetings by SF members became common, with Michael O'Kelly actively participating.[8] Initially the hunt managed to dodge the protestors in some areas, but on 20 February at Davidstown in south Kildare the IRA made hunting impossible by sounding horns close to coverts. Hunting was then abandoned for the season.[9] The row over hunting soon pitted SF and the IRA against farmers and traders who benefitted commercially from the equine industry. The Kildare Hunt Club, which was infuriated by SF's successful efforts, retaliated by cancelling the Punchestown races in April. The meeting was of vital importance to the local economy and to the equine industry in the county, and had been curtailed by the conscription crisis in 1918. In Meath the Fairyhouse and Navan races were likewise abandoned.[10] The Kildare Farmers' Union tried to persuade the Hunt Club to alter its position on Punchestown and collected 1,532 signatures from farmers.[11] The Hunt Club was unmoved. On 6 March the situation was eased with the sudden release of the German Plot prisoners following the death from influenza of Pierce McCann, a Tipperary TD.[12] Suffering from flu, Art O'Connor was confined to the prison hospital in Durham and was one of nine prisoners unable to travel home due to illness.[13] Following his release the following month, he lost no time in returning to politics by involving himself in Dáil business.[14]

Although the prisoner issue was somewhat resolved in March, two incidents in April triggered a fresh cycle of arrests in Kildare. On 23 April the RIC was refused entry to a Naas SF concert in the town hall. Three days later, at another SF concert in Ballymore Eustace, the police were requested to leave.[15] This was prompted by de Valera's appeal in the Dáil for a boycott of the RIC.[16] Thomas Patterson and Jimmy Whyte, SF members in Naas, were fined, and when they refused to recognize the court or pay up were given sentences in Mountjoy.[17] Likewise, following the episode at Ballymore Eustace, William McGrath of Kilgowan, secretary of the South Kildare SF executive, and Dr Thomas F. O'Higgins, brother of Kevin O'Higgins, TD for Laois, were imprisoned for one month.[18]

Incidents like these were useful for propaganda purposes, enhanced the standing of the republican movement in Kildare and led to great rejoicing following release of the prisoners. McGrath's release was celebrated with a large reception at Newbridge railway station on 19 July. The IRA marched triumphantly through Newbridge and through part of the Curragh on to Athgarvan.[19] The sight of Volunteers marching through Newbridge, past one of the largest cavalry garrisons in the country, then proceeding to the Curragh and passing within one mile of the largest military camp in the country, celebrating the release of a republican prisoner was clearly an embarrassment to the authorities. Receptions had now become a common occurrence for released political prisoners in Kildare. J.J. O'Byrne was released in late May due to ill-health after serving ten months and was given a public reception in Athy on 30 June.[20]

Receptions for released prisoners in Athy were not always peaceful occasions. Official celebrations on 20 July to mark the Peace Treaty (which was signed on 28 June 1919) were cancelled as a protest against the government. A homecoming reception also on 20 July for Seán Hayden, a political prisoner who had been court-martialled the previous January for being in possession of a seditious document, was marred by scuffles between SF supporters and ex-soldiers. The following night the ex-soldiers marked Peace Day before running amok and damaging a bicycle shop. The five local policemen were powerless to intervene.[21] This resulted in calls by Athy UDC to enrol local citizens to preserve the peace.[22] The incident prompted the CI to obtain military assistance from the Curragh to forestall any further potential trouble.[23] At Athy petty sessions those prosecuted for the trouble were described by the magistrates as a pack of savages 'fighting like mad dogs about the streets of Athy.'[24] Peace Day celebrations did not go according to plan in the Curragh camp either. When fireworks caught fire, and rockets went off like machine-guns, thousands of people on the green stampeded and fifty-three were injured.[25] In the aftermath of the Peace Day trouble, extra police were drafted into north Kildare to deal with labour troubles in the region.[26]

A local farm labourers' strike in late June in the Celbridge area soon spread throughout the entire county and created a delicate and complicated situation for SF and the IRA.[27] Kildare farmers were a very powerful lobby with 1,100 affiliated to the Farmers' Union, which had an organization in every district.[28] Farm labourers were by far the largest workforce in the county and were equally well-organized with the majority having joined the ITGWU. Politically, farmers, especially those who belonged to the strong farmer class, were not supporters of SF while their employees, the farm labourers, largely supported the republican movement. The Agricultural Wages Board recommended an increase from £1 8s. per week to £1 12s., but the ITGWU sought £2 5s. per week, which was the going rate for labourers in Dublin city.[29]

The all-out strike posed a dilemma for the Kildare IRA. With farmer pitted against labourer and with intimidation by the strikers a common occurrence, the farmers found themselves driven to seek protection from the RIC. This alarmed the IRA, which had portrayed itself as the army of the republic. Patrick Colgan, commandant North Kildare Battalion and a member of the ITGWU, informed the farmers that if they sought RIC protection, he would encourage the strikers to attack both those needing protection and the police. In return for cooperation on this issue, he offered to assist in keeping order. The farmers accepted Colgan's advice and he told the BMH that the IRA leadership kept both sides within bounds.[30] In south Kildare, Art O'Connor, who came from a strong farmer background, assisted in mediation, but his efforts were unsuccessful.[31] Inevitably, many arrests were made during the strike. At Celbridge assizes, when suspects accused of intimidation appeared in court, the authorities took no chances and fifty armed soldiers were drafted in to keep the peace.[32] The strike was not confined to Kildare. In Meath, an estimated 1,600 ITGWU members were in dispute with the local Farmers' Union.[33] By contrast, in Carlow farmers and their labourers successfully settled their differences.[34] On 20 August, to the relief of all concerned, a compromise was reached between the Farmers' Union and the ITGWU. Agricultural labourers in the Celbridge area and much of north Kildare received an increase of 2s. more than the wage recommended by the Wages Board.[35] One of the ITGWU signatories to the agreement was Michael Smyth in his capacity as a senior union negotiator. With labour difficulties settled, the republican movement could concentrate on extending its electoral mandate at the local elections.

In spring 1919 the government introduced proportional representation for local elections, which, it was hoped, might limit SF's progress.[36] The elections took place in two stages: the towns of Naas, Athy and Newbridge that had municipal status in January 1920 and other councils, such as county councils, district councils and boards of guardians, in June. Nationally, 126 urban centres voted in the first round, and, in contrast to the 1918 general election, only nine of the councils or corporations went uncontested.[37]

In the January urban elections the nine-seat Naas UDC was hotly contested. Eight outgoing Redmondites went forward as independent nationalists. They were opposed by six candidates standing under the collective banner of SF and Labour who cooperated to maximize their vote. This group included Thomas Patterson who had been imprisoned in 1919. The occupations of the various candidates varied, with the outgoing nationalist candidates mainly self-employed merchants and auctioneers, while the republican candidates, who were younger men, included insurance agents and clerks.[38] The turnout was high at sixty-nine per cent; six outgoing nationalists were returned (with a combined sixty-six per cent of the vote) and three from SF and Labour were elected (on thirty-one per cent). The Naas result went against the national trend. It represented a significant victory for the still-sizeable remnants of the

IPP and an underperformance by SF, which claimed that 'the military population had been marched down to the polling booths four deep for the purpose, and they had the police officials' votes, which was not a vote for
republican principles'.[39] The status of Naas as a garrison and county town was
a factor in SF and Labour's poor showing. There was much tension at subsequent meetings of Naas UDC between republican and nationalist members.

In Athy there were fifteen seats to be filled. The turnout was seventy-two
per cent. Labour won seven seats, SF four, independent nationalists two and
unionists two (with a respectable twelve per cent of the vote).[40] This result was
a surprise given Athy's First World War connection. The election for
Newbridge Town Commission proved to be one of the most divisive within the
republican movement with SF and Labour competing against one another and
well-known individuals such as Michael Smyth and Jack Fitzgerald on opposing sides. Although Smyth was a leading IRA and SF figure, he contested the
election as a Labour candidate. Surprisingly, the outgoing nationalists who controlled the town commission conceded without a fight despite the advantage of
the proportional representation system.[41] Four days before the election,
attempts to forge a pact between the two sides ended with an altercation
between the leaders.[42] In a mainly working–class and garrison town, Labour
emerged as the real winners, obtaining a majority of the votes and gaining five
seats to four for SF.[43] After the election in Newbridge, SF refused to support
William Cummins, the Labour nominee for the chairmanship of the town commission. Newbridge became the only town in Ireland where this position was
contested. Labour won, with Cummins defeating Jack Fitzgerald.[44]

The Kildare urban results contrasted sharply with figures at national level.
Excluding Ulster, SF obtained forty-one per cent of the vote, Labour seventeen per cent, Nationalists fourteen per cent, independents twenty-one per
cent and unionists seven per cent.[45] With thirty-three seats available in the
three Kildare towns, Labour was the most successful party with twelve seats.
SF won eight seats, and those under the banner of SF and Labour obtained
three. The level of Labour's success in Kildare was unusual. To the surprise
of many, the expected overwhelming defeat of outgoing nationalists and
unionists who obtained eight and two seats respectively did not materialize.

The June elections in Kildare were contested in every electoral area with
the exception of Clane, where three members were returned unopposed.[46]
Kildare County Council accepted an offer by the IRA to keep order at polling
stations. The RIC, whose remit this would ordinarily be, were withdrawn to
the larger barracks for the day.[47] Apathy was widespread with an unusually
low turnout in many areas of below fifty per cent. The IRA presence at
polling stations, and the fear of their influence on voters, may have deterred
nationalist supporters. Indeed, the extent to which the election was dominated
by republicans could be seen everywhere, even in the garrison town of

Kildare where the tricolour was flying from the polling station with the red flag of Labour nailed to the mast above the tricolour.[48] Predictably, SF gained control of the administrative machinery of the entire county of Kildare, as indeed it did in practically every county in Ireland outside the north-east. Only one outgoing independent nationalist, Michael Fitzsimons, was returned in the county council election; SF won fifteen county council seats and Labour five.[49] The republican success in Kildare County Council was repeated throughout the south of the country. One major difference between the 1918 election and the local elections was a reduced clerical involvement. Most notable was Fr Matthew O'Brien's diminished role in SF politics. In August 1919 he was transferred from Kill to a curacy in Laois.[50] The involvement of Fr John James, curate in Balyna in north-west Kildare, also faded. There is no record of a public chastisement by Bishop Foley, but episcopal censure was probable given their republican credentials.

The success of SF and Labour in Kildare resulted in interesting personnel at the helm at council and board level. Patrick Colgan and Thomas Corcoran were elected chairmen of the Celbridge and Athy Boards of Guardians as Labour nominees, while Thomas Harris and Thomas Patterson, both active IRA members, became chairs of Naas No. 1 RDC and Naas Board of Guardians respectively.[51] A tricolour was attached to the flag pole over Naas courthouse, even though it was adjacent to the CI's office, for the first meeting of Kildare County Council on 24 June.[52] Ua Buachalla was elected chairman and Éamon Ó Modhráin vice chairman. The latter proposed that the council acknowledge the authority of Dáil Éireann with only Fitzsimons dissenting. The new council included five members who had Easter Week connections and, unsurprisingly, a motion to rescind the condemnation of the Easter Rising was carried.[53]

The council's allegiance to the Dáil government soon brought it into conflict with the Local Government Board (LGB), which cut off government grants to the council on 1 October 1920. The following month, the RIC, supported by the military, raided a council meeting and confiscated council records including rate collectors' lodgement abstracts. Although the collection of rates was difficult as many withheld payments, the council continued to function with a loan from the Hibernian Bank. The council denied accusations made by the Dáil and the *Leinster Leader* that compromises made during the dispute were repudiations of the Dáil's authority.[54]

In the aftermath of the local elections, unionism in Kildare continued to fracture with support drifting to yet another splinter group, the Irish Dominion League, formed by Sir Horace Plunkett in June 1919 to promote dominion status for Ireland within the empire as a compromise alternative solution to partition and republicanism.[55] A conference organized largely by the league in Dublin in August 1920 was well supported with a strong representation of Kildare unionists, including Revd Lionel Fletcher, rector of Straffan, Major Henry de Courcy-Wheeler, now an ex-army officer, and George Mansfield, deputy lieutenant, JP and a Catholic unionist member of the landed gentry.[56] Support for the aims of the Irish Dominion League from Kildare was reinforced by magistrates from the south of the county at a meeting in Athy the following month. Twelve magistrates passed a motion that called on the government 'to adopt a measure of the fullest and most comprehensive colonial home rule, if our country is to be saved from ruin'.[57] Many had previously opposed even the most watered-down measure of home rule. The change of stance belied a fear of isolation from the numerically strong Ulster unionist population in a partitioned Ireland. Dominion status also found favour among the military in the Curragh. During a chance conversation between General Jeudwine, O/C 5th Division, and Paddy Mullaney, an IRA officer from Leixlip, at the scene of a minor automobile accident in south Kildare in May 1920, the general indicated that he was in favour of 'colonial home rule'.[58] The exchange took place while the league was introducing a dominion of Ireland bill in the House of Lords which was defeated during its second reading on 1 July 1920.[59]

Opposition to the Government of Ireland bill of 1920, which proposed to establish a northern and southern parliament and would marginalize southern unionists, continued unabated throughout the second half of 1920 with Kildare unionists prominent at executive level of both the IUA and the IAPL.[60] In the House of Lords, Mayo claimed the bill would introduce partition and asked: 'what is to become of the minorties in the south and west ... who gave their sons and daughters' lives during the war, and were they to be left to the tender mercies of a SF parliament?' Mayo suggested that a SF parliament would 'get rid of them [unionists] and tax them out of the country'.[61] Despite considerable support in the Lords, southern unionists failed to muster enough support to block the bill.[62]

To some degree, politics resumed in late spring 1921 when elections to the parliament for southern Ireland held under the Government of Ireland Act necessitated constituency reorganization. Paudeen O'Keeffe TD, general secretary of SF, encountered difficulties when proposing a new five-seat constituency encompassing Kildare and Wicklow (see map 4). When SF in Kildare proved unable to arrange a joint convention, O'Keeffe threatened to allocate all five seats to the better-organized Wicklow side. He also asserted that Domhnall Ua Buachalla did not even know the names of the SF branches in the constituency.[63] The election scheduled for May 1921 did not take place in any meaningful sense, but was used by SF to elect members to the second Dáil; all candidates were returned unopposed. This included Ua Buachalla and Art O'Connor, the sitting TDs for Kildare, together with Wicklow-based Erskine Childers, Robert Barton and Christopher Byrne.[64]

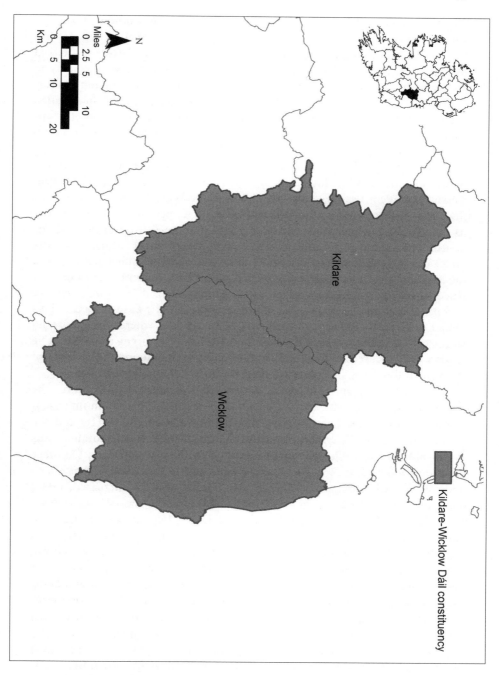

**4** Parliamentary constituencies in 1921 and 1922

The Government of Ireland Act also created a senate for southern Ireland on which Kildare unionists were represented by Lord Mayo, Lord Cloncurry, Sir William Goulding and Sir Bryan Mahon. The latter settled at Mullaboden, Ballymore Eustace following his retirement from the army in 1921 and became involved in County Kildare affairs. The election of May 1921 contributed indirectly to bringing the fighting to an end. Michael Laffan argues that with Ulster unionists now satisfied following the creation of a separate assembly in Northern Ireland, their Conservative mentors were ready to display some flexibility towards nationalist Ireland.[65]

The War of Independence was in large measure a conflict between the police and the IRA. In his classic *The British campaign in Ireland,* Charles Townshend identifies three distinct phases of the War of Independence. The first from 1918 to winter 1919–20 comprised a long period of low-level activity by the IRA which involved boycotting and social ostracization of the police. The second phase during 1920 saw the more direct influence of IRA GHQ being brought to bear in respect of attacks on larger police barracks and the emergence of Dáil courts. The third phase from autumn 1920 until the truce saw a reorganization of the IRA, which engaged in more offensive actions, and an intensification of countermeasures by the Crown forces. This model only partly reflects the experience in Kildare where there were no large-scale attacks on police barracks and few significant engagements. The Kildare IRA focused on smaller operations aimed at hindering the mobility of the Crown forces. It also played a pivotal role in the intelligence war.

As major road and rail networks passed through north Kildare, the Kildare IRA, periodically assisted by Cumann na mBan, played an important communications role by conveying dispatches between IRA GHQ and the south and west of the country. Patrick Colgan, O/C Kildare Battalion, was responsible for dispatch delivery operating from his place of work. On other occasions, letters from Michael Collins were sent to him using his brother's address in Carton demesne.[66] When the volume of work increased, GHQ appointed Michael Fay, an activist from Celbridge, as a special courier from the Kildare Battalion. A medical student in UCD, Fay was able to travel to and from Dublin unnoticed.[67] A system for communication between GHQ and the south of Ireland through central Kildare was also devised. From Dublin, dispatches would proceed through Naas to Kildare and on to the next destination. Dispatches for Dublin came through Kilcullen to Naas and eventually to the city. Various activists were in charge of delivery, with Alphonsus Sweeney responsible in Naas where six couriers were available to convey them.[68] From a communications perspective, it was advantageous to GHQ that north Kildare remained largely peaceful. It was also a safe haven for men on the run. The most famous example occurred in May 1919 when five members of the Tipperary IRA involved in the Soloheadbeg ambush and

Knocklong rescue, including Dan Breen, Seán Treacy and Seán Hogan, were given refuge in Maynooth.[69]

The IRA in Kildare excelled at intelligence-gathering and provided vital assistance to IRA GHQ. In early 1919, Alphonsus Sweeney, intelligence officer in the Naas company, was tipped off by Sergeant Jeremiah Maher, a clerk in CI Supple's office, about his impending arrest due to involvement in the anti-hunt protests. Advised to leave Naas, Sweeney moved to Dublin.[70] Maher continued to pass intelligence to the IRA through Thomas Harris, but grew uneasy given Harris' IRA profile. For this reason, in August 1919 Seán Kavanagh, a Waterford native who moved to Naas as an Irish teacher, became the sole intelligence officer who liaised with Maher.[71] Michael Collins was anxious to obtain secret police cypher codes and directed Maher to assist in this endeavour. Kavanagh obtained police telegrams in cypher from Maher along with decoded copies. Together they decoded the cypher. Subsequently, deciphered RIC messages were passed to Collins. Each month a new cypher was issued, which the CI kept in his safe. Maher succeeded in passing an impression of a key to unlock the safe to Collins who had a duplicate made. This allowed Maher ready access to the safe and the monthly cyphers. Kavanagh visited Maher two or three times a week and passed on every piece of information that might be of interest to the IRA as well as replies to Collins' queries. Maher also recruited Constable Patrick Casey, a fellow policeman in Naas barracks, to assist in intelligence work. One of their most valuable pieces of intelligence concerned a scheme of cooperation between the police and military in the event of major activities on the part of the local IRA. The information pertaining to the military was of considerable importance to Collins.[72] Collins and Kavanagh established a network by which messages were sent through railway employees in Kingsbridge and Sallins. Secret messages and police codes could reach Collins within hours.[73] Messages for the IRA were also conveyed occasionally by Fr Patrick Doyle, a curate in Naas and a close friend of Collins.[74] The intelligence from the CI's office in Naas changed the course of the War of Independence and an analysis of the Kildare IRA's pivotal role has been largely overlooked in the broader historiography.

In mid-August 1920, the RIC discovered that the IRA was obtaining secret police cyphers because when Terence MacSwiney was arrested, he was in possession of the newly issued cypher that had not yet reached the Cork CI. Kavanagh had acquired it from Maher in Naas.[75] The police authorities immediately changed the key but not the type of cypher used or the mode of delivery. Inevitably, Maher came under suspicion from his superiors. He had been offered promotion to head constable, which would have necessitated his transfer from Naas. He declined and continued with his intelligence activities.[76] Maher came under renewed suspicion when, following the Kill ambush in August 1920, firearms permits were withdrawn and the police were ordered to collect the weapons to prevent them falling into the hands of the IRA. However, in many cases the IRA had already collected the arms and clearly had insider information.[77] Although there was no evidence implicating Maher, Collins advised him to resign from the RIC.[78] Unbelievably, Maher was succeeded as clerk to the CI by Casey, who continued to supply intelligence to Kavanagh, including the secret cyphers. In November 1920 Kavanagh learned of his impending arrest and went on the run. He became adjutant Kildare No. 2 Battalion and participated in armed raids on the Dublin to Cork train searching for Dublin Castle mail until his arrest in January 1921.[79]

With the IRA still able to obtain the secret codes, the efficiency of CI Kerry Supple was called into question, and in January 1921 his retirement was announced. Aged 59, he had not been due to retire for another six years.[80] Supple was succeeded by Major Victor Henry Scott, who had been adjutant of Gormanston Black and Tan camp. He proved more efficient than Supple and within a month of his appointment changed his office staff. Casey was transferred to the Down CI's office in Downpatrick and continued to supply intelligence to the 3rd Northern Division IRA.[81]

In January 1919 *An tÓglach*, the IRA organ, declared that every IRA Volunteer was entitled to use 'all legitimate methods of warfare against soldiers and policemen, and to slay them if necessary'.[82] By late 1919 the scale of violence directed against the RIC by the IRA was beginning to have a detrimental effect on the force generally.[83] Although the attacks were initially confined to the south and Dublin, by the late autumn the activity had spread to Meath with attacks on Ballivor and Lismullen RIC barracks.[84] Shortly afterwards, a number of outlying barracks in north Kildare were vacated, including Sallins, Donadea and Ballinadrimna.[85] The Meath IRA was more militant than the Kildare Battalion and posed a danger to isolated barracks close to the Meath–Kildare county boundary. According to the IG, by November 1919 'the police were confronted with almost insuperable difficulties ... owing to the state of terror organized by the Republican Party'.[86] One civilian was shot dead by a military sentry near the Curragh, but little occurred in Kildare until late November when members of the Naas company severed the gas connection to the town hall.[87] More seriously, on 22 December shots were fired into the home of CI Supple on Sallins Road in Naas.[88] This was the first engagement involving the use of firearms and was followed by a second incident at the house on 3 January 1920, when five activists, with Thomas Patterson in charge, fired shots that hit a lower window.[89]

An assault on Baltinglass RIC barracks in County Wicklow in late January, situated two miles from the county boundary with Kildare, sent shock waves throughout the RIC in Kildare. The operation involved up to fifty men, including many from south Kildare.[90] It was a hit-and-run encounter with the perpetrators making no attempts to capture the building. Nevertheless, one constable died and another was wounded. The shooting and the wave of violence were condemned by Bishop Foley, who intimated that the perpetrators faced excommunication.[91] The closure of smaller police barracks was now accelerated in Kildare, beginning with Leixlip in early March (see map 5, p. 82).[92] Practically all the police barracks in rural districts of Kildare had been vacated by mid-March. As a result, large stretches of the countryside were without any police presence. When Robertstown barracks closed, west Kildare became one of the most unpoliced regions in the east of the country, with Edenderry being the nearest barracks to the north, Celbridge to the east and Naas to the south. Art O'Connor, who on occasion did not see eye to eye with the local IRA, refused to cooperate with the destruction of the Mill complex in Celbridge, which housed the local RIC.[93] The three garrison towns of Naas, Newbridge and Kildare were served by larger RIC barracks, with Kilcullen near the Curragh camp also remaining open. The smaller barracks at Kill and Monasterevin on the main Dublin to Cork/Limerick road also continued to operate. The only barracks remaining in south Kildare was at Athy.[94] The number of RIC barracks decreased from twenty-five in the autumn of 1919 to just eight by the summer of 1920 as the preservation of law and order in large areas of rural Kildare had passed from the RIC to the local IRA. The IRA's policing function in Kildare was reported in the *Kildare Observer* in late April 1920.[95]

In late March 1920 rumours that the barracks in Maynooth was to be re-opened prompted the local IRA to burn the building on 3 April.[96] Care was taken to find alternative accommodation for the wife of Sergeant Dunne who resided in the barracks. The destruction prevented re-occupation of the barracks.

That week it was reported that the RIC had returned temporarily to the vacated barracks at Rathangan.[97] At Easter 1920, IRA GHQ authorized the destruction of all vacated barracks and 300 were destroyed throughout the country.[98] The Kildare IRA burned six vacant barracks from Ballinadrimna in the north to Ballitore in the south. In all cases a large number of armed and disguised men took part and the raids were carried out with the greatest speed.[99] The only difficulty was at Leixlip where the local RIC sergeant and his family resided in the building. They were allowed to salvage some belongings before being removed.[100] During summer 1920 the remaining vacated barracks were burned. Sallins required three attempts to complete the task.[101] The consideration shown to the families of RIC in north Kildare was extended to the south of the county. Before the IRA burned Castledermot barracks, arrangements were made for the safe removal of the sergeant's wife, family and furniture. However, the job did not go to plan as an IRA Volunteer was accidently trapped in the burning building and had to be rescued by Paddy Cosgrave, the IRA leader and first cousin of W.T. Cosgrave, a member of the Dáil government.[102]

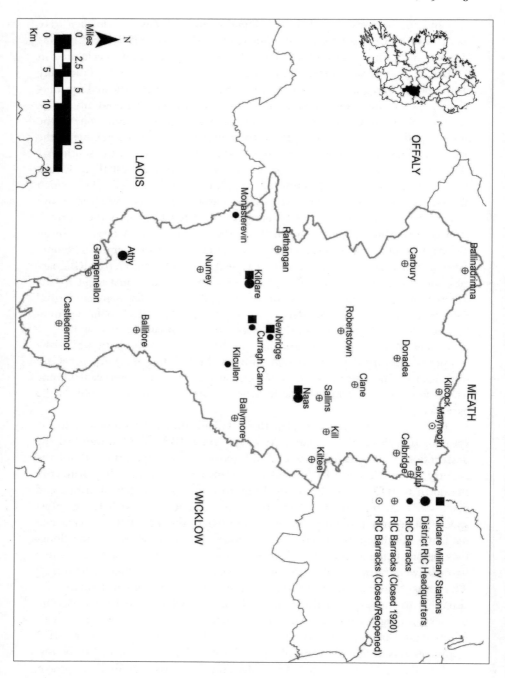

**5** Distribution of the Crown forces

1 (*above, left*) John O'Connor, MP for North Kildare, 1905–18.
2 (*above, right*) Denis Kilbride, MP for South Kildare, 1903–18.
3 Lord Mayo, Kildare unionist leader in the House of Lords.

4 Curragh camp, the largest British army camp in Ireland.

5 (*above*) Michael O'Kelly, editor
of the *Leinster Leader*, 1912–22.
6 Ted O'Kelly, Irish Volunteer
organizer for Kildare, 1915–16.

**7** Group photo of Kildare Easter Week participants from 1938. *Back row, from left*: Patrick Weafer, Tom Byrne, Joseph Ledwith, Thomas Mangan, Matthew Maguire. *Front row, from left*: Pat Kirwan, Thomas Harris, John Maguire, Patrick Colgan, Domhnall Ua Buachalla, Tim Tyrrell, Liam O'Regan. Domhnall Ua Buachalla, TD for North Kildare, 1918–21; Kildare–Wicklow, 1921–2; Kildare, 1927–32; governor general, 1932–6. Thomas Harris, IRA commandant, 1920–2 and ATIRA commandant, 1922–3, he served as a TD from 1931 to 1957. Patrick Colgan, IRA commandant, 1917–21.

8 Eve Burke, Volunteer nurse in the GPO, 1916.

9 Naas RIC barracks, HQ of Kildare RIC. Note, semi-fortified building, barred windows ground floor and projecting window for defensive purposes first floor.

10 Colonel Bertram Portal, commander of the Curragh Special Reserve and operational commander in Dublin, Easter Week, 1916.
11 Captain Henry de Courcy-Wheeler, assistant to General Lowe during Easter Week, 1916 in Dublin.

12 Michael Smyth, SF and Labour councillor and IRA commandant.
13 Art O'Connor, TD South Kildare, 1918–21 and Kildare–Wicklow, 1921–2.

14 Éamon Ó Modhráin, vice chairman Kildare County Council, 1920–2, with his wife Margaret, who was also an activist during the revolution.

**15** (*above*) Sir William Goulding,
leading Kildare Unionist.
**16** Patrick Foley, bishop of
Kildare and Leighlin, 1896–1929.

17 Naas courthouse.
18 Lieutenant General Sir
Hugh Jeudwine, GOC 5th
Division, 1919–22.

**19** Jeremiah Maher, IRA mole in Naas RIC barracks.
**20** Seán Kavanagh, senior Kildare IRA intelligence officer, 1919–20.

**21** Patterson family, Naas. *Left to right*: John, Daisy, Thomas; *front*, Kitty. Daisy and Kitty were members of Cumman na mBan while Thomas was prominent in the IRA.
**22** Ulster Bank, Kilcock, burned during the Belfast boycott, 1921.

23 Hugh Colohan, TD for Kildare–Wicklow, 1922–3, and Kildare, 1923–31.
24 Lieutenant J. Wogan-Browne, killed while resisting an armed robbery in 1922.

**25** Newbridge British army barracks.

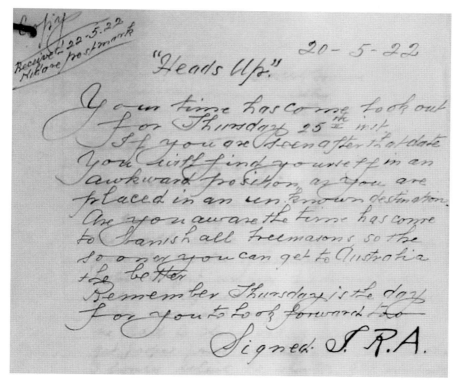

"Heads Up."

Your time has come look out for Thursday 25th inst. If you are seen after that date you will find yourself in an awkward position, as you are placed in an unknown destination. Are you aware the time has come to banish all freemasons so the sooner you can get to Australia the better

Remember Thursday is the day for you to look forward to

Signed. I.R.A.

26 (*above*) A threatening letter from the IRA dated 1922, to Robert Eccles, a loyalist from Athy.
27 Paddy Mullaney, ATIRA commandant during the Civil War.
28 Monsignor Pádraig de Brún (Patrick Browne), professor of mathematics, Maynooth College, pictured with his niece, Máire Mhac an tSaoi (MacEntee). He was arrested for ATIRA sympathies during the Civil War.

29 Tom McHugh with his wife, Lily. McHugh was the longest-surviving Kildare ATIRA commandant.
30 George Wolfe, TD for Kildare, 1923–32.

With the RIC largely neutralized throughout rural Kildare, the local IRA targeted other areas of British administration by destroying a number of courthouses and raiding customs offices. The extent to which the IRA controlled rural towns in Kildare during the late spring and early summer of 1920 was illustrated by the ease with which Maynooth town hall was destroyed when it was believed that the RIC intended to use it to re-establish a police barracks.[103] Stephen O'Reilly, attached to the transport section of the Dublin Brigade, carried out the operation, travelling by train to Maynooth with 30lbs of gelignite. After reporting to Ua Buachalla, he was assisted by the local IRA, including Patrick Colgan. The explosives did not destroy the building, which had to be set on fire.[104] With no British security presence in the area, Michael Collins was able to travel to Maynooth shortly afterwards to inspect the damage.[105]

The closure of Celbridge barracks in August 1920 left only six RIC barracks operating in the county: Naas, Newbridge, Kildare, Kilcullen, Monasterevin and Athy. Unionists felt exposed, but there were only two significant incidents between Kildare unionists and the IRA. The first occurred in late July at Ballindoolan, a remote area of north-west Kildare, when William Tyrrell, an executive member of the IUA and a grandmaster of Edenderry Orange lodge, successfully resisted an attempt by the IRA to seize his firearms.[106] The following month the IRA raided the Hendy family home at Kilcrow House, Athy. The family's submission to the Irish Grants Committee revealed the trauma endured by them. Jane Hendy suffered a nervous breakdown and gave birth prematurely to twins, John and Robert. Her health never recovered and she died in June 1922; her twins predeceased her.[107]

The need to bolster numbers in the RIC was a matter of urgency and the government initiated a recruitment drive in Britain of mainly ex-servicemen. The new force, officially known as the RIC Special Reserve, but nicknamed the Black and Tans, made their appearance in Kildare on 12 April 1920 at a new training depot in Hare Park camp, the Curragh.[108] Two companies of the Auxiliary Division, recruited from ex-army officers, were formed at Hare Park camp in June and July 1920. The RIC Hare Park depot was relocated to Gormanston in October 1920.[109]

From the spring of 1920 the legal system underwent a transformation with the administration of justice carried out by a new republican courts system instigated by Dáil Éireann.[110] Until June 1920, they only provided for arbitration courts but had greater powers thereafter. Two types of courts emerged, parish courts with powers to deal with claims of under £10 and district courts for more serious offences.[111] By May 1920 republican courts were reported in the garrison towns and surrounding areas. In Newbridge, three men who pleaded guilty to stealing oats were fined and ordered to make immediate restitution.[112] When cattle were reported missing in the Kilcullen area and sheep from the Curragh borders, the IRA investigated the matter and arrested five men. Subsequently, it was indicated that some of the cattle had been returned to the owners.[113]

As the summer of 1920 progressed, republican police recruited from the ranks of the IRA emerged. An order issued by Richard Mulcahy in June 1920 provided for a police officer to be appointed at company, battalion and brigade level.[114] On 18 July, a SF meeting was held publicly in Athy workhouse to elect republican magistrates and to arrange for courts that would oust the Crown court system.[115] By this point, IRA or republican police had all but replaced the RIC in north Kildare, where 'volunteer police patrols' were active nightly in Maynooth and Kilcock enforcing an order issued by Dáil Éireann that public houses should only supply drink from 7 a.m. until 10.30 p.m.[116] Republican police were also vigilant at various outdoor social events, and on one occasion in early July at an aeridheacht in Ballitore, two policemen in plain clothes were detected and removed by the IRA.[117] In the first week of August two republican courts which were open to the public were held in the Christian Brothers school in Kilcock with solicitors representing the plaintiffs and the defendants in attendance.[118]

One of the most remarkable achievements of SF was to make the administration of justice through the Crown courts unworkable in large areas of Kildare and instigate a parallel mechanism in the form of republican courts from the spring of 1920. However, the scale of apparent public acceptance of republican courts outside the major towns was not surprising due to a gap left by the withdrawal of the RIC from rural areas. Successful policing by the IRA, which prevented a breakdown of law and order particularly in rural areas, further reduced the acceptability of the RIC among nationalists in the county. This was illustrated during the trial of Joseph Cusack, a SF county councillor from Robertstown, arrested for being in possession of seditious documents. Cusack admitted that he settled small differences at republican courts in the absence of any other authority and stated that 'If they did not keep the blackguards down they would be over-run by them'. Cusack was found not guilty and discharged.[119]

In tandem with the campaign against the RIC was an attack on the prison system with a surge of hunger strikes in Irish and English jails. Since January 1919 IRA prisoners had been under orders to defy the prison regulations and generally to subvert prison discipline if denied political status.[120] On 2 October all DORA prisoners in Mountjoy sought full political status through their spokesman, Kildare 1916 leader Ted O'Kelly, who was serving a two-year sentence for political activities.[121] When the authorities refused, many of the prisoners, including O'Kelly, went on hunger strike. A riot in the prison involving forty-four prisoners ensued on 5 October. Two days later, O'Kelly, the ringleader, was transferred to a prison in Derry, but his health deteriorated and he was released under the Cat and Mouse Act on 11 October, which meant that he was liable to re-arrest if he re-offended. Under the same provision the first batch of prisoners on hunger strike in Mountjoy was released on 14 October and over the next week all were freed.[122] Kildare IRA activist, Richard Higgins, who had been arrested in September when two pounds of gunpowder were found in his premises, subsequently joined the hunger strike, but was released in early November when his health deteriorated.[123]

The hunger strike continued to be used by the IRA in 1920. In April Athy's Éamon Malone was part of the leadership group behind the hunger strike in Mountjoy led by Peadar Clancy.[124] Malone was commandant 5th Battalion and later O/C of the Carlow Brigade. On the run since September 1918, he was arrested in November 1919 and had been intermittently on hunger strike since Christmas. He was commandant of the prisoners in the jail before and during the strike.[125] Within a week, 101 men were refusing food. Thousands gathered outside the prison and scuffles with the troops on guard became menacing.[126] By the beginning of the second week the city's attention seemed directed entirely upon the prison and the Catholic hierarchy intervened, condemning the government.[127] The two prelates with authority in Kildare – Archbishop Edward Byrne and Bishop Foley – issued several statements during the War of Independence. Although they stopped short of recognizing Dáil Éireann, they continually reaffirmed the right of the Irish people to self-determination.[128]

In this highly-charged atmosphere labour leaders called for a general strike on 12 April.[129] This was observed throughout the country, apart from Belfast and Derry. In many cases it led to workers taking control of their towns. Even Naas, which had elected a majority of independent nationalists three months previously, was virtually taken over by local trade union activists who formed a strike committee (council) headed by Thomas Patterson, president of the local branch of the ITGWU.[130] Thomas Foran, who participated in the Naas protest, recalled that 'if a shop had dared to open there would have been murder'.[131] A procession through the town was attended by almost 1,000 people of all classes and creeds. For the third year in a row, Punchestown races was a casualty of the civil unrest.[132] The strike in Naas was a remarkable success.[133] Newbridge and Kildare were also taken over by strikers. Businesses were closed and work suspended, including the Newbridge fair. In Kildare, strong pickets were mounted each night as the police were withdrawn from the streets.[134] The local strike committee styled itself 'The Kildare Soviet' and there were accusations of intimidation of army employees.[135]

Rail communications were closed down on 13 April when workers of the Great Southern & Midland Company refused to move any trains. The use of the main Dublin to Cork road was seriously curtailed as Naas was firmly controlled by labour activists and Newbridge was also in the hands of the strikers. The British army in Kildare was therefore virtually cut off from the out-side world. At Easter 1916, regiments from Kildare could reach Dublin within five hours, but this was not possible in April 1920 as the crisis in Mountjoy unfolded and rumours of a new rising circulated. With strike com-mittees controlling virtually every town outside the north-east, the country was fast receding into the equivalent, as Conor Kostick suggests, of the Russian Revolution of February 1917.[136] In most places the police abdicated their responsibilities and the maintenance of order was taken over by the local workers councils.

Lord French and General Nevil Macready, GOC of the British army, knowing that the government was shaken by the militancy of the general strike, decided to release the hunger strikers on parole.[137] The official who wrote the release order failed to note that half the strikers, as sentenced men rather than internees, were not entitled to parole.[138] The error delivered a dra-matic republican triumph.[139] Celebrations greeted the released men through-out the country. In Athy, Éamon Malone was given a hero's welcome by 3,000 well-wishers, including a large contingent of ex-army men.[140] During the crisis, SF politicians, both nationally and locally, were sidelined by the events. According to Kostick, the two days of general strike did more to undermine British authority than months of armed struggle.[141] Lieutenant General Sir Hugh Jeudwine, commander of the 5th Division based in the Curragh from 1919 until 1922, regarded the wholesale prisoner release as having a detrimental effect on relations between the army and civilians which up to that point had been good.[142] Furthermore, the outcome was a severe blow to the police, the prison system and the Dublin Castle administration.[143]

The munitions strike of 1920 also created difficulties for the British army. From 1 June railwaymen in Kildare refused to handle munitions or operate troop trains and the strike continued until December. It generated an unusual unity of support for the railway workers from politicians and clergy.[144] For General Jeudwine the strike caused a great inconvenience and steps had to be taken to convey armed personnel and munitions by road.[145] The strike, which lasted for eight months, resulted in the widespread dismissal of workers and was not broken until December of 1920.[146] The terrain of the 5th divisional area, especially the Bog of Allen, was covered with a haphazard network of narrow secondary and third-class roads. The poor state of the roads assisted the IRA who, as discussed below, successfully interrupted army communica-tions from December 1920.[147]

The second phase of the War of Independence, as outlined by Townshend – the ambushing of police patrols to obtain arms – was slow to begin in Kildare. Kill barracks, which was manned by twenty-two men, was the only Kildare police establishment located outside the towns. A party of RIC regularly cycled from the barracks to take up guard duty at the Naas residence of the CI, a distance of almost four miles. On the night of 21 August, four policemen were ambushed at Greenhills near Kill. Sergeant Reilly and Constable Haverty subsequently died of their wounds and the two others were captured. The IRA seized two revolvers and two carbines.[148] Evidence differs as to whether the police were given adequate opportunity to surrender. At the inquest, one of the survivors stated that a call to surrender was accompanied by a volley of shots, whereas James Dunne told the BMH that Reilly opened fire when called on to surrender, which led to general firing.[149] Haverty was 39 years old, single and had been in the force for nineteen years. Reilly was married, and after twenty-six years' service was just three weeks from retirement. In 1916 he had been in charge of Swords barracks, which was captured by the Irish Volunteers.[150] The ambush was widely condemned, with the most vocal criticism coming from Bishop Foley, who referred to the encounter as assassination and murder.[151] However, the horror was quickly overtaken by acts of retaliation by the police when, on 26 August, a party of twenty heavily armed Black and Tans arrived in Kill by lorry and looted and shot up Broughall's public house.[152] The following night they turned their attention to Naas and burned Boushells' shop. Despite the proximity of the RIC barracks, the police did not intervene.[153] The incident caused hysteria among the civilian population of Naas, with some families leaving their homes and staying with friends. The incident damaged the reputation of the RIC in Naas and ended any sympathy that had existed for the RIC fatalities at Kill.[154]

After the Kill ambush, Celbridge and Kill barracks, the last remaining RIC barracks in north Kildare, were vacated and subsequently burned by the IRA.[155] The ambush also led to an increasing number of resignations from the RIC.[156] David Fitzpatrick has shown that in the country as a whole, 1,590 RIC men resigned during 1920 and 1,428 in 1921. However, Terence Dooley records only eight policemen resigning in Kildare between January 1920 and July 1921.[157] Kildare magistrates also resigned with seven resigning in one week in early September.[158] Attacks on the Kildare RIC continued in September when Constable Everard who was off-duty and James Doyle, an ex-soldier from Baltinglass suspected of being a spy, were ambushed at Coolrake, near Moone. Both suffered gun-shot wounds but escaped.[159]

As 1920 progressed the IRA became better organized and trained. In July, a training camp was established at Ladytown, Naas, under the control of Peadar McMahon, a GHQ organizer. The following month, Dowdingstown House, four miles south of Naas, was taken over as battalion headquarters, and fortnightly meetings of the battalion council were held there.[160] A reorganization of the Kildare Battalion, which controlled an extensive area of northern Kildare and some adjoining areas, was undertaken by McMahon in September when two new battalions were formed: the Kildare No. 1, encompassing the northern region with Patrick Colgan in charge; the remaining area became Kildare No. 2 under Thomas Harris.[161]

In October the Kildare IRA experienced a major setback when an arms and ammunition dump close to Monasterevin was discovered. This at least partially explains the lack of militancy in late 1920.[162] Another reason was a reluctance by some in the local leadership to engage in ruthless activities, and for very good reasons. In the wake of the death of Terence MacSwiney, Éamon Ó Modhráin, a senior figure in both SF and the IRA, was discharged from the Volunteers by GHQ for refusing to kill unarmed RIC men. Ó Modhráin, who knew the situation on the ground far better than his superiors in Dublin, was fully aware of the sympathies of many RIC members to the movement, and argued that the IRA were obtaining vital intelligence from friendly policemen. He was reinstated on appeal.[163] The spate of arrests after Bloody Sunday, 21 November 1920, was another major factor that contibuted to the lack of militancy in Kildare. Throughout the country, over 500 arrests were made and this included virtually the entire IRA leadership in Kildare, notably Thomas Harris, Thomas Patterson and Jack Fitzgerald.[164] The authorities also tracked down IRA figures on the run such as Colgan, Ó Modhráin and Éamon Malone, O/C Carlow Brigade.[165] They were held in Hare Park, the military prison camp in the Curragh. Vice commandants had to step up with Michael Smyth becoming O/C Kildare No. 2 Battalion and Frank Purcell O/C No. 1 Battalion.[166] The Bloody Sunday arrests filled Ballykinlar internment camp and a new internment centre called Gibbet Rath camp was established at the Curragh for prisoners from the 5th Division and the Dublin District. In due course there were inmates from every area of the 5th Division, and every parish in Kildare.[167] The most prominent were Desmond Fitzgerald and Rory O'Connor. Escape attempts from Rath camp were a regular occurrence. One of the first to succeed was Rory O'Connor who escaped with another prisoner disguised as construction workers.

The second phase of the War of Independence saw the attempted enforcement of the Belfast boycott in Kildare. This was initiated in August 1920 in response to the outbreak of sectarian violence in Belfast. Resolutions in favour of boycotting goods from Belfast and later from Britain were passed by local government bodies in Kildare between mid-August and mid-September.[168] The organized destruction of Belfast goods began on 8 October when forty bags of bran were taken from a Kildare town railway goods store and burned. Two days later, five cases of boots from a Belfast firm were taken at Maganey station.[169] English Sunday papers were also targeted with a consignment burned at Sallins.[170] After an initial upsurge, interest in the boycott declined until the spring of 1921 when a re-escalation of activity began. By April, many shops in Kildare stocking goods from Belfast had been raided.[171] Flax crops grown on land rented by Belfast merchants were also targeted and in

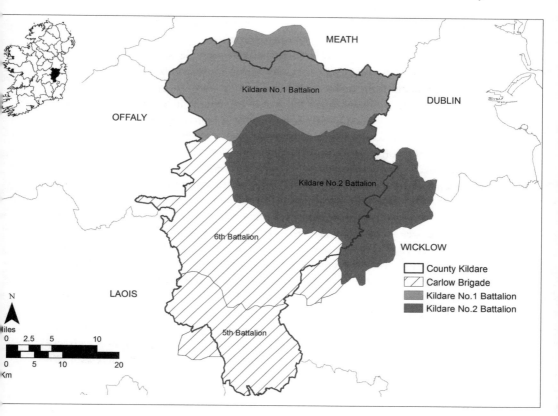

**6** Kildare IRA battalion areas, September 1920

many cases the crops were destroyed.[172] In addition, some food destined for the military was targeted. For example, twenty tons of flour was taken off a barge at Robertstown and thrown into the canal by the IRA.[173] Overall, however, enforcement of the Belfast boycott in Kildare was well below the level that obtained in other counties. According to a Dáil report it was the sixth lowest.[174] The most serious incident during the boycott campaign was the burning of the newly built Ulster Bank premises in Kilcock on 15 March 1921. The IRA believed the building was due to be used as a barracks for the Crown forces, but this was discounted by the CI. There followed a concerted effort by the IRA to force Ulster Bank account holders throughout the county to withdraw their business from the bank.[175] Some were even threatened with having their houses burnt. In most cases this had the desired effect. The boycott caused considerable hardship for local traders while depriving the public of much-needed commodities that were not available in the south.

During the third phase of the War of Independence the Crown forces stepped up counterinsurgency measures. One indication of this was the commencement in October 1920 of a three-day guerrilla warfare course at the Curragh consisting of lectures and practical exercises.[176] There was greater coordination between units of the military at the Curragh and the police. Under DORA, military courts operated in several locations including the Curragh.[177] The Curragh garrison provided a GHQ reserve called 'The Curragh Mobile Column', which comprised one convoy regiment and one squadron of cycles, a composite battalion of three companies of infantry cycles, a section of royal engineers (cycle and motor transport), one section of eighteen pounders and a supply of baggage column of motor vehicles. Military duties included provision of guards and escorts, conducting patrols, searches and arrests. Between 1 January 1921 and the truce in the 5th Divisional area some 1,600 arrests were made.[178] One of the most spectacular military drives took place between 27 May and 16 June 1921 in the north-midlands where the 5th Division employed four regiments, reinforced by local infantry units, to traverse eight counties. The operation began and ended in the Curragh.[179] Jeudwine later admitted that the drives produced little results beyond providing excellent training operations.[180]

Although these operations increased popular discontent with the military, the army was not targeted to the same degree as in several other counties. One incident in the spring of 1921 shows the extent to which the military and IRA co-existed in the Curragh region during this period. On the night of 13 February three masked men armed with revolvers approached while a private from the 12th Lancers and his 24-year-old girlfriend from Newbridge were courting on a by-road. They requested the soldier to leave the scene and for the girl to remain. The private, suspecting their intention was to cut the girl's hair as a punishment for keeping company with a soldier, refused to comply. The armed men, at that point, warned them not to return to that area again and departed without harming the couple.[181] This is one of the many examples of the IRA in Kildare acting in a more lenient manner when compared to Munster.

In early 1921 the policing presence in Kildare was increased. Larine House in Maynooth became the Black and Tans headquarters for north Kildare.[182] Police patrols were restored throughout the town. On the night of 21 February a six-man patrol was ambushed near the Catholic church and Sergeant Hughes was fatally wounded. The 34-year-old was a native of Wolfhill, County Laois, with twelve years of service.[183] According to Paddy Mullaney, vice commandant Kildare No. 1 Battalion, it was a big operation carried out by the Kilcock company with other contingents assisting in outpost duty, but it failed in its principal aim to capture weapons. Mullaney revealed how poorly armed his men were. They had only shot-guns and due to dampness, the cartridges had to be heated before use.[184] Once again, ordinary people bore the brunt of this serious ambush when fears of retaliation by the Black and Tans led to an almost complete evacuation of the civilian population from Maynooth.

There was also a psychological toll on serving policemen with the violence they both feared and experienced leaving many disturbed and unsettled,[185] including in quiet counties such as Kildare.[186] On 19 February Constable Thomas Bradshaw committed suicide in a stable at the rear of the Monasterevin barracks before he was to take part in a patrol.[187] On 7 March Constable Harold Stiff, originally from London and stationed in Maynooth, likewise committed suicide in the barracks.[188] Coming two weeks after the Maynooth ambush, this tragic event bore similarities with the suicide of Cadet Henry Spenle in Dublin on Bloody Sunday, which his comrades believed was the result of the terror he experienced that morning.[189]

For a short time in the spring of 1921 Séamus Finn, director of training for the Eastern Division of the IRA, was sent to Kildare. He noted that the Kildare battalions were not as well developed as in other areas and that the county posed more challenges in comparison to other counties for engaging in a successful campaign. He described Kildare as

> honeycombed with police and military. Naas was chuck full and the Curragh was right in our centre. The country was as flat as a proverbial pancake and the cavalry [motorized security forces] were operating in rather strong forces. The curfew was at 10 p.m. while there was a complete ban on the use of bicycles.[190]

The military presence was more significant than in any other county. In May 1921 there were 5,348 men of all ranks in Kildare, of which 4,177 were stationed in the Curragh camp, 651 in Newbridge, 452 in Kildare town, and 68 in Naas.[191] This was in marked contrast to other neighbouring counties such as Meath where 563 soldiers were stationed, Offaly with 536, and Laois with 76.[192] Nonetheless, under Finn, Kildare No. 2 Battalion became more active, but the focus was on the RIC not the military. Three ambushes were scheduled for Easter 1921 but failed to transpire. The most significant was an ambush of a police tender on the Hill of Allen, but this failed when the lorry did not appear at the expected time.[193] An IRA Active Service Unit (ASU) was formed in the Kildare No. 2 area in April 1921 under the command of Martin O'Neill, an ex-British soldier from Ballymore Eustace.[194] The CI believed that the ASU assisted the Carlow No. 6 Battalion which was responsible for firing at Athy RIC barracks on 22 May and Kilcullen barracks four days later.[195] These incidents followed an unsuccessful IRA ambush at Barrowhouse in Laois close to Athy, just outside the Kildare county boundary, on 16 May in which two IRA Volunteers were killed.

Kildare No. 1 Battalion assisted GHQ with attempts to hamper troop trains. In June 1921, King George V opened the new Northern Ireland parliament and substantial numbers of soldiers were drafted into Belfast including many from the Curragh. Troop trains returning to Dublin were attacked at Adavoyle in south Armagh and at Killester near Dublin. Another train carrying 700 soldiers of the King's Own Yorkshire Light Infantry to the Curragh was targeted with Michael Collins personally choosing Stacumny, close to Celbridge, as the ambush point, where the tracks would be blown up as the train passed. This was the biggest planned IRA operation in Kildare during the War of Independence with Volunteers from Meath, Dublin and Kildare mobilized for the job. Seán Boylan, O/C Eastern Division, was in overall command.[196] Paddy Mullaney, who provided local knowledge of the area, reported afterwards that there were more than 120 men present.[197] As with other planned ambushes in Kildare, Stacumny ended in failure. Alerted by fallen trees in the area, the authorities scrambled a patrol of the South Lancashire Regiment from Baldonnell, which surprised the IRA as the train, accompanied by a spotter plane, was approaching. There was a brief exchange of fire before the entire IRA contingent escaped.[198]

Following Stacumny, attacks on troop trains continued with a raid on 8 July at Ballyfermot bridge on a train carrying an advance party of the 2nd Gordon Highlanders to the Curragh. At this point, due to the IRA offensive against troop trains, transport of troops by rail was temporarily suspended. This caused considerable inconvenience for the army. The main body of the 2nd Gordon Highlanders had to travel on foot to the Curragh and did not arrive until 10 July.[199] The Stacumny ambush was the only incident during the War of Independence in which shots were fired at regular British soldiers in Kildare. Significantly, however, no shots were fired by Kildare IRA members on that occasion.

The Cumann na mBan in Kildare were active throughout the War of Independence and did much useful work by carrying dispatches, arms and ammunition, fund raising and distributing food parcels to interned or imprisoned IRA members.[200] Branches were present in all the big towns with membership ranging from fifteen in Castledermot to seven in Leixlip. They also flourished in rural areas such as Maganey in the southern tip of the county which had six members fronted by Mary Malone.[201] Another rural branch was located at Two-Mile-House, where Molly Curran studied Morse code.[202] Many of the most prominent members were close relatives of well-known SF and IRA activists such as Bridget and Fanny O'Connor, sisters of Art O'Connor TD. May and Fanny Dunne were daughters of Patrick Dunne of Kill. Mary Cosgrave was a sister of Paddy Cosgrave of Castledermot. Kitty Patterson, who served as adjutant of the North Kildare executive, was a sister of Thomas Patterson, and another sister, Daisy, was active in both Kildare and Dublin.[203] Peggie and Lucy Daly from Kildare town were sisters of Katie Daly who was active during Easter Week.[204] Claire Moran from Naas served as president of the North Kildare executive.[205] The best-known Cumann na mBan activist associated with Kildare was Brigid O'Mullane who was sent to the county by the executive of the movement in late 1920 as an organizer.[206] However, her work came to an abrupt end when she was mistaken by the locals for a spy during the mass arrests that followed Bloody Sunday. She was obliged to leave Kildare for her own safety as the local IRA had plans to kill her.[207] O'Mullane learned afterwards from Máire Comerford that there was a female spy operating in Kildare. The spy was sentenced to leave the country following a republican court-martial.[208] Only one member of Cumann na mBan was arrested in Kildare – Nelly Wallace, daughter of a Newbridge shopkeeper, who was detained overnight on 8 April 1921.[209] The Crown forces were hampered by a lack of female searchers. According to General Jeudwine, throughout 1920 there were practically no female searchers in the whole of the 5th Divisional area, and by June 1921, there were only twelve.[210]

Fianna Éireann was not as strong in Kildare as in other counties. During the War of Independence a branch emerged in Newbridge under Patrick Fullam for which some records have survived. In general, the Fianna were regarded as a recruitment body for the local IRA. Accordingly, Fullam and James Clancy progressed to full membership of the IRA. By mid-1921 membership of the Newbridge Fianna stood at thirty-six, with 17-year-old James Sheehan in charge.[211] An examination of census records indicates that most of the members were aged between sixteen and seventeen with two as young as fourteen. Some were siblings of other republican activists. For example, Patrick Wallace was a brother of Nelly Wallace.[212]

Small operations such as disrupting communications, severing telephone and telegraph wires, and raiding mails achieved greater success than bigger and more violent operations. Trenching roads, felling trees and damaging bridges involved considerable risk and required greater manpower than ambushes. The first road-cutting to impede the mobility of the Crown forces was recorded at Christmas 1920 in Rathangan.[213] Until the truce in July 1921 there were regular and numerous reports of IRA efforts to disrupt communications. For example, in March 1921 there were thirty-six reported incidents.[214] By June, so many roads and bridges had been blocked or destroyed that even horse-drawn cavalry had difficulty travelling. One cavalry officer wondered: 'if it is like this within twenty miles of the Curragh, what is it going to be like in Cork (the rebel stronghold)?'[215]

As IRA activity escalated, the military authorities, on two occasions, imposed restrictions under the Restoration of Order Act in Kildare. The first was in response to a series of road trenchings and the demolition of bridges in the Castledermot area in early February. The order signed in the Curragh on 15 February prohibited the holding of fairs and markets within a five-mile radius of Castledermot. Following the ambush in Maynooth, a similar order was issued on 25 February banning fairs and markets within a two-mile radius of the town.[216] This restriction was another example of the effect the ongoing unrest had on civilians' lives. After the March incidents, the RIC responded by arresting a number of individuals in the Naas area, which included Michael O'Kelly, who until that time, despite his active behind the scenes involvement, had escaped detection.[217] Michael Smyth's March report to GHQ detailed an intensification of activities. However, his superiors' response was mixed. While they supported measures such as road blocking that required few men, they expressed concern about mustering large numbers without proper training, citing the example of the abortive Hill of Allen ambush in which fifty-five men were mobilized.[218]

The disruption to mail courier services prompted the military to initiate an air mail facility, which was undertaken three times weekly from Baldonnell to the Curragh and other stations in the 5th Divisional area. A daily postal lorry service between the Curragh and GHQ Dublin was also introduced during this period.[219] In addition, by 1921 all the major barracks in the division were connected with the army's wireless transmitting service including Coolmany in the Glen of Imaal.[220] The disruption to communications also inconvenienced the civilian population of Kildare. Dorothea Findlater, daughter of Captain de Courcy-Wheeler, recalled having to climb 'over two or three trees getting from our house in Robertstown to church in Kilmeague two miles away on Sundays'.[221] When the truce was declared, numerous roads were impassable. The Crown forces left it to Kildare County Council to clear them.[222]

Inevitably in a garrison county, activity by informers was a cause of concern to the IRA.[223] At the second attempt Philip Dunne, who lived close to the Hill of Allen, was fatally wounded by the IRA in mid-June 1921.[224] Michael Power, an ex-serviceman from Nurney, was another identified as a suspected spy. Initially, he took refuge in the nearby Curragh camp when sentenced to banishment by a republican court. But on 10 June, while visiting the house of a relative close to the Curragh camp, he was shot dead by a party of IRA.[225] As a result, some other suspect spies, including a woman, who were under observation by the IRA, took refuge in the Curragh camp. Suspected spies were also punished in other localities such as in Castledermot where a man was paraded in front of the congregation emerging from Mass with a placard indicating that he had given information to the authorities.[226] Lists of suspects were forwarded by the IRA in Edenderry and Naas to GHQ.[227] Although the IRA took effective measures against a small number of suspected informers, they did little to weed out such activities. Dooley suggests that they did not seem to have had the necessary callous streak to exterminate them.[228] The fact that only two suspected spies, a civilian and an ex-serviceman, were killed, demonstrates further how quiet Kildare was during this phase of the conflict. A number of other individuals suspected of being spies were threatened with violence or ordered to leave the country.[229] One example of the latter was 26-year-old Paul Goodwin from Fontstown, Athy, who was ordered to leave Kildare in June 1921. After a one month in England, he moved to Longford and returned home some months later.[230] Violence directed against unionists in Kildare was not as widespread or fatal as in the more violent counties, with the IRA more inclined to give warnings in advance, which obtained the desired results. According to Peter Hart, areas which experienced a low level of IRA violence witnessed a low level of state violence: violence was cyclical.[231] This certainly applies to Kildare where the pattern of IRA activity was low-key and violence by the Crown forces was notably lower than in other counties.

The King's speech at the opening of the Northern Ireland parliament in June set in motion a series of contacts and meetings that led to a truce. This came into effect on 11 July 1921. During the War of Independence there were eleven fatalities attributable to political violence in County Kildare: no British military, five police (this includes two suicides), five civilians and one IRA member. One civilian, Patrick Gavin, appears to have been accidentally shot in February 1919 by a British army sentry on the approaches to the Curragh camp.[232] Two other civilian deaths occurred in Newbridge on 7 July when the IRA burned the Navy and Air Force canteen, killing (unintentionally) Bridget Doran and her 13-year-old step-son, John.[233] Jack (Seán) Sullivan, a Kildare IRA volunteer, died outside the county in Ballykinlar following an assault after his arrest; he was the only Kildare IRA man to die during the conflict.[234]

The low number of fatalities illustrates the sharp difference in IRA effectiveness between Kildare and the adjacent midland counties. Nonetheless, the IRA was virtually able to gain control of much of the countryside and smaller towns in the county due to the abandonment of rural RIC barracks. They also successfully established Dáil courts. SF's political progress at local government level saw various councils and boards transfer their allegiance to Dáil Éireann – an important aspect of sustaining the Dáil counter-state. The Kildare IRA had little success in acquiring arms. Of the four attempted or actual ambushes, only one yielded captured firearms. Although small quantities of firearms were obtained from the Curragh camp, no serious attempt was made to acquire weaponry from the ordnance store there, the largest store of military equipment in the country. Despite facing a sizeable military presence which severely restricted movement and organization, the Kildare IRA certainly made enough of a nuisance of itself to disrupt communications and pin down Crown forces that might have been deployed elsewhere. The most significant contribution during the War of Independence was in the acquisition of high level intelligence from the CI's office in Naas. While engaging in low-level militancy, the IRA in Kildare managed to avoid any serious defeat at the hands of the vastly superior Crown forces and despite the arrests of key figures, they remained a strong force as the country entered a new phase.

# 7 From truce to Civil War, July 1921–June 1922

The period between the truce negotiations in the summer of 1921 and the outbreak of Civil War in late June 1922 saw the most radical transformation of the country's political system in over seven centuries. This chapter examines in turn the political and military developments in Kildare during the period. Kildare overwhelmingly supported the Anglo-Irish Treaty. In the June 1922 general election more than eighty per cent of the vote favoured pro-Treaty candidates. Labour were the real winners, with the constituency recording the fourth-highest percentage of Labour support in the country and returning the only deputy from Kildare county to the third Dáil.[1] The withdrawal of the British army from Kildare was the defining development of this period. With the emergence of the new state, a new army and Civic Guard were instituted; both had strong early connections to Kildare. The beginnings of the National army in Celbridge in January 1922 are not well known. Eight years after the Curragh incident, Kildare was once again at the centre of a mutiny when the Civic Guard in Kildare barracks was involved in a potentially explosive stand-off with the Provisional government. A majority of the IRA remained loyal to the government.

The truce was announced simultaneously by the British and Irish sides. The IRA would cease all attacks and the British would end military manoeuvres, raids and searches. An undefeated IRA was allowed retain its arms and activists on the run were permitted to return home without fear of arrest. Generally, the IRA viewed the truce as a form of victory. As General Jeudwine put it, IRA leaders 'came out of their hiding places – convincing themselves and the population generally they had won the war'.[2] Similarly, the CI in Offaly reported the jubilation of the republican movement.[3] The general public in Kildare welcomed the truce. The local press reported celebratory bonfires in several areas, including Newbridge, Kildare and Athy. While the IRA endeavoured to ensure that the conditions for the truce were being observed, the military, likewise, displayed an eagerness to keep its side of the agreement.[4] To ensure that the agreement operated smoothly, truce liaison officers were appointed by both sides. Thomas Lawler from Naas, who succeeded Michael Smyth as O/C Naas Battalion, was appointed liaison officer with responsibility for north Kildare; in the Carlow Brigade area of south Kildare, Liam Stack, O/C Carlow Brigade, was appointed.[5]

Reaction to the truce among the Crown forces was mixed. The RIC greeted the news with uncertainty and were suspicious that the force would be let down by the British government.[6] The Kildare CI reported that the IRA behaved in an exemplary way, but, nonetheless, the police were still subjected to intimidation when travelling outside the county.[7] The British military did not relax general precautions. According to Jeudwine, his

> officers could not but feel humiliation and disappointment at the necessity for treating on equal terms with those whom they regarded as callous and treacherous murderers, and among those victims were reckoned many of their friends.[8]

The military authorities also found it unpalatable to be forced to refer to the armistice as a truce. General Macready preferred the term 'agreement' and regarded its effects as a 'Suspension of Activities'.[9] There was also a distaste for dealing with the IRA liaison officers, a class which Jeudwine asserted 'left much to be desired'. He referred disparagingly to Liam Stack as merely a chemist's assistant. The rank and file were relieved at the truce which promised if not a quick release from duties in Ireland then at least more uninterrupted sleep. The British army complied promptly with the truce regulations and by 14 July all restrictions, besides curfew, had been removed from the 5th Division area. People could once again move freely.

    Although Kildare unionists welcomed the truce, there was an inherent fear that the release of IRA prisoners might result in revenge attacks on them. Such fears were justified. As Brian Hughes has shown, the IRA could achieve 'cooperation' from local communities through fear and intimidation rather than by generating support.[10] Soon after the truce, intimidation of unionists, particularly those who had regular contact with the RIC, the army, or the Dublin Castle authorities, began.[11] Claims made to the Irish Grants Committee (IGC) indicate that unionists in south Kildare were more likely to suffer intimidation than those in north Kildare, which was closer to Dublin. In some instances, government agencies issued warnings and offered advice to persons in danger. For example, four days after the truce came into force Leonard Wilson-Wright, high sheriff of Kildare and a cousin of Sir Henry Wilson, received an urgent telegram from London advising him to leave Ireland immediately as his life was in danger. Wilson-Wright, who lived in Timahoe, an isolated area of west Kildare where the nearest RIC barracks was twelve miles away in Edenderry, left Ireland as directed.[12]

    From the beginning the terms of the truce were interpreted differently by the opposing sides. As a result, breaches occurred and the liaison officers were kept busy. The IRA seemed to test the water initially, but gradually flexed its muscles and eventually controlled the countryside outside the big towns in Kildare. By mid-July the RIC reported that the IRA was engaged in drilling at various locations in the county.[13] The military authorities were aware of the situation. Within a week of the truce they received news of drilling and training by the IRA on an extensive scale. On 18 August it was reported that an

IRA training camp had been established at Duckett's Grove on the Carlow–Kildare county boundary.[14] The IRA was also enlisting new members (so-called trucileers), which was clearly a breach of the truce. According to the RIC, the local liaison IRA officer gave the impression of being annoyed over the matter and reprimanded his followers.[15] In Meath, two IRA training camps were established. One was close to Maynooth at Ballymacoll, but the IRA confined activities to within the precincts of the camp.[16] By September the IRA in Kildare also openly held republican courts.

As the IRA continued to strengthen its position, its members became more daring, establishing large training camps. Within the county Dowdingstown House emerged as the official training camp. Other camps included vacant big houses such as Kildangan Castle, owned by the More O'Ferrall family, which accommodated sixty IRA members on two weekends during September. Harristown House, owned by the La Touche family, was occupied for a week until a local loyalist, Pim Goodbody, reported the matter to Andy Cope, the undersecretary, who duly arranged for the IRA to vacate the premises. Goodbody was subjected to intimidation when the IRA established a new camp closer to his house than the previous base.[17] In north Kildare an additional training camp was established in Celbridge Union under Robert Crone of Leixlip for which the IRA truce liaison officer was bluntly unapologetic when challenged by the RIC.[18] The IRA camps acquired provisions from the local inhabitants, men were billeted and levies were imposed to pay for running costs. In the Carlow Brigade area, levies of one shilling in the pound on all valuation were imposed as well as a demand of a fixed monthly payment in support of the Republican Prisoners' Fund. In practically all the cases, the sums were paid.[19]

By late September, the IRA in Kildare had greatly increased in strength, although claims by the CI that it had grown by 5,000 in Kildare alone seem excessive. Jeudwine suggested that the IRA nationally numbered 200,000 men.[20] Military intelligence reported that large quantities of rifles and ammunitions had been landed on the coast and rifles were seen at IRA parades in Kildare.[21] Greater numbers of men and arms allowed the IRA to gain almost complete control of the Carlow Brigade area, which included much of south Kildare.[22] RIC authority in Kildare was further restricted with the closure of Monasterevin and Kilcullen barracks, reducing the number of police barracks in the county to five.[23] The republican police had stepped into the breach and effectively took over policing from the RIC in most of the small towns, villages and rural areas. However, they did not function in Naas or Maynooth, and had a limited role in the other big towns.[24]

With the IRA engaged in military preparations, the British army took precautionary steps lest the truce break down. A month's reserves of non-perishable food as well as ammunition were collected by the army for the police.

Following serious hitches in the peace negotiations on 14 August and 5 December, troops were ordered to be prepared for a breakdown of negotiations. On 25 October 1921 it was agreed by both sides that seventy-two hours' notice would be given should there be a termination of the truce. In that scenario troops would be directed to engage organized parties of rebels, undertake raids for known members of the IRA, assist the RIC and re-impose curfew regulations pending the coming into force of martial law.[25]

While the truce held, one of the main functions of the army in Kildare was management of Rath camp in the Curragh. Prisoners were not provided for in the truce agreement. Internees were, therefore, instructed by the IRA that they were free to escape.[26] A series of escapes from both the Curragh's Hare Park camp and Rath camp caused tensions. The number of escape tunnels prompted Jeudwine to describe Rath camp as a 'regular rabbit warren'. Due to the escapes, the internees had their privileges curtailed and accusations of mistreatment followed.[27] Responding, the military authorities allowed three members of the British press to visit the Rath camp. Their report in the *Manchester Guardian* gave a mainly even-handed account.[28] Despite a tightening up of security by the prison authorities, escapes continued. As the Anglo-Irish negotiations progressed, many men were released on parole. By 7 November, eighty-nine internees had been released from the Rath and other camps. Two Kildare county councillors, Éamon Ó Modhráin and Thomas Harris, had been freed by the end of that month.[29]

From July until September the Dáil and the British government continued their diplomatic though unproductive dealings. On 30 September de Valera accepted an invitation to negotiate a settlement. On 7 October five plenipotentiaries were appointed, one of whom was Robert Barton, TD for the Kildare/Wicklow constituency. The feeling in Kildare at this time was that 'peace is at hand'.[30] In the Curragh, signs of army disengagement were evident, with some of the military works closing down.[31] While the negotiations were taking place, politicians refrained from comment and local politicians continued with business in the local bodies throughout the county. The Anglo-Irish Treaty was signed on 6 December 1921. The Irish delegation won a considerable measure of sovereignty with the status of a dominion but were forced to accept an oath of allegiance (bound into article 4), partition (masked by a Boundary Commission) and various concessions on security. The Treaty was greeted with celebrations throughout Kildare. The *Leinster Leader* described the agreement as a truly remarkable achievement while observing that the terms fell short of the 'standard of republican government'.[32] Bishop Foley officiated at a peace thanksgiving service in Carlow cathedral for the successful conclusion of the Anglo-Irish negotiations.[33] The celebrations became even more intense following the release of hundreds of internees from Rath camp and Ballykinlar camp within two days of the signing of the Treaty. According to Jeudwine, there were nearly 1,400 internees in the Rath camp prior to their release.[34]

As the Treaty debate began in the Dáil amid a divided political leadership, an intense wave of support for the Treaty spread throughout Kildare. Almost all public bodies and organizations called meetings to lobby their representatives. In Athy, Art O'Connor was urged by both constituents and the local UDC to support the Treaty.[35] A special sitting of Kildare County Council debated the Treaty on 30 December. The degree of unanimity was not as strong as other public bodies with Éamon Ó Modhráin, who chaired the meeting, opposed to ratification. Thomas Harris argued that the Treaty was not what the men of Ireland gave their lives for and abstained from the vote. A resolution in favour of the Treaty was passed, however.[36] The North Kildare executive of SF unanimously passed a motion on 1 January 1922, calling on the TDs for the constituency to vote for the Treaty. Kildare Farmers' Union, one of the few organizations in the county that included both nationalists and unionists, unanimously favoured ratification. Bertram Barton, a unionist and second cousin of Robert Barton, told a meeting that the time had come to bury past feelings of animosity.[37] The two Kildare TDs, Ua Buachalla and O'Connor, gave their views on the Treaty at the resumed session of the Dáil after the Christmas break. O'Connor opposed the Treaty and mocked his own constituents. He denounced the lobbying as 'howling at us and telling us where our duty lay'. He seemed to be most irritated by the Farmers' Union and claimed 'people of that ilk never did an hour's honest work'.[38] He was forced to apologize to the farmers for this slur. Ua Buachalla also opposed the Treaty, arguing that the plenipotentiaries had signed for something less than the freedom of Ireland. While wisely refraining from making personal attacks on supporters of the Treaty, his reference to 'stampeding the representatives' may have been a veiled reference to the pro-Treaty lobbyists in his constituency.[39] Three deputies in the constituency voted against the Treaty. Erskine Childers joined Ua Buachalla and O'Connor, while Barton and Christopher Byrne voted in favour. The Treaty vote caused a political split in SF at a national and county level but, as will be shown, the more significant split occurred in the IRA.

The first opportunity for the SF grassroots to express its viewpoint on the split came on 18 January at a meeting of the Naas branch, hitherto the largest in the county with 400 members. Neither Ua Buachalla nor O'Connor were present, but Christopher Byrne spoke in favour of the Treaty. A motion giving instructions to the ard fheis delegates to support the Treaty was passed with only three of the 150 in attendance voting against. Athy gave delegates no mandate relative to the Treaty.[40] Smaller SF clubs that voted on the Treaty issue included Clane which gave its unanimous support, while nearby Timahoe was an example of a split vote, with fifteen for and eight against.[41]

Anti-Treaty activists came out in force to a North Kildare SF executive meeting in Prosperous on 21 January at which eleven SF clubs were represented. Surprisingly, by a two to one majority the meeting voted to oppose the Treaty. It was attended by Barton, Childers and Ua Buachalla. Barton explained his reasons for signing and then renouncing the agreement.[42] However, it subsequently emerged that the meeting had been illegally packed with anti-Treaty members and did not reflect the actual viewpoint of the branches.[43] Ua Buachalla attended a number of SF meetings at which he maintained that the minority who went out to fight for freedom in 1916 were proven right, and in 1922 that same minority would also be proven right.[44] Over the following month the split in the SF movement widened with the anti-Treaty side strengthening its position. At the ard fheis on 21 February a weakened pro-Treaty camp agreed to delay a proposed general election and that the ard fheis would reconvene in three months.[45]

Pro-Treaty SF candidates launched their election campaign in Kildare on 14 March with Naas town hall as headquarters.[46] Distinct divisions had become apparent at a local level. In Athy a pro-Treaty election committee was formed while the local Cumann na mBan campaigned for the anti-Treaty side.[47] The campaign in south Kildare began with a pro-Treaty meeting in Athy on 9 April that was followed by heckling and disturbances. Anti-Treaty SF organized election committees in all the local towns and distributed literature at chapel gates.[48] In mid-April the pro-Treaty side in Kildare received a major boost when Michael Collins and several Provisional government ministers attended an election rally in Naas. Collins argued that the alternative to the Treaty involved the return of the British forces, the renewal of warfare, and the improbability of further negotiation with the representatives of a country whose delegates were already repudiated by a minority.[49] Pro-Treaty SF nominated Thomas Lawler and James Kavanagh to represent respectively the north Kildare and west Wicklow districts of the constituency. Simon Malone from Rathangan was selected for the south Kildare area.[50]

On 20 May Collins and de Valera approved an election pact, which provided for an agreed list of candidates from both sides to fight the general election jointly and form a coalition government afterwards.[51] The pact was described by Townshend as pure election-rigging in which the contours of the split would be artificially preserved.[52] In Kildare the two anti-Treaty TDs would have a free run in the county with no pro-Treaty SF candidate opposing them, although pro-Treaty SF supporters would have the opportunity to support Wicklow-based Byrne. The candidates selected at pro-Treaty conventions in Kildare were required to stand down and all four anti-Treaty TDs – O'Connor, Ua Buachalla, Barton and Childers were selected to contest the constituency. On 14 June de Valera spoke at public meetings in Athy, Kildare town and Naas where a crowd, estimated at 3,000, attended. Many of the best-known anti-Treaty activists in the country addressed the Naas meeting such as Barton, Harry Boland and Austin Stack. Art O'Connor used the opportunity to mend fences with farmers.[53] Under pressure from the British government, which regarded the pact as a violation of the Treaty, Collins virtually ended the pact at an election meeting in Cork when he specifically urged support for pro-Treaty candidates.[54]

The Labour movement emerged in the post-Treaty period as the most efficient political organization in the county. On 26 March a meeting of the Trades Council, with eight unions represented, was held in Newbridge and a decision to contest the election was carried.[55] Athy was the venue for the next Labour gathering when the local branch of the ITGWU and Labour Party members of different councils unanimously voted to nominate James Everett from Wicklow as the Labour candidate for south Kildare. He was joined by Hugh Colohan in north Kildare.[56] By pitching Labour against two anti-Treaty SF candidates in Kildare, the pact was advantageous to Colohan, particularly as the county was strongly pro-Treaty. Unlike other counties, where anti-Treaty supporters intimidated Labour candidates into withdrawing, there was no intimidation of this kind in Kildare.[57] Colohan indicated that it was time for the country to get on with practical work by suggesting that 'the rule of the gun should give way to the rule of the spade'.[58] The Farmers' Union, which included former Redmondite nationalists and unionists, was not affiliated to any political party. It sought to obtain a strong representative political voice for farmers.[59] Farmers were not normally supporters of SF, but had strong links with the Ratepayers' Association, an urban movement that campaigned for a reduction of rates.[60] In May 1922 the Farmers' Union held public meetings at nineteen locations throughout Kildare. The outcome was the selection of candidates for a Farmers' and Ratepayers' Party: J.J. Bergin from Athy, Patrick Phelan, a county councillor from Timahoe, and Richard Wilson who had been nominated by County Wicklow constituents.[61] Unlike other counties, there were no reports of intimidation being used to force farmer candidates to withdraw in Kildare and Wicklow.

On 19 January Lord Mayo organized a meeting of fellow unionists in Dublin to endorse the new Provisional government.[62] He was supported by a sizeable number of southern unionists, including a large contingent from Kildare such as Lord Cloncurry and General Bryan Mahon. Mayo urged the gathering to realize that the union and the past were dead. Archbishop John Gregg of Dublin pointed out that it would be a serious mistake for former unionists to withhold their cooperation from the new constitutionally appointed government. A resolution declaring that southern unionists recognize the Provisional government was passed unanimously.[63]

A general meeting of the UAPL, chaired by Lord Midleton, was held on 21 January and attended by Mayo, Sir William Goulding, Col. T.J. de Burgh,

H.J.B. Clements and W.T. Kirkpatrick. In view of the altered situation it was decided to drop the term unionist from the party name and adopt the title 'Constitutional Anti-Partition League' instead. It was also agreed to make every effort to secure cooperation of all classes in establishing stable and constitutional government in the country. The more hard-line Irish Unionist Alliance met in Dublin on 26 January, but resolved, due to the uncertainty of the whole position, not to take any definite action.[64] Despite this, within two months, Protestants in many parts of the south were subjected to intimidation and murder.[65] On 12 May, a deputation from the General Synod of the Church of Ireland, comprising Archbishop Gregg and Bishop Miller as well as Sir William Goulding, met the Provisional government to discuss the violence.[66] The problem was prevalent in Kildare. Claims submitted to the IGC reveal that many unionists were forced from their homes, among them Charles Bury who lived three miles from Goulding's residence.[67] The deputation demanded to know if the government 'wanted to keep the Protestant community in Southern Ireland or to expel them'. While Collins gave assurances that the government would protect its citizens and ensure civil and religious liberty, he claimed that sectarian violence in Belfast had a bearing on the situation.[68]

The election on 16 June 1922 was generally peaceful except for one tragic incident when Thomas Dunne, an anti-Treaty IRA Volunteer, was accidentally shot dead in Castledermot by government forces.[69] The total electorate of 58,584 eligible voters was almost evenly divided between the two counties, with Kildare totalling 29,505 or 700 more than Wicklow. The turnout was low at sixty-two per cent or 35,674 voters; this included 1,160 spoiled votes.[70] Turnout was four per cent lower than in December 1918. As expected, the election produced a resounding victory for pro-Treaty candidates who won eighty-one per cent of the vote. Christopher Byrne topped the poll with 9,170 first preferences – more than one and a half quotas. Both Hugh Colohan and James Everett for Labour also exceeded the quota.[71] Colohan's 6,522 votes almost matched the combined total of the four anti-Treaty candidates who had a disastrous day. Only Robert Barton was elected for anti-Treaty SF. The combined Farmers' Party obtained a respectable vote of 6,261, a mere 307 votes less than the anti-Treaty vote, which was enough to elect Richard Wilson.[72] Of the five TDs, Hugh Colohan was the only Kildare resident. A substantial pro-Treaty SF vote from Kildare went to Christopher Byrne. Preferences from Kildare farmers helped to elect Wilson.

While a bitter loss for O'Connor, Ua Buachalla and Childers, the result was not unexpected. Childers and Ua Buachalla stayed away from the count centre. Support for anti-Treaty candidates in Kildare reflected the average vote received nationally which was twenty-one per cent or two per cent more than in Kildare and Wicklow. The Labour Party's vote of thirty-six per cent was the fourth highest in the country, while the Farmers' Party, with eighteen per cent, was substantially higher than the national average of seven per cent.[73] The message from the voters was clear. Four out of five people supported the Treaty. The combined Labour and Farmers vote of fifty-eight per cent signified an economic message. While Labour championed the issue of unemployment, the Farmers' Party highlighted rising rates brought on by the War of Independence.

One of the most momentous consequences of the Anglo-Irish Treaty was the withdrawal of the British army from Ireland and Kildare. The evacuation began on 16 January 1922 when notice was received that the Treaty was officially ratified.[74] That night, ninety-three RAF personnel from Baldonnell aerodrome and an advance party of thirty artillerymen were shipped out from the North Wall, Dublin.[75] The withdrawal was conducted in three phases. The first was to move out of the country all troops not required for the garrisons in Dublin, Cork and the Curragh; the second phase involved evacuating Cork and the Curragh, and the final phase was the evacuation of Dublin. This was to avoid leaving units in potential flashpoints where they might be called on to aid the civil power.[76] The military authorities in the 5th Division planned to evacuate in two stages. All stations outside County Kildare would be vacated first; departure from Kildare, Newbridge, Naas and the Curragh would form the second stage. As divisional troops were withdrawn, they passed through barracks in Kildare before embarking for Britain.[77] As a result, the Curragh camp was heaving with activity as units and surplus equipment were funnelled through the camp.[78] On 25 January Clogheen in County Tipperary and Baltinglass were the first stations to be evacuated. The following day it was the turn of two stations in the Glen of Imaal.[79] On 7 February Carlow barracks, garrisoned by 437 Northumberland Fusiliers, was vacated and handed over to the Carlow Brigade adjutant, James Lillis.[80] On the same day the RDF departed from the depot in Naas, the secretary of state for war having announced the disbandment of the regiment.[81] The Provisional government had pressed for an early evacuation of Naas barracks, which they wanted to use as a military officer training college. However, the British army authorities decided to retain Naas until the transfer of the Curragh.[82] The Leicestershire Regiment were posted to Naas, which continued to house troops in transit until 16 May.[83]

An incident in early February temporarily halted the withdrawal. The British army in Kildare had not been seriously targeted until after the signing of the Treaty. On 8 January 1922, Lieutenant Bevin of the King's Own Yorkshire Light Infantry, a plain clothes intelligence officer, was fired on three miles south of the Curragh.[84] Following the incident, pre-truce precautions requiring officers to be armed or provided with an escort were restored. These orders had not reached the O/C of the artillery barracks in Kildare when on 10 February Lieutenant John Wogan-Browne, serving in the Royal

Field Artillery in Kildare, was shot dead as he tried to resist the attempted robbery of the regimental pay of £135, which he had collected from a local bank.[85] Wogan-Browne was from Naas, the only surviving son of Colonel Francis Wogan-Browne, a leading Catholic unionist. His death was the most serious incident during the evacuation. Although the local IRA were not directly involved and assisted in the pursuit of the killers, feelings of resentment were high among the military. On the evening following the shooting, six soldiers from Kildare barracks broke some windows in the local cinema where John Breslin, who was suspected of involvement, was caretaker. Immediately, republican police opened fire on them, wounding three soldiers. The serious situation developing in Kildare was defused when Seán Kavanagh, liaison officer, contacted Commandant-Colonel Percy Skinner, O/C Curragh command, to have soldiers confined to barracks, while he endeavoured to deal with unauthorized persons possessing firearms.[86] The War Office suspended the evacuation of troops and moved the 1st Royal Dragoons from Ballinasloe to the Curragh camp for a period.[87] Fortunately, the killing did not escalate into a crisis. Within days Collins contacted Winston Churchill, secretary for the colonies, informing him that suspects had been arrested. This enabled Churchill to give a favourable report to the House of Commons.[88] The evacuation programme resumed on 27 February after a 15-day hiatus.[89] Three IRA men from the Suncroft area on the southern fringes of the Curragh were believed to have been responsible. The accused never went on trial for the Wogan-Browne shooting and they were released from Mountjoy in May 1922 due to the unwillingness of any party to testify.[90] Wogan-Browne was the only serving British soldier to be shot dead in Kildare during the Irish Revolution in what was a botched robbery rather than a politically motivated killing.

In addition to the evacuation of army personnel, a vast quantity of property and equipment was removed and a considerable volume of non-fixtures, temporary structures and stores was sold by public auction. This included all huts and other military stores. The first of a series of auctions took place in Naas barracks on 2 February with various household furniture and a quantity of timber on offer.[91] The biggest sale was held in the Curragh camp on 16 and 17 February, with the contents of the Frenchfurze and Rath camps, which included, among other items, 250 huts, kitchen ranges and boilers. The personal property of army officers was also sold at this time, including dwelling houses and horses.[92] On 23 February, Richard Mulcahy visited the Curragh camp and held discussions with senior British army officials regarding preparations for the final evacuation which was planned for late May.[93]

All wives and children of both officers and other ranks from the army stations in County Kildare were ordered to depart Ireland by 15 April.[94] Kildare artillery barracks was the first station to be evacuated. The 4.5 inch Howitzer battery was transferred to Newbridge; personnel moved to both Newbridge and the Curragh. Some minor incidents took place prior to evacuation. A safe that contained a considerable sum of cash was robbed from a canteen in the barracks and three days before departure, Connacht Lodge, owned by an army officer, was burned maliciously.[95] The deployment of some 1,800 men of the Royal Field Artillery on Saturday 15 April completed the evacuation. The extensive military barracks was then taken over by a body of 300 National army soldiers supervised by Captain Cotter and Lieutenant Roe who were appointed by GHQ.[96] The majority of the Irish soldiers came from the National army camp at Celbridge.

Arrangements for the handover of the Curragh, Newbridge and Naas were handled by Lieutenant-Colonel Francis Elphinstone-Dalrymple of the 5th Division and General Emmet Dalton, chief liaison officer National army.[97] Some weeks prior to the Curragh evacuation Ballyfair House, the residence of General Jeudwine, was transferred and used as an assembly area for Irish troops destined to take over the Curragh camp.[98] Considerable preparatory work had to be undertaken by the British army in the Curragh. All ordnance and barrack stores belonging to the Royal Engineers and Royal Army Service Corps – about 1,000 tons – had to be moved to Britain or Northern Ireland. The Royal Scots Fusiliers departed from Hare Park on 4 April together with the remaining disbanded RIC.[99] Certain civilian employees from the various administrative departments were selected by the British army to take over installations and stores in the camp. But the fire brigade, which was often of service to the local community, was withdrawn to Dublin.[100] The Curragh military hospital was closed on the first day of the evacuation, but provision was made for patients who were unfit to travel.[101]

On the morning of 15 May troops of the 30th Brigade RHA, and 2nd Royal Welsh Fusiliers marched out to the Curragh siding and departed for Dublin. Later, an advance party of about eighty National army troops, commanded by Commandant Patrick Cronin, arrived by train from Beggars Bush barracks, Dublin, and settled in overnight in Hare Park.[102] Two of the officers, Captain Hugh McNally and Lieutenant Éamon Prendergast, were from Monasterevin and veterans of the War of Independence in Kildare who had been detained in the camp for two weeks in 1920. Later that night they were joined by General J.J. O'Connell, Commandant Bissette and Captain O'Byrne.[103]

The British forces had an early start the following morning. By 9 a.m. all roads from the camp were filled with lines of marching troops, accompanied by over 300 motor lorries and armoured cars, all making their way to Dublin. The infantry, composed principally of Leicesters and Northampton Regiments, proceeded to the railway sidings.[104] The official handover took place at 10.30 a.m.[105] O'Connell, at the head of his staff, met Elphinstone-

Dalrymple who was accompanied by other British officers at the staff house. The two senior officers of each group proceeded to Beresford (now Ceannt) barracks where the handover took place.[106] There was no ceremony to mark the surrender of 'England's greatest military stronghold in Ireland'.[107] Elphinstone-Dalrymple then escorted O'Connell around the south perimeter road for an inspection while Lt-Col. Stockwell of the divisional staff escorted Commandant Cronin along the north perimeter road for a similar inspection.[108] The withdrawal of the last troops was supervised by Commandant-Colonel Percy Skinner who waited for the two platoons of Northamptonshire Regiment to form up, as a trumpeter sounded the last call. They were followed shortly afterwards by Elphinstone-Dalrymple and Stockwell. As the British troops marched out, detachments of Irish troops arrived from Kildare and Newbridge railway stations. Commandant Barra Ó Briain, with a contingent of Irish troops, passed the last of the British column to leave the Curragh. He observed that some in the British cavalcade engaged insensitively in catcalling and cautioned his own men to keep calm.[109] As was the custom, the British removed the flagpoles before their final departure. It was not until 12 noon that a flagpole was obtained by the National army and the tricolour was hoisted by O'Connell over the water tower in the camp.[110]

Newbridge was also vacated at the same time on 16 May with entry routes for the National army and exit routes for the British army agreed in advance. The British troops marched out of the barracks at 10:30 a.m. and proceeded to Newbridge station where two trains transported 209 men to Dublin.[111] At 10:30 a.m. the barracks was formally taken over on behalf of the Provisional government by Captain O'Kelly and Captain Joseph Rowan.[112] Naas was the last British army station to be vacated in County Kildare. The same procedure was adopted with the company of Leicesters marching out at mid-day, one-and-a-half hours after the evacuation of the Curragh and Newbridge. Following the departure, the depot was taken over by Brigadier Thomas Lawler, with Captain J. Joyce appointed O/C in charge of the barracks.[113]

The departure of the British army in early 1922 had severe economic consequences throughout Kildare. Days after the departure, forage prices collapsed with hay fetching only £9 a ton instead of the usual £14. The substantial reduction in the number of horses not alone harmed the breeders and suppliers of fodder but caused hardships for tillage farmers and vegetable growers who had utilized manure from military camps.[114] During the period between April 1921 and April 1922 almost all agricultural commodities recorded double digit price reductions of between ten and forty-six per cent.[115] The residents of Newbridge and the Curragh lobbied the Provisional government to choose the Curragh and Newbridge as the headquarters of the new Irish army and for the creation of light industry in the barracks.[116] In March 1922, Naas UDC requested assistance from the minister for labour for individuals who had become unemployed after the withdrawal of the British army. Following the evacuation of Kildare artillery barracks in April 1922, the deployment of the new Civic Guard to the complex provided a short-term boost to the area, but did not compensate for the commercial loss to the town. The Curragh camp was described by a contemporary as more like a modern industrial estate with large workshops and stables.[117] In late December 1921, the weekly wage paid to the large workforce in the camp amounted to £7,000 and it was estimated that between £90,000 and £100,000 a month was circulated by the military in the Curragh district.[118] Following the British evacuation in mid-May 1922, the local economy was decimated. Normal business practically ceased. Only a fraction of those previously employed by the British military were retained by the National army. It was reported that in the Curragh region no less than 1,100 men were unemployed.[119] No town in Kildare was more dependent economically on the British army or more adversely affected by the withdrawal than Newbridge. As a local resident put it

> One lived off the army; no matter what one had to sell the army bought it, from a horse to a chicken. One could poach a salmon or shoot a pheasant, anything, the army would buy it, hay, straw, logs. There was no fear in the town, very little violence and no sectarianism, they were part of society and they were welcome.[120]

Owing to the severe economic consequences, all of the garrison towns experienced a notable decline in population.

Against the background of the British army withdrawal, a serious division occurred in the IRA over the Treaty. On 11 January at least three anti-Treaty members of GHQ and some divisional commanders called on Richard Mulcahy, chief of staff of the IRA, to hold an army convention to discuss their opposition to the Treaty. Six days later the 2nd Southern Division repudiated the authority of the GHQ. The leadership of the 1st Eastern Division in north Kildare and the 2nd Eastern Division in south Kildare both accepted the Treaty.

While the IRA leadership wrangled over the Treaty, the Provisional government took steps to form the National army. The nucleus came from the Dublin Guard, a combination of Collins' old squad and the Dublin ASU, which in late January were assembled at Celbridge barracks to 'train and equip' as the first unit of the National army.[121] Pádraig O'Connor, who had been a member of the Irish Volunteers in Celbridge in 1914, was one of the National army officers in Celbridge. He described how recruits in their new uniforms paraded around Celbridge charming 'the female hearts in the manner of soldiers the world over'.[122] Collins went to Celbridge to inspect the men as they were the first to be issued uniforms. On 31 January the Celbridge unit, under Captain Paddy O'Daly, took charge of Beggars Bush barracks in Dublin – the first barracks to be handed over by the British army.[123] During an intensive recruitment drive, some new members of the National army came from Kildare. In early April, for example, twenty-two men who recently joined the IRA from Newbridge and Castledermot were reported to have gone to Celbridge and Beggars Bush for training.[124]

At this time the anti-Treaty IRA (ATIRA) grew disillusioned, feeling they had been duped by Collins. At a meeting in Newbridge on 5 February, chaired by Éamon Ó Modhráin, more than 100 ex-prisoners from the county expressed their grievances.[125] Men who were in senior positions in the IRA prior to their arrest did not regain their positions on release as the pre-truce command structure of the battalions in Kildare remained in place. An ex-internee association was formed with Thomas Harris, who was opposed to the Treaty, elected as commandant in charge.[126]

In March the RIC were evacuated from the last five police barracks in the county which were then transferred to the local IRA. The handover was smooth and low-key with only trusted pro-Treaty IRA personnel installed in the barracks by GHQ. This meant that the most experienced IRA companies, such as Maynooth which had fought the RIC for six years, were excluded. Resentment was inevitable. Athy was the first to be vacated on 10 March; it was taken over by personnel appointed by IRA headquarters. In Maynooth the barracks was taken over by Captain McKenna from GHQ and Seán Kavanagh, liaison officer. The barracks in Newbridge was passed to republican police loyal to GHQ; likewise Kildare town.[127] On 24 March the final and most important evacuation occurred of Naas barracks, the headquarters of the RIC. It was handed over to Brigadier Thomas Lawler, O/C Naas (7th Brigade). Under CI Murphy, the RIC moved to quarters in Hare Park, Curragh, which was used as a demobilization centre.[128]

The split in the IRA became more pronounced following the convention on 26 March at which a resolution stated that the IRA be maintained as the army of the Irish Republic under an executive appointed by the convention and headed by Liam Lynch. Two days later, the executive renounced the Provisional government's control over the IRA and ordered an end to recruitment for the National army and Civic Guard.[129] In Kildare the resolution shattered the fragile unity that held the pro- and anti-Treaty wings of the IRA together. Almost immediately, the anti-Treaty side took the initiative by firing on Newbridge police barracks on 4 April with a second incident in Monasterevin.[130] There were also a number of arms raids by anti-Treaty units. On 8 April a daring raid, planned by Paddy Mullaney, O/C Leixlip Battalion, and Andrew Cooney, O/C Eastern Division anti-Treaty IRA, was made on the headquarters of the official IRA Eastern Division in Dunboyne. A large quantity of arms was captured.[131] On the same day General Eoin O'Duffy visited Naas to put the Treaty position before officers of the local 7th Brigade, 1st Eastern Division. While the meeting was in progress, James

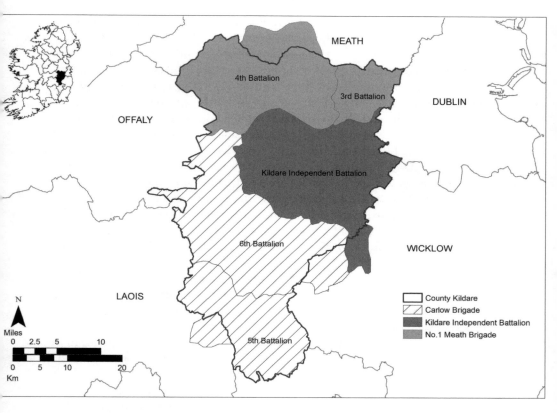

7 Kildare IRA battalion areas, 11 July 1921

Dunne, vice O/C 1st Battalion, together with eight men, raided the police barracks in Naas and made off with about twenty shotguns, some revolvers, ammunition and explosives.[132]

The IRA split in Kildare replicated the pattern identified by Hopkinson where rank and file tended to follow their commander's position on the Treaty, although this was not universal.[133] The largest territorial area in Kildare was that of the 7th Brigade, 1st Eastern Division, which stretched from near Rathcoole to Rathangan. This area, formerly the Kildare Independent Battalion, was rearranged as a brigade area by GHQ (see map 7, above). The new brigade consisted of six battalions and controlled the key locations of Naas, Newbridge, Kildare and the Curragh. This brigade was Thomas Harris' old division prior to his arrest; he was elected O/C of the rival anti-Treaty 7th Brigade in mid-April 1922 which claimed to have 400 men. New leaders were appointed in the various battalions. In the 1st Battalion covering the Naas-Kill area, 19-year-old James Dunne was appointed O/C. In other areas such as the 4th Battalion, Edward Tracy O/C and Thomas McHugh vice O/C, having chosen the anti-Treaty side, simply renounced the authority of the Thomas Lawler-led official IRA brigade and transferred allegiance to Harris.[134] Almost the entire leadership of the Eastern Division chose the pro-Treaty side with only Mullingar and Leixlip taking the anti-Treaty side.[135] The battalion staff in Leixlip and the Maynooth company followed the anti-Treaty stance of Paddy Mullaney.[136] Most, but not all, of the battalion based at Kilcock (4th Battalion, Meath No. 1 Brigade), and led by Michael Flynn, chose the pro-Treaty side with headquarters in the re-built Ulster Bank building. In Carlow there was little sign of dissention at first. The brigade staff, including James Lillis, the adjutant who had served in the IRA close to the Curragh, chose the pro-Treaty side.[137] Among the rank and file, approximately half the members adopted a neutral path, and the remainder took positions for and against the Treaty.[138] Seán Hayden from Athy, a senior ex-internee IRA officer, became O/C 5th Battalion, Carlow Brigade ATIRA based in Athy.[139]

The divisions within the IRA and the departure of the RIC resulted in a virtual breakdown of law and order throughout the county in the late spring and early summer of 1922. In Kill attacks on the homes of former RIC members, raids and inspections of canal boats for boycotted Belfast goods became the order of the day.[140] Elements within the ATIRA engaged in a campaign of intimidation of pro-Treaty SF supporters and unionists. Near Robertstown the house of Joseph Cusack, a pro-Treaty county councillor, was fired on and his farm buildings burned.[141] This area of west Kildare was virtually controlled by the ATIRA and criminal gangs were rampant.[142] In an effort to enforce law and order, an ATIRA unit, commanded by Harris, commandeered a vacant house in the area and established a barracks with Paddy Brennan in charge.[143]

The level of intimidation directed against unionists was low when compared to other counties such as Cork or Cavan.[144] A meeting of Athy Protestants adopted a resolution expressing abhorrence at the sectarian violence in Northern Ireland and recording their appreciation of the good feeling that existed between themselves and their Catholic neighbours.[145] Nevertheless, in early April a number of houses belonging to Protestants in the area of Kildare town were burned. This prompted the local IRA to issue a statement denying involvement.[146] In Athy in early June, the windows of several Protestant houses and the Methodist church were broken.[147] Sarah Giltrap from Ballymore Eustace had her gun taken and a number of cattle stolen. She believed these cattle were driven to the ATIRA camp at Kilbride and were earmarked to feed the occupants of the Four Courts garrison in Dublin.[148] During a raid on a Protestant household in Moone in south Kildare in May 1922 by men claiming to be members of the IRA, Thomas Glynn suffered serious injuries from which he died four years later.[149] Some of the victims of intimidation left the country. Robert Eccles, an ex-serviceman and a Freemason, was a successful chemist in Athy. He emigrated with his family to Australia after receiving a threatening letter (see plate 26).[150] Harry Andree, a photographer in Newbridge, likewise moved with his family to England due to threatening letters.[151] In west Kildare intimidation of Protestants prompted Fr Michael Kelly, curate of Staplestown, to describe the perpetrators as vile cowards who 'remained quiet while the foreigners stalked the country, and now when the danger was over, they came out to pursue their own country-men – their own neighbours'.[152]

The divisions in the IRA also contributed to a crisis that marked the early weeks of the newly formed Civic Guard, later to be known as the Garda Síochána. In February 1922 Collins appointed a committee to oversee the establishment of a police force, which recommended that the Civic Guard be essentially modelled on the RIC.[153] According to Brian McCarthy, the com-mittee failed to anticipate the degree of suspicion and resentment among ex-IRA men, the main source of recruits, towards former RIC men as 'the mood of the country at the time demanded the replacement of the RIC, rather than the enshrinement of it'.[154] Discontent increased in late April when some 800 Civic Guard recruits were moved from Ballsbridge into the evacuated British army artillery barracks in Kildare town. They were unhappy at being instructed by their former enemies in the RIC who were continually appointed to positions of every rank above that of sergeant. By mid-May, apart from Michael Staines, the commissioner, and Patrick Brennan, the deputy commis-sioner, both prominent members of the IRA, virtually all the remaining head-quarters staff comprised ex-RIC men.[155] Resentment came to a head in mid-May when five ex-RIC were promoted: Patrick Walsh to deputy com-missioner, Jeremiah Maher to private secretary, and three to superintendent. All five had assisted the IRA during the War of Independence.

On 15 May a protest committee issued an ultimatum to Commissioner Staines demanding the immediate expulsion of the five appointees.[156] This was mutiny and Staines mishandled the developing crisis by resorting to con-frontation rather than diplomacy. Unwisely, he called a full parade of all 1,250 recruits in the barracks. A confrontation between himself and the signatories of the ultimatum ensued, and the vast majority chose the side of the protest committee, which took control of the barracks.[157] Staines reported the mutiny to the Provisional government and sought military assistance. Fortunately, when the National army soldiers arrived at the barracks they were persuaded by the armed Civic Guards to withdraw.[158] Negotiations between the govern-ment, Staines and Walsh from the Civic Guard management and two mem-bers of the protest committee did not end the dispute. Neither did a visit by Michael Collins to the barracks on 26 May to address the mutineers. A stand-off now ensued with the Provisional government halting supplies, cutting off pay and diverting new recruits to a new headquarters in Dublin.[159] For almost two months the new Civic Guard was divided into two rival groups, one in Kildare under virtual siege and the other in Dublin.

On the night of 17 June an anti-Treaty faction within the depot, led by Thomas Daly and Seán O'Brien who were secretly in contact with the leadership of the anti-Treaty forces in the Four Courts, openly joined the ATIRA.[160] Rory O'Connor, Ernie O'Malley and Tom Barry led a party from the Four Courts garrison, and with the assistance of Daly and O'Brien, held up a number of the Guards, first on the Curragh and also in the Kildare depot where they raided the armoury, acquiring the entire supply of weapons. Several of the Guards who assisted Daly and O'Brien left the Kildare depot and joined the Four Courts garrison.[161] The incident led to the reopening of talks on 24 June when Arthur Griffith and Éamonn Duggan visited Kildare barracks and an agreement was reached. The men were granted all monies due to them for past services and an undertaking was given that an inquiry would be held without delay.[162] This was headed by Kevin O'Shiel and Michael McAuliffe, two senior administrators in the Provisional government, who were also tasked with providing recommendations relating to the future structure of the Civic Guard.[163] The findings acknowledged that the mutiny was engineered by the Four Courts leadership with a small number of anti-Treaty men identified as provoking the hostility. Jeremiah Maher was singled out as a man wrongly listed on the ultimatum as a demobilized member of the RIC, even though he joined the IRA. The key recommendations included the disbandment of the Civic Guard and selective re-enrolment of current-men, the creation of an unarmed force and the appointment of a new commissioner.[164] Eoin O'Duffy succeeded Staines and Patrick Walsh was re-deployed in a non-commissioned capacity.[165]

In the period following the truce, with the army and police largely confined to barracks, the extent to which a new order had emerged was evident by the growing authority exercised by the Kildare IRA, particularly in rural areas. The split that emerged in the aftermath of the Treaty produced an unusual scenario in Kildare whereby a strongly pro-Treaty county was at odds with the two Dáil representatives. The 1922 election consolidated public support for the Treaty, but the electorate also adopted an independent line by voting on economic issues rather than personalities. The contest saw the emergence of a four-party political system which was to become a permanent feature in the future political configuration of the county. This was set against the evacuation of the British army from Kildare and the handing over of the barracks to the National army in May 1922. Arguably, this was one of the most profound events in Kildare for centuries. The Curragh camp was destined to continue its role as an important military base as the country slid inexorably towards civil war.

# 8 Unpopular militancy: Kildare during the Civil War, 1922–3

During the Civil War, the level of militancy and violence surpassed that of the War of Independence in Kildare. In June 1922 the country was divided politically, with the SF movement split into two opposing camps. Separate armies had emerged, and Kildare was no exception. Following the departure of the RIC and the British army from the county, two factions of the IRA had emerged. However, as a strongly pro-Treaty county the divide in Kildare was not evenly matched as the pro-Treaty side was far superior both numerically and in terms of arms. Furthermore, the new National army was dominant in the Curragh and Naas while the new Civic Guard controlled the other big towns such as Kildare, Newbridge and Athy. In addition, the pro-Treaty IRA which was now aligned to the National army remained a strong powerful force. Nonetheless, well-organized ATIRA units emerged and were prepared to fight to defend their political viewpoint. The Irish Revolution produced a body of prisoners well experienced in opposing the prison administration. Many were to find themselves back in prison during the Civil War and through successive hunger strikes and prison escapes, they opposed the pro-Treaty authorities. At one point, two-thirds of the entire political prison population in the Irish Free State (IFS) were confined in jails in County Kildare. This was due to the availability of evacuated British barracks. As a result, the county featured in a number of prison escapes and hunger strikes of national significance during this period of the conflict. Kildare also appeared prominently in the policy of executions carried out by the Provisional government.

The Civil War began with the attack on the Four Courts in Dublin on 28 June 1922 and, almost immediately, the National army in Kildare set about rounding-up prominent ATIRA activists. Checkpoints were set up on all the main roads and a barricade opposite the police barracks in Naas netted Thomas Harris, ATIRA O/C 7th Brigade, Eastern Division.[1] The following day, three of the leading republican activists in north Kildare – Domhnall Ua Buachalla, Paddy Mullaney, O/C 1st Meath Brigade ATIRA, and Michael O'Neill – were arrested at Kilcock. The arrests illustrated how previous loyalties had been severed by the Civil War. Captain Michael Flynn, who was in charge of the checkpoint at Kilcock, had served under Mullaney and alongside the other two during the War of Independence. The prisoners were initially held in the local barracks, formerly the Ulster Bank.[2] Intelligence relating to ATIRA militancy was passed on to army authorities by Patrick Colgan, who spent five days on holidays in Maynooth during the early days of the conflict. According to Colgan, the ATIRA in Maynooth established a base in a house on the Main Street in the town and were holding a brother of Captain Flynn in their custody. This group had also been responsible for railway disruption close to Maynooth.[3] The first exchange of fire in north Kildare in the Civil War occurred at the end of June in Maynooth.

The arrest of Harris and Mullaney reduced the capacity of the ATIRA during the early weeks of the conflict. However, numerous roads were blocked by fallen trees to disrupt army transport between Newbridge and Naas. In the Curragh area the rail line at Cherryville was dismantled. This did not hamper the National army to any great extent.[4] Paddy Brennan took over command of the ATIRA 7th Brigade with headquarters established at Timahoe in Coolcarrigan House, the residence of Leonard Wilson-Wright. This unit held up vehicles and sniped at National army posts in Naas and Robertstown.[5] Activity levels increased with the arrival of James Dunne and his unit from Kill. To acquire badly needed rifles, Brennan targeted Rathangan barracks, some twelve miles south-west of Coolcarrigan House. After three hours of heavy fighting on 5 July, the 35-man garrison surrendered. There were no fatalities on the ATIRA side but a number of National army troops were wounded. Brennan did not leave a garrison in the town and returned to Coolcarrigan. As the superiority of the ATIRA in west Kildare was now apparent, the National army garrison at Robertstown withdrew to the safety of Naas.[6]

Blessington on the fringes of County Kildare was earmarked as a staging point for the ATIRA to provide assistance for their hard-pressed comrades in Dublin. On 30 June, the day the Four Courts fell, Oscar Traynor, O/C ATIRA forces in the capital, sent a mobilization order to Andy McDonnell, O/C South Dublin Brigade based in Bray, and Paddy Brennan of the 7th Brigade.[7] Responding, McDonnell moved his entire contingent, numbering 150–200 men, to Blessington, which was already occupied by men of the 3rd Battalion commanded by Gerald Boland. Brennan sent forty Kildare men to Blessington, including the brigade adjutant Richard Harris and Willie Byrne, O/C 6th Battalion.[8] Ernie O'Malley assumed command of the assembled men. To defend Blessington and enable ATIRA contingents to move freely, O'Malley ordered the occupation of Baltinglass and Ballymore Eustace, two strategic towns south of Blessington. On 2 August, an anti-Treaty force, commanded by Larry O'Brien of the South Dublin Brigade, which included Willie Byrne and thirty Kildare men, captured Baltinglass. There were no fatalities, but three ATIRA and one National army soldier were slightly wounded.[9] The following day the small barracks at Ballymore Eustace was captured. The ATIRA, centred in Blessington, now controlled an area extending along the Dublin-Tullow road from Brittas to Baltinglass. O'Malley, having directed a defence scheme in Blessington, moved on to Carlow and instructed Andy McDonnell to keep pressure on Naas and to cut off communication between the Curragh and Dublin.[10]

The civilian population in Naas were fearful due to persistent rumours of a republican attack on the town. The rumours were not without foundation. A planned attack was drawn up by Captain James Dowd of the South Dublin Brigade, which involved exploding a bomb against the wall of Naas military barracks.[11] Harry Boland was privy to these plans, and on 4 July he linked up with an ATIRA unit led by Con O'Donovan, vice O/C 3rd Battalion, South Dublin Brigade, outside Naas. However, the attack was abandoned as news of the National army converging on Blessington forced the republicans to go on the defensive.[12]

The National army offensive began on 5 July by targeting Ballymore Eustace. Reinforcements from the Curragh, under the command of Commandant Bishop, were required before the ATIRA garrison under Larry O'Brien was forced to withdraw.[13] This was followed by a three-pronged attack on Blessington directed by Brigadier Niall MacNeill, son of Eoin MacNeill. Initially, outposts were established on all roads leading to the town to prevent the escape of the ATIRA. The first advancing column with Commandant Heaslip in charge headed south from Dublin; the second contingent from the west under Commandant McNulty converged from Kilbride. The third force deployed units of the Curragh Brigade under Commandant Bishop with supporting units advancing from the south through Carlow and Wicklow. They were also assisted by a contingent led by Barra Ó Briain who made a forced march cross-country from the Curragh. Estimates of the number of troops involved vary from 500 to 1,000 in one of the biggest operations of the opening phase of the Civil War.[14] As the forces were about to march out from Ballymore Eustace, spiritual assistance was rendered by the local parish priest 'who took up a position on the turreted armoured car and gave a general absolution to the entire force'.[15] Having learned of the National army's pincer movement, Traynor travelled to Blessington on 7 July. He was unimpressed with the defences and ordered an immediate evacuation.[16] Richard Harris, one of the last defenders in the town, recommended that the ATIRA should 'dump all arms in safety, give men some rations, and let every man mind himself'.[17] On 8 July 1922 National army troops entered Blessington without opposition. Although the majority of the garrison escaped, the episode was a disaster for the republican war effort; 100 men were arrested, including Andy McDonnell and Gerald Boland.[18]

The National army employed a similar strategy in respect of the ATIRA based in Coolcarrigan and their arsenal even included an eighteen-pound gun. A hurried evacuation of Coolcarrigan took place on 12 July. The main contingent of forty men, led by Brennan and Dunne, while retreating, formed a defensive barricade at Corduff cross. An unfortunate case of friendly fire occurred at the cross when three men in army uniforms, who were on their way to join the ATIRA, were fired on by the retreating republicans. Thomas

Reilly from Valleymount died at the scene, while Paddy Tierney and William Rooney were wounded.[19] A second ATIRA party retreating from Coolcarrigan encountered a National army contingent at the entrance to Knockanally House. Following an exchange of fire, some were arrested while others escaped.[20] Many of the dispersed Kildare ATIRA ended up in Baltinglass, which was captured by the government forces on 17 July. Some managed to escape, but Byrne and a number of Kildare men were taken prisoner.[21]

The early stages of the conflict took a different course in south Kildare. The leadership of the IRA in the Carlow Brigade, which included two battalions in the south Kildare area, were strongly pro-Treaty, and, as a result, the National army was firmly in charge of main towns such as Carlow and Athy. The two battalions in the period prior to the outbreak of hostilities did not split into separate pro- and anti-Treaty units to the same extent as in north Kildare. However, with many of the headquarters staff of the Carlow Brigade such as Liam Stack and James Lillis moving to positions in the police and National army respectively, other IRA officers moved into senior positions in the brigade command. At the outbreak of the war, Tommy O'Connell, who emerged as O/C Carlow Brigade IRA, took the ATIRA side.[22]

When hostilities began, the National army in this region was to some extent unaware of the political viewpoint of many IRA personnel such as Christopher Murphy, quartermaster 5th Carlow Battalion who had anti-Treaty sympathies. Murphy was in charge of all the battalion arms, which were stored at his residence in Moone, and at the commencement of the Civil War, Commandant Tom Finn of the National army had the arms removed. In the last week of July Murphy openly involved himself in militant republican activity. Fronting a small unit based in a disused house close to Ballitore, he managed to escape an attack by about fifty troops. Murphy went on the run and assisted various ASUs operating in the Baltinglass area. With other republicans from the 5th Battalion, Carlow Brigade, he joined another group from the 2nd Battalion of which James O'Toole was O/C. This unit operated in Wicklow, Carlow and Kildare.[23]

Republicans were strong in some areas such as Monasterevan where they held the local barracks and in the early stages of the conflict disrupted communications by blowing up bridges in the locality.[24] Activists in the region, including Peter Lamb and Sylvester Shepherd, joined an ASU and on 2 July vacated and burned the local barracks before engaging in operations in the Athy area. One section of the ASU, which included men from Monasterevan and Athy led by Michael Bryan of Carlow, came into collision with a National army patrol at Rosetown on 4 July. Shepherd was fatally injured and the others forced to surrender.[25] With a large force, including some Tipperary men, Ernie O'Malley was active in south Kildare at this time. Having left Blessington on 3 July on a sortie, he initially made an unsuccessful attempt to secure the surrender of Carlow barracks before retiring to Castledermot. O'Malley's force left before the arrival of the National army which entered the town with two armoured cars. Unaware of O'Malley's departure, two motorcars conveying republicans were fired on by the National army. Joseph Sweeney from Dublin was killed and Harry Esmond severely wounded. It was reported that up to twenty arrests were made.[26] The National army made several arrests in south Kildare; official accounts suggest that forty-seven republicans were rounded-up, including senior figures such as Seán Hayden, O/C 5th Battalion Carlow.[27] Éamon Ó Mordháin, vice chairman of Kildare County Council, was captured on 5 August.[28] Shepherd and Sweeney were the first Civil War fatalities in Kildare. Shepherd was buried in Monasterevan without ceremony. By contrast, Seán Nolan, a National army vice commandant killed in Meath on 6 July, was given an elaborate military funeral at Grey Abbey, Kildare. The cortège was accompanied by 600 Civic Guards in uniform and units of the army under Brigadier General Lawler.[29]

In July 1922 the ATIRA reverted to guerrilla tactics that had been successful during the War of Independence. With many republican officers in prison, new personnel were appointed to senior positions. Following the imprisonment of Paddy Mullaney, Mick Price, O/C Eastern Command, appointed Thomas Gallivan acting O/C 1st Meath Brigade. Derry-born Gallivan, who resided in Leixlip, took over command of an area where activities were hampered by a lack of weaponry and men. Price visited the 1st Meath Brigade area on 5 August, and a downbeat Gallivan reported the collapse of the company and battalion organization; there were only twenty-five men armed with four rifles, two revolvers and ten bombs.[30] A command structure consisting of a joint command of the 1st Meath Brigade commanded by Gallivan and the 7th Brigade commanded by Paddy Brennan was formed.[31] The two brigades concentrated on destroying communications. One of the most spectacular planned operations was the demolition of the railway bridge close to Sallins where the Great Southern & Western Railway crossed the canal. James Dunne and thirteen men were, however, surprised by a National army patrol and forced to surrender. The loss of the most active members of the ASU in the brigade area, together with their rifles, was a serious setback.[32]

Gallivan did not enjoy the full cooperation of republicans in his area for two reasons.[33] First, he had not come up through the local ranks and was not a member of the brigade staff in early July. Second, Thomas Mangan, vice O/C of the brigade, had been given authority by Mullaney, but this had not been sanctioned by headquarters.[34] Because of this, Gallivan had to recruit activists from outside the locality.[35] His unit was responsible for a number of engagements, including the partial destruction of Leixlip bridge on 25 August and the explosion of a mine on the railway at Hazelhatch on 1 September which closed the line for two days.[36] On 9 September they ambushed a

National army convoy of two tenders and a lorry near the Catholic church in
Leixlip. Three National army soldiers were wounded and three ATIRA were
arrested by reinforcements who arrived from Lucan.[37] The ambush represented a major set-back for the ATIRA which may have miscalculated the
strength of the convoy. A disillusioned Gallivan was not optimistic about the
potential of the 1st Meath Brigade, claiming that the five men brought into
the area had been responsible for all of the recent activity; the group was
reduced to two as three had been arrested and poorly armed with just five
rifles, two revolvers and nine bombs.[38] O'Malley contemplated transferring
Gallivan but in the event he was arrested.[39]

As the Civil War progressed, increasing numbers of ATIRA were captured and many were imprisoned in Kildare. A number of prisons were established in the Curragh camp and also in Newbridge military barracks. These
prisons became the centre of various protests by republican prisoners. The
first occurred in July 1922 in the Curragh when James Lennon, a former TD
from Carlow, went on hunger strike to obtain political prisoner status. The
hunger strike was quickly resolved when the Curragh was designated a political detention prison.[40] Two months later, attention focused on a hunger strike
by James Smith, a 16-year-old from Grangebeg near Dunlavin, and Frank
Driver, a 14-year-old from Ballymore Eustace, in Keane barracks, Curragh
camp. They were the youngest prisoners to engage in this form of protest.[41]
They had been detained for ten weeks even though neither had been in possession of arms. Following promises of imminent release, they ended the
hunger strike and were removed to the Curragh military hospital. However,
the deal did not materialize as they refused to sign the 'form of undertaking',
which required prisoners not to engage in anti-government activity.[42]

Faced with hunger strikes, the prison authorities were determined not to
grant concessions. On 1 September 1922, Richard Monks, a republican prisoner from Kilkenny, was shot dead as he allegedly tried to escape from custody in the Curragh camp.[43] This was the first fatality in any of the Kildare
prisons. This heavy-handed approach also extended to other prisons such as
Maryborough prison, Portlaoise, where, six days later, Patrick Hickey, a prisoner, also died in a shooting incident. According to the inquest, Hickey was
shot by a sentry who believed he was attempting to escape.[44] The two incidents represent a trigger-happy approach in the period following the death of
Michael Collins. After the Monks shooting, sentries in Newbridge were given
orders to shoot, but not to kill.[45]

Initially, republicans from the north of the county were imprisoned in
Dundalk. The capture of the jail by Frank Aiken on 14 August resulted in
the release of almost 200 prisoners, of which eighty-five were from Kildare,
including Domhnall Ua Buachalla, Michael O'Neill and James Dunne.[46] The
freed men were given arms and ammunition before setting out on foot back

to their native counties.[47] For those living in central Kildare this was a 70-mile journey. James Dunne of the 7th Brigade commanded sixty men from his brigade while Michael O'Neill led twenty men from the 1st Meath Brigade.[48] The first leg of their journey south took them to Dunleer. The authorities used aerial reconnaissance to track the freed prisoners. Flying from Baldonnell, Brigadier General W.J. Sweeney described Dunleer at 12.55 p.m. on 15 August as full of irregulars with about 200 on the street. He also indicated that the bridge south of Dunleer was partially damaged.[49] This was almost certainly the bridge in Dunleer blown up by Patrick McGee, the 7th Brigade engineer, acting under instructions from local republicans in Dundalk.[50] Under cover of darkness, the Kildare contingents crossed the River Boyne at Oldbridge.[51] National army troops from Drogheda and Navan were scrambled to recapture the escaped prisoners who were trapped in a triangular area between Kentstown, Rathfeigh and Screen.[52] As National army units closed in, there were running battles over several miles of countryside. Dozens of prisoners surrendered with their arms.

In one engagement at Rathfeigh, the National army, complete with a Lewis machine-gun mounted on a Lancia, flushed out a party of forty Kildare men. The majority surrendered, but about ten, including Michael O'Neill, escaped. The prisoners were all from the Maynooth and Celbridge areas and eighteen rifles and a number of revolvers were recovered.[53] Another encounter near Oberstown cross resulted in the death of Private Patrick Keogh.[54] According to James Dunne, twenty men under his command escaped due to the rearguard action of Patrick McGee and a small party who remained behind to keep the National army engaged.[55] The running battle lasted from 4 p.m. to 8.30 p.m. and led to the re-capture of at least eighty republican prisoners.[56] Dunne and O'Neill, with their parties of approximately twenty and five men respectively, avoided capture and returned to Kildare by different routes.[57] Ua Buachalla managed to board a train for the capital where he spent the remainder of the Civil War, keeping out of view in safe houses and not engaging in the militant side of the conflict.[58] In Kildare the escapees were joined by Paddy Mullaney who, with others, had escaped from the Curragh on 20 August by sawing through a dining room window and concealing himself in a Board of Works laundry lorry.[59] These hardened, experienced, well-armed determined activists would soon make their presence felt with a significant increase in activity throughout the northern section of Kildare.

Michael O'Kelly, the versatile republican activist, provided sanctuary to some of the escapees and this led to his arrest. His anti-Treaty sympathies surfaced in September when he published a letter in support of a wages and employment issue concerning a republican internee. Furthermore, he was serving as intelligence officer for his local battalion. On 11 November, while a republican meeting was taking place in O'Kelly's residence, the house was raided and Gus Fitzpatrick and Walter Halligan, two freed Dundalk prisoners, were found on the premises. O'Kelly and the escapees were placed under arrest.[60]

Many of the recaptured Dundalk prisoners were sent to the *Arvonia* prison ship anchored off Dun Laoghaire before they were moved to a new military prison in Newbridge barracks.[61] Shortly afterwards, some found themselves at the centre of another prison breakout. By September 1922 the prison population of the barracks was 1,100.[62] Many prison veterans from the War of Independence period were experts at plotting and carrying out escapes. They discovered that sewer traps ran in a line from the buildings where the prisoners were housed for approximately 500 yards to the Liffey, and that if a tunnel of approximately thirty feet in length was cut from one of the blocks, a connection could be made to the sewer. Despite difficulties, the trench was completed, with inmates using a saw manufactured from a dinner knife, a pointed poker as a pick, and a fire shovel. A second tunnel out of the sewer was dug leading to a sawmill and the River Liffey.[63]

The escape took place on the nights of 14 and 15 October 1922. On the first night, thirty men who lived furthest away from the prison escaped undetected.[64] The following night men from Kildare were among those hoping to escape, but the attempt did not go smoothly. Just after midnight sentries noticed movement and opened fire. Many of those in the tunnel were recaptured. Of the 149 men who broke out over the two nights, thirty-seven were quickly recaptured, but 112 made good their escape.[65] Commandants Thomas Harris and Willie Byrne, the Breslin brothers from Kildare, Thomas J. Williams from Naas and Patrick Bagnall from Kildare were among thirty-three escapees from Kildare.[66] For six of the Kildare escapees it was a case of second time lucky. The O'Keeffe brothers from Kilcock and James Dempsey from Celbridge had been recaptured after escaping from Dundalk jail.[67] The breakout from Newbridge was one of the biggest mass escapes in modern Irish history. It was more remarkable than Dundalk as it was initiated and executed by the internees alone without any outside assistance. The return to active service of key activists resuscitated a flagging republican campaign in Kildare.

In early August, the 7th Kildare Brigade ATIRA, despite widespread arrests, was regarded as one of the strongest numerically in the Eastern Division; Paddy Brennan reported that he still had 140 men under his command. However, they possessed only nine Lee Enfield rifles and 2,000 rounds of ammunition.[68] The return of twenty escapees from Dundalk on 20 August was a double boost, bringing James Dunne and an additional fourteen rifles.[69] A restructuring of the 7th Brigade saw Brennan given a role in Mick Price's headquarters staff as acting brigadier, 1st Eastern Division.[70] He was arrested following a botched raid on Oriel House, headquarters of the Provisional government detective division, on 17 September.[71] Mick Kelly, the divisional training officer, was sent to the 7th Brigade to oversee restructuring and training.[72] James Dunne was appointed acting O/C under Kelly's authority and in September, Kelly became O/C while Dunne remained commander of the brigade ASU.[73] Other changes in personnel followed. Tom McHugh became O/C of the ASU 4th Battalion when Edward Tracy was arrested on 13 September.[74] After the Newbridge prison escape, Thomas Harris and Willie Byrne resumed their roles as brigade O/C and O/C 6th Battalion respectively.[75]

The leadership changes injected a new dynamism in the republican campaign in Kildare which witnessed attacks on the railway infrastructure and sniping of National army patrols in October and November.[76] An ASU under Bryan Moore was quite active on the northern fringes of the Curragh. For example, on 9 October it sniped a National army patrol; two days later it blew up a railway bridge outside Kildare and commandeered two train engines, which were driven westwards; one overturned outside the town and blocked the line.[77] On 14 October an attempt to blow up the Curragh railway bridge was unsuccessful as the detonator failed. On 26 October the railway line at Cherryville was torn up and an engine derailed, which held up rail traffic for several hours.[78] Not content with targeting the railways and bridges, the ASU became even bolder. On 28 November it attacked a troop train on its return to the Curragh siding in Rathbride with four officers and 100 men on board. Two soldiers were wounded and, in the confusion, a policeman was accidentally shot by a soldier.[79]

Obviously, the National army needed to eliminate the serious military threat in the Curragh region and it stepped up efforts to capture the ASU. One member of the column, Thomas Behan, who was also the brigade intelligence officer, was concerned at the danger of capture and requested instructions from the O/C and Divisional HQ. On 13 December, Bryan Moore's house, where the ASU was based, was raided.[80] A military report indicated that during a search of the farmyard, a dugout was discovered underneath the floor of a stable. It contained ten men, ten rifles, ammunition, cables and a quantity of food.[81] Eleven individuals were taken into custody, including Moore, his sister Annie, Thomas Behan and Patrick Bagnall, an escapee from Newbridge prison.[82]

On the eastern side of the brigade area, James Dunne's ASU also caused difficulties for the National army. In the early hours of 3 November, telegraph and telephone wires were cut at Sallins railway station and the signal cabin was damaged.[83] When a patrol of eight National army rushed to the scene, Private Francis Crampton was killed and Private Whittle wounded.[84] The ASU suffered no casualties. Another gunfight occurred on 17 December when a dance in Johnstown close to Naas was searched by the National army. Dunne had advance knowledge of the search and ambushed the army party. Lieutenant John Keogh was killed.[85] The National army had been searching for members of the Dunne ASU and misjudged the danger posed in Dunne's home territory. In December Dunne took charge of 7th Brigade following the resignation of Thomas Harris who felt that a continuation of the armed campaign had become impossible.[86] The loss of large numbers of activists had taken its toll.

While there were two fatalities in north Kildare, the bloodiest encounter took place in south Kildare. From August to October the two battalion areas of the Carlow Brigade seemed the least disturbed section of the county. National army garrisons at the Curragh to the north and Athy and Carlow to the south contained ATIRA activity in the region. The apparent tranquillity was shattered on 24 October when an eight-member National army patrol was ambushed at Graney cross. Three soldiers – Pat Allison, Edward Byrne and James Murphy – died at the scene. James Hunt, the driver, died some days later, and four others were wounded. The republican ASU suffered no casualties.[87] This ambush was the bloodiest military encounter in Kildare during the Irish Revolution.[88] It had far-reaching consequences, not only in Kildare, but also in Wicklow and Carlow.

An extensive search for the assailants was hampered by an increasing level of republican militancy. Following the ambush, in an effort to hamper National army activity, the ATIRA laid several strands of wire across the road mid-way between Athy and Ballitore.[89] During the weeks following the ambush some enraged soldiers became trigger-happy. One unlucky motorist was fired on by the army when driving into Castledermot; in Carlow barracks a soldier drew his revolver and wounded a prisoner whom he accused of participation in the ambush.[90] The ASU suspected of involvement was tracked down on 7 December near Myshall in Carlow. After a shoot-out at Sheean, Myles Carroll from Borris was killed and James O'Toole, O/C of the ASU, was fatally wounded. Two other members of the ASU were captured.[91] In addition, Jim Lillis, thought to be a member of the ASU, was arrested in County Carlow on 12 December.[92]

While the ATIRA ASU in south Kildare gained notoriety due to the Graney ambush, in north-east Kildare during the autumn, a new ASU engaged in the most successful guerrilla warfare campaign in the county.[93] Thomas Gallivan was succeeded by Paddy Mullaney. Linking up with Michael O'Neill, who had also returned to the area after his escape from Dundalk, Mullaney began the difficult task of forming a new ASU, and together with Jack O'Connor and Tim Tyrrell, the company captains respectively of Celbridge and Maynooth, a new ASU, known as the Mullaney (or Leixlip) column, emerged. Local support denied to Gallivan was now freely given to Mullaney.[94] Anti-Treaty militancy increased and, within a month of taking over, Mullaney had shaped the ASU into an effective fighting force of fifteen fully armed men based largely in Castletown estate, Celbridge. Arms dumps were also prepared in four locations in the area.[95] The ASU proposed ambitious targets such as the capture of Baldonnell aerodrome and commandeering an aeroplane to bomb government buildings.[96] Throughout the autumn, Mullaney made contacts with up to thirty disgruntled members of the National army at Baldonnell who promised to desert and join the ATIRA. There were two attempts to capture Baldonnell. On the first occasion, John Dowling was to take charge, but the operation was postponed for a week. The second attempt on 9 October, with Tom Derrig in overall command, was spearheaded by the Mullaney ASU and assisted by men from the Dublin Brigade and Kildare 7th Brigade. In total, about eighty Kildare men took part. In the event, however, the operation was cancelled by Derrig on the basis that insufficient numbers had assembled.[97] In the early hours of 10 October, Mullaney, always the strategist, attacked Lucan barracks as a diversion to enable the safe return of the republican units.[98] Mullaney then concentrated on destroying communications infrastructure and was impressively successful during the remainder of October and November. The long list of activities included various endeavours at severing communication to the west on the main Dublin to Galway road and the Great Southern & Western railway line. Telegraph communications were cut or destroyed at several locations in the general area between Maynooth and Lucan, while bridges at Straffan, Leixlip and Celbridge were blown up.[99] The ASU largely avoided ambushes with the exception of one engagement on 14 October when a military car was over-powered just as the remainder of the ASU was blowing up Louisa bridge in Leixlip.[100] One of the biggest operations was the destruction of the Liffey bridge at Celbridge on 25 October.[101] The townspeople were forewarned and the destruction caused severe traffic disruption.[102] On 6 November the old fever hospital in Celbridge Union was burned down, apparently to prevent its use by the National army.[103] As November progressed, the Mullaney column became more daring. On 9 November it occupied Leixlip for two-and-a-half hours, apparently planning to ambush a National army party.[104] On 28 November, the ASU virtually held up the town of Maynooth in a similar exercise.[105] On that occasion they were fresh from a successful raid on Baldonnell camp earlier that evening. Assisted by sympathetic National army personnel, the ASU captured a Lewis gun, together with spare parts and ammunition, three rifles and fifteen rounds of .303 ammunition. Two soldiers deserted and joined the ASU.[106]

Success bred overconfidence. On 30 November the ASU ambushed Commandant Christopher Lynam and two soldiers who had left Lucan barracks with rations for a larger National army party that was searching trains. Lynam and one of his men were captured, but the third soldier escaped and raised the alarm.[107] A National army party under Captain Joseph Ledwith was reinforced by troops under Commandant-General Hugo MacNeill, a nephew of Eoin MacNeill.[108] Mullaney, now based in Grangewilliam house close to

Maynooth, had miscalculated the extent of reinforcements and, following a fire-fight in which one soldier had been killed, withdrew, but the ASU was being slowly encircled by a big body of troops with an armoured car and a tender patrolling the roads.[109] At 4 p.m. the ASU was spotted at Ballygoran and after a ten-minute exchange of fire the Mullaney column, comprising twenty-two experienced men, surrendered.[110] This was the most extensive gunfight during the entire Irish Revolution in County Kildare with exchanges of heavy weaponry from both sides lasting four hours. The encounter exemplified the division among former comrades. Captain Ledwith of the National army and Tim Tyrrell of the Mullaney ASU were both members of the Maynooth company that participated in Easter Week, while Mullaney and Lynam were both residents of Leixlip. General MacNeill acknowledged that Mullaney 'fought a damn good clean fight'.[111] Mullaney's capture ended the career of the most successful military activist in Kildare during the Irish Revolution. Overnight, organized resistance to the National army in Kildare ended.

Throughout the summer and early autumn both Church and state condemned anti-Treaty militancy and it was apparent that some special powers by the government were needed to discourage ATIRA activity. Bishop Foley argued that assisting the ATIRA was a violation of the Fifth Commandment: 'when they shoot their brothers on the other side they are murderers, when they commandeer public or private property they are robbers and brigands'.[112] In August, Archbishop Edward Byrne of Dublin was accused of ordering chaplains in Mountjoy to refuse absolution to some republican prisoners. However, following a letter from Art O'Connor, who broke the story to the media, the archbishop allowed additional priests not connected with the prison to attend every week for confessions.[113] Parliamentary politics at national level resumed when the third Dáil met on 9 September, and it was obvious that some form of legislation was needed to deal with the militancy.[114] The government introduced the Emergency Powers Resolution, otherwise known as the Public Safety bill, which empowered military tribunals to impose life imprisonment and the death penalty for a variety of offences.[115] The bill was passed on 27 September 1922, by forty-one votes to eighteen. All four TDs from the Kildare-Wicklow constituency attended; Christopher Byrne and Richard Wilson voted in favour while Hugh Colohan and James Everett voted against.[116] The four TDs also voted similarly for an amendment the following day which gave greater effect to the measure.[117] In a coordinated manoeuvre, at the prompting of the government, the Catholic hierarchy issued a pastoral on 10 October 1922 that gave the appearance of credibility to government policy. It also coincided with an offer of an amnesty to republicans to put down their weapons.[118] The pastoral threatened to excommunicate any ATIRA member who continued their campaign against the National army.[119] Read in churches, it highlighted the destruction caused by the republicans in the Civil War.

Following the passage of the Act, the first executions took place at Kilmainham Gaol on 17 November 1922 when four anti-Treaty activists from the capital were executed for firearms possession. The execution of Erskine Childers, a former TD for the constituency, followed on 24 November.[120] At the first meeting of Kildare County Council following these events, due to pressure from Labour councillors, a resolution expressing regret that it should be necessary for the government to carry out executions was adopted.[121]

Within three weeks the execution policy effected Kildare to a greater extent than any other county. The Rathbride ASU was the first group of Kildare prisoners to face a military court. Controversy has surrounded the treatment of the ASU with the trial held in secret, an apparent cover-up and conflicting accounts of the facts. It appears that official records of the trial have either been lost or destroyed. Following the arrests at Rathbride, Annie Moore was imprisoned in Mountjoy and the ten men were taken to the Glasshouse prison in the Curragh. Before any trial could take place, Thomas Behan died in suspicious circumstances. The official army account was that he was shot when attempting to escape.[122] A more probable explanation is that he died as a result of a serious assault inflicted by his captors. It was alleged that Behan suffered a broken arm during his arrest and was assaulted when unable to climb into the army lorry.[123] Another account suggests that he was shot following his arrest. Behan's remains were returned to his relatives in Rathangan.[124] Seven of the nine remaining men were convicted by a military court for being in possession of rifles, ammunition, detonators and exploders, and were sentenced to death.[125] Patrick Moore and James White, whose brothers were convicted, escaped execution, apparently due to the National army's reluctance to execute two sets of brothers.[126] The condemned men were allowed to write letters to family members and were ministered to by Father Donnelly, the Curragh chaplain.[127] On 19 December at 8.30 a.m., the seven men, who included Bryan Moore and Newbridge escapee Patrick Bagnall, were executed by firing squad in the military detention barracks, Curragh camp.[128] These were the first executions to take place outside of Dublin and the largest individual set of executions during the Civil War. The men's remains were not passed on to their respective families, but were buried in the grounds of the detention barracks. In 1924 they were exhumed and re-buried in Grey Abbey cemetery, Kildare.[129] The haste with which the executions took place and the numbers involved shocked the whole country, but particularly Kildare. Although the ASU had successfully hampered rail communications in the Curragh area, the punishment seemed excessive as no members of the National army had been killed.

By contrast, following their arrest at Ballygoran the Leixlip ASU was not subjected to mistreatment. In fact, one National army officer, Jack Logie, who had served under Mullaney, destroyed papers taken from Michael O'Neill.[130]

The prisoners were taken to Wellington barracks and Hugo MacNeill made sure that no unauthorized soldiers were allowed access.[131] Nevertheless, some soldiers sought access to the prisoners on their first night of captivity. The following day they were interrogated separately, and, with the exception of Mullaney and O'Neill, all suffered assaults.[132] Five were identified as army deserters who had left their posts in Baldonnell.[133] Two were from Kildare: Leo Dowling from Carna near the Curragh and Anthony O'Reilly from Simmonstown, Celbridge. On 11 December the five were tried by court martial in Kilmainham. They were found guilty of treachery in that they assisted certain armed persons in using force against the National troops and of a second charge of consorting with the armed persons mentioned in the first charge. Surviving details of the trial are scant. All five were executed on 8 January 1923 in Keogh barracks, formerly Richmond barracks.[134] Fr Fitzpatrick travelled from Celbridge to attend the men and gave some of them absolution.[135] The bodies were interred in unconsecrated ground and there was no known public outcry until 1924 when the remains were exhumed and returned to their families for re-burial.[136]

The remainder of the column were removed to Mountjoy on 2 February without being tried.[137] At this stage most of them had also signed the government undertaking, but Mullaney, O'Neill, Bertie Hawney, John Curley and Thomas Cardwell held out against signing. In mid-March the five were notified they would be tried by military court on 25 March. James Brady, a solicitor who had been instructed by some friends of the prisoners, held a meeting with Mullaney and O'Neill and informed them that Charles Casey, the prosecutor at the military courts, indicated that the five would be executed unless they signed the undertaking form. At this, Mullaney consulted every officer and person of importance in the wing, but none would give a definite opinion although most favoured signing. Robert Barton, the only republican representing the constituency of Kildare–Wicklow, could not give a decided opinion.[138] Liam Deasy was another senior figure in the wing and had initiated an unsuccessful appeal to his comrades to end the war, but his action had no effect in influencing Mullaney's decision.[139] The view of Ernie O'Malley, who was a patient in the hospital section of the prison, was also sought, but his instruction not to sign was not received by Mullaney until the deadline had expired. The O/C of A wing, Seán Lehane, in the absence of O'Malley's reply, advised them to sign. At the eleventh hour Mullaney and the other four signed. Mullaney later gave three main reasons for signing: first, he was responsible for the lives of his comrades who would be entirely guided by what he did; second, those in charge of waging the war at GHQ were not serious, and he emphasized their faintheartedness to support the Baldonnell operation, and third, with the war practically over, having men executed would be a needless sacrifice of life. Mullaney stressed, however, that had a definite order been given by GHQ or O'Malley against signing he would have obeyed it. The death sentence was commuted to seven years penal servitude.[140]

The last prisoner executed for an offence committed in Kildare was Carlow man, Jim Lillis, who was linked to the Graney ambush. He was tried by military court in Dublin on 12 December and, according to James Nolan, O/C of the ATIRA, Carlow Battalion, one of the National army officers testified that he was a participant at Graney.[141] Lillis was convicted of being in possession of a rifle when arrested at Knocksquire, County Carlow, on 14 December 1922 and also of having taken part in the Graney ambush. He was executed in Carlow barracks on 15 January 1923.[142] In all, some eighty-one officially sanctioned executions were carried out between 17 November 1922 and 2 May 1923. Four of them were civilians who were not ATIRA members, and as their offences were regarded as non-political, it is generally accepted that seventy-seven was the correct number of state-imposed executions of republicans.[143]

The importance of the Kildare connection to the executions cannot be overstated. It is not widely known that both Dublin and Kildare share in equal terms the highest numbers executed for political offences committed in their respective counties. According to a list compiled by Breen Timothy Murphy, eighteen executions, by far the highest number per county, were carried out in Dublin. However, this number does not take into account the location where the offence that warranted execution was committed. The list includes five of the Mullaney ASU whose offences occurred in Kildare, and Erskine Childers whose offence occurred in Wicklow. The number executed for offences committed in Dublin is actually twelve.[144] Equally, twelve were executed for offences committed in Kildare which includes seven of the Rathbride ASU and five of the Mullaney ASU. This accounts for 15.5 per cent of the total executed during the Civil War. Although eight prisoners were executed in Galway, two were regarded as civilians for non-political offences. Likewise, in Westmeath where seven were executed, two are regarded as civilians. The county with the highest number of officially sanctioned executions after Dublin and Kildare is Kerry with seven.[145]

Many republicans claimed that the bishops' pastoral had given the government a licence to execute. While the hierarchy of the Catholic Church did not publicly condemn the executions, they privately opposed the measures.[146] Archbishop Byrne regarded the executions as unjustifiable from a moral point of view, and in November 1922 privately protested to the government. In reply, Cosgrave used wording from the bishops' pastoral to justify the government's actions.[147] Bishop Foley made no public reference to the Rathbride executions or the execution of Jim Lillis, which happened less than a mile from the bishop's residence in Carlow. According to Patrick Murray, Foley did not seem to have been unduly troubled about the moral aspect of the government's reprisal executions, but was worried that they might have been politically inopportune.[148] Monsignor Pádraig de Brún, professor of mathematics in Maynooth College from 1914 to 1945 and a future president of University College Galway, while constrained by the bishops' pastoral, found a way of commemorating executed republicans.[149] In late July 1922, Cosgrave complained to Archbishop Byrne, accusing a number of priests in the diocese, including de Brún, of treasonable acts. The latter was suspected of visiting republicans and hearing their confessions thereby encouraging them in the early days of the war. Prior to his execution, Childers requested a Catholic priest, naming either de Brún or Capuchin, Fr Albert Bibby. The request was denied.[150] De Brún regarded the quiescence of the bishops during the executions as 'the blackest stain on the Irish priesthood since the coming of St Patrick'.[151] Powerless to publicly condemn the executions, he penned poetry to express his views. His elegy, 'In memoriam', a commemoration of O'Connor, Mellows, Barrett and McKelvey, four anti-Treaty prisoners executed on 8 December 1922, was widely circulated as a broadsheet in 1923.[152] During a raid on SF headquarters in Dublin in February 1923, de Brún was taken into custody, accused of possessing seditious documents, using unpriestly language and being uncooperative. The document in question was a poem he penned that extolled the activities of the five members of the Mullaney column who were executed in January 1923.[153] He was released after four days in Mountjoy and cautioned by the embarrassed Maynooth authorities.[154]

The Civil War adversely affected the unionist population in Kildare. When the IFS came into existence on 6 December 1922, Seanad Éireann (Senate) was instituted to form with Dáil Éireann the new Oireachtas. Three Kildare men with a unionist background – Lord Mayo, Sir Bryan Mahon and Henry Greer – were appointed by the government to serve for a six-year period.[155] Due to a vacancy in February 1923 William Cummins, a prominent Labour activist in Kildare, was also appointed to the Seanad.[156] Kildare's unionist senators were to pay a high price for participation in the new institutions; however, loyalists in general did not suffer the same degree of persecution as in other counties such as Cork.[157] Applications to the IGC reveal that every class of former unionists in society were victimized, with more than forty loyalists from Kildare suffering violence and intimidation at the hands of the ATIRA or those claiming to be republicans.[158] In many areas of Kildare, Protestants were relatively safe, but intimidation was more widespread in south and west Kildare. Revd L.M. Hewson, who lived at Ballinafagh close to Prosperous in west Kildare, gave the following description to the IGC:

> Altogether both the English government and the Free State government have shown a totally incapable ability to keep that particular

corner quiet: any decent law-abiding man or woman be he a member of the Church of Ireland or Roman Catholic in politics 'Loyalist' (whatever that means) or 'Republican' or 'Free State' got it in the neck <u>unless</u> they kept their gun handy and used it.[159]

A number of families were forced to vacate their farms due to intimidation and boycott during the period. In December 1922, Pim Goodbody from Ballitore, with his wife suffering from depression, sold his 300-acre farm and left Ireland.[160] Charles Bury from Downings House, Prosperous, was forced out of his house in early 1922 and was unable to obtain normal rent due to an IRA boycott. Stables and farm implements on his estate of 624 acres were destroyed by fire and the land was used as commonage. Bury moved to Dublin and his daughters emigrated to London. He claimed that in early 1923 between forty to fifty republicans were in the house at one time and he was required to enter the dwelling by way of a republican sentry.[161] Although the southern part of the county was the most severely affected, where a number of Protestants were targeted by an IRA boycott, other areas throughout the county suffered violence and theft from groups claiming to be republicans.[162] In the general state of lawlessness that prevailed in many areas of the county, all sections of the civilian population were impacted, with shops, post-offices and even isolated farmhouses targeted. In some districts, there were arson attacks and land-grabbing was attempted. This may not have been entirely the work of the IRA as general criminality was widespread at the time.[163]

Lord Mayo, regarded as the leader of Kildare unionists, had not been subjected to intimidation or violence until January 1923, when he was targeted as a result of Liam Lynch's order to destroy houses belonging to senators; a total of thirty-seven properties were destroyed, including two in Kildare.[164] The order was accompanied by a categorization of senators. Those on the A list, which included Mayo and Mahon, were earmarked to be shot in retaliation for executed republicans. Those on the B list, such as Henry Greer, were to have their houses burned only.[165] On the night of 29 January a small party of the 7th Brigade ASU burned Mayo's Palmerstown House, and informed the staff that they had come to burn the house as a reprisal for the execution of men in the Curragh. Lady Mayo was specifically asked to verify the fact that her husband was a senator.[166] When Mayo queried whether he would be shot, he was informed that the orders were to burn the house only. Mayo suspected that local men were involved in the operation, a view subsequently confirmed by James Dunne who indicated that members of his column from Kill and Kilteel were involved.[167] On 16 February, it was the turn of Sir Bryan Mahon whose residence, Mullaboden House in Ballymore Eustace, was burned. Mahon had taken the death threat seriously and vacated the premises.[168] As at Palmerstown, the building was totally destroyed. One of the raiders mockingly dressed up in General Mahon's British army uniform.[169] The arsonists, who belonged to the 2nd Dublin Brigade, had come from west Wicklow where members of an ASU known as the Plunkett column were implicated.[170] Curragh Grange outside Newbridge, the home of Sir Henry Greer, the third senator from Kildare, was not targeted, and neither were the mansions of two previous senators under the Government of Ireland Act, Lord Cloncurry or Sir William Goulding – Lyons House and Millicent House respectively. The vacant Coolcarrigan House also escaped destruction probably because it was a working farm and provided local employment.[171] However, James Johnson, the farm steward, and his family were subjected to intimidation.[172] While the burning of senators' houses in Kildare was in response to the execution policy of the government, it was not essentially sectarian. One of the houses targeted belonged to a Protestant while the second belonged to a Catholic. However, in other areas of the country such as Munster, where arson was more widespread, the motivations were more complex. Gemma Clark argues that in addition to the burning of senators' houses due to their support for the IFS government, there was widespread burning of Protestant houses motivated by an attempt to purge religious minorities and force redistribution of land.[173] The burning of senators' houses in Kildare was the final act of serious militancy carried out by the ATIRA in the county.

The final episodes of the Civil War in Kildare involved the prisons. With a large prison population in the Curragh region and many of the internees having experience of successful escapes in the past, it was inevitable that other jail breaks would be attempted. On Saturday 21 April 1923, seventy-one prisoners tunnelled their way out of the Curragh camp. Although local activists provided assistance, unlike previous mass escapes when very few were located, on this occasion the authorities recaptured several in areas close to the Curragh: at Ballymore Eustace, at Harristown and at Naas. While the dragnet throughout the county was taking place, James Dunne and his column guarded fifteen men who were from the west and north of Ireland. One batch of ten men was brought to Cardwell's house in Celbridge but was surrounded by a National army column from Naas. Dunne and Tom Kealy of Celbridge, one of the Mullaney ASU still at large, who were the only men armed in the house, managed to keep the troops engaged for an hour while some of the ex-prisoners got away. According to an army statement, a patrol of nine troops recaptured six prisoners following a short engagement at Cardwell's house in Celbridge on 25 April. Leo Cardwell, son of the occupant of the house, who was a minor, was also arrested.[174] The issue of his arrest was raised in the Dáil by Hugh Colohan who asked Richard Mulcahy if he aware that Cardwell was only thirteen and a half and was admitted to the military hospital with a neck wound.[175]

Although the Civil War officially ended on 23 May 1923, by the following autumn the government had not put in place a definite release programme. Discontent among the prison population increased. By October, with 8,349 still imprisoned, the hunger strike weapon was again contemplated.[176] The strike began on 14 October in Mountjoy and escalated four days later when 1,858 prisoners at Tintown A in the Curragh camp joined in the protest. The following day the strike spread to nearby Tintown B where the entire 1,346 prisoners on the roll refused food. By 21 October, prisoners in the remaining jails in Kildare and throughout the country joined the protest. The official figures suggest that 7,570 went on hunger strike, a figure supported by republican sources.[177] Of that total, 5,221 hunger strikers (sixty-nine per cent) were incarcerated in Kildare, something which has not been adequately acknowledged in the historiography.[178] The government faced a crisis of gigantic proportions.

A number of Kildare men detained in Mountjoy had joined the hunger strike from the beginning. They included Art O'Connor, the highest-profile prisoner from the county, who was moved with a number of other well-known prisoners such as Ernie O'Malley and Austin Stack to Kilmainham on 19 October. Éamon Ó Mordháin, Paddy Mullaney and a number of other Kildare prisoners in Mountjoy had also joined the protest from the beginning.[179] By mid-November reports on the health of many of the strikers were causing concern. Ó Mordháin, who was on the thirty-fourth day of his hunger strike, was described as 'weak'.[180] The large numbers participating militated against the success of the hunger strike and within days many abandoned the protest. On 27 October, the government suspended the release of prisoners engaged in the protest and it was made clear there would be no concessions.[181] Figures started to dwindle rapidly. By 2 November, 239 prisoners in Newbridge internment camp had abandoned the hunger strike as well as sixty-six in Tintown A.[182] The next day, the overall number had fallen to 5,067.[183] In Newbridge, some internees decided to sign the undertaking form while a list from Tintown showed that some forty-two had signed during the hunger strike.[184] The strike finally came to an end with the death of two of the participants. The first was Denis Barry, an inmate of Newbridge who died in the Curragh military hospital on 19 November. Fr Doyle, the prison chaplain, reluctantly administered the last rites, having initially refused the request.[185] After the inquest, the coroner gave the relatives an order for the burial of the body, but the military authorities refused, and Barry was interred in the Curragh camp. However, following a successful High Court action by the Barry family the remains were exhumed.[186] There was a large attendance at the removal to Newbridge town hall which included members of Cumann na mBan and ATIRA Volunteers.[187] When the remains reached Cork, Bishop Daniel Cohalan refused a religious funeral.[188] With the death of

Andy Sullivan in Mountjoy three days after Barry, and with no prospect of concessions from the government, the ATIRA ordered an end to the protests on 23 November.[189] While the strike itself failed in its objective, it did, however, activate a slow process of prisoner release – the state being worried of the political impact of more deaths.

An analysis of militancy in Kildare during the Civil War reveals that the ATIRA were never in a position to rival the pro-Treaty forces, unlike their colleagues in Munster. From the beginning of the conflict, the National army held a vastly superior position. It held all the towns and military barracks in the county. ATIRA militancy was nipped in the bud by the arrest of most of the leaders in the early days of the conflict. The activity of Ernie O'Malley in the Blessington area resulted in a short phase of conventional warfare with barracks at Ballymore Eustace and Rathangan falling briefly to the ATIRA. Republican resistance petered out given the strength of the major garrisons in the county, not to mention the Curragh. Just when it seemed that Kildare was reverting to its noted quiet county status, in the early autumn the various escapes of key ATIRA activists led to a resumption of guerrilla activity and two ASUs produced a level of militancy far greater than that witnessed during the War of Independence. Fatalities were low until the Graney ambush, which was the only seriously bloody encounter in Kildare. The county was centre stage in three significant national events during the Civil War and its immediate aftermath: the great escape from Newbridge in October 1922, the largest mass prison escape in Irish history, the executions, and the mass hunger strike of October 1923, in which the vast majority of participants were in Kildare jails. Politics during the Civil War in Kildare was marked by a three-way divide. Pro-Treaty SF and anti-Treaty SF were engaged on opposite sides of the conflict while Labour occupied a more neutral position.

# 9 A return to its Redmondite roots: Kildare in 1923

The general election in August 1923 provided an interesting barometer of public opinion in Kildare after the grim tragedy of fratricidal Civil War. Perhaps unexpectedly, former Redmondite nationalists such as George Wolfe and John Conlon were returned. The Kildare electorate rejected members of both SF and the IRA. The election was not fought in normal circumstances, with republicans to some degree hampered. Nevertheless, their vote increased slightly, and this reflected a declining degree of support for the government due to the executions and prison policy.

With the principal function of the third Dáil now fulfilled, a general election was necessary. In preparation, constituency revisions were undertaken and the number of Dáil seats increased from 128 to 153. As a result, Kildare county became a three-seat constituency as the unwieldy Kildare-Wicklow constituency was broken up. The franchise was also extended and 35,000 new voters were eligible to vote. For the first time this included both males and females aged twenty-one and over.[1] Although republicans were at a disadvantage, every constituency was contested by a variety of parties and candidates.

In early 1923 the four parties that had contested the 1922 election – Pro-Treaty Sinn Féin, Anti-Treaty Sinn Féin, Labour and the Farmers' Party – began preparations. Pro-Treaty Sinn Féin became a distinct party with the launch of Cumann na nGaedheal on 27 April 1923. New branches were established throughout the country and, on 7 June, a Cumann na nGaedheal branch was formed in Naas under the presidency of the local curate, Fr Patrick Doyle. Notably, it was supported by the remnants of the Redmondite nationalists such as D.J. Purcell and Michael Fitzsimons. But the biggest boost to the new branch was support from George Wolfe, the much-respected Protestant nationalist who joined the committee and worked alongside former IRA personnel such as Thomas Lawler and Stephen Garry.[2]

A public rally in Naas to launch the new party in the county was held on 15 July. Several leading Cumann na nGaedheal politicians addressed the gathering. They included three cabinet ministers: Kevin O'Higgins, vice president of the executive council; Éamonn Duggan, minister without portfolio; and Ernest Blythe, then minister for local government. Senator Jenny Wyse Power, one of the leading female politicians in the party, also spoke.[3] The new organization was now extended throughout the county and, within two weeks, twenty branches had been formed.[4]

A total of nine candidates from the four parties were nominated to contest the election. Labour, boosted by a rally in Newbridge with Big Jim Larkin as the keynote speaker, was the first to choose candidates, selecting Hugh

Colohan, the out-going TD and Michael Smyth as his running mate.[5] Cumann na nGaedheal was next in the field on 2 August and put forward three candidates.[6] Thomas Lawler and Simon Malone were regarded as front runners having stood down on the last occasion due to the pact election. Both represented different levels of opinion in the party with Lawler belonging to the militant section of the movement, whereas Malone identified with the political side. To add even greater appeal, George Wolfe was also selected.[7] As a long-term Redmondite supporter and a prominent member of the Farmers' Union, his addition aimed to influence the farmers' convention that was due to take place the following evening.[8] The convention was highly representative with almost 100 delegates from sixteen clubs in attendance.[9] As the three candidates chosen by Cumann na nGaedheal were farmers, former county council chairman, Stephen J. Browne, proposed that a Farmers' and Ratepayers' candidate should not be nominated as this might split the farmers' vote. However, this motion was overwhelmingly rejected, and former county councillor, John Conlon, was selected on behalf of farmers and ratepayers.[10] A native of Newbridge and a former nationalist councillor, before taking up farming he had been editor of the *Carlow Nationalist*.[11] Conlon's supporters included former Redmondite nationalists and unionists. On the republican side, Domhnall Ua Buachalla, Art O'Connor and Thomas Harris were announced at a rally in Naas on 8 August.[12] Harris, an escaped prisoner, chaired the meeting and at its conclusion was arrested.[13] Both Ua Buachalla and O'Connor were also in prison. Ua Buachalla, having been on the run earlier, was re-arrested between the ending of hostilities and the election.[14]

The election campaign was lacklustre with none of the scenes of violence typical of previous campaigns. The republican campaign was hampered by censorship and the imprisonment of many of its activists. The prisoner issue was highlighted at meetings by Muriel MacSwiney, widow of Terence MacSwiney; James O'Connor, brother of Art O'Connor; and Michael Smyth, who argued that the prison gates should be thrown open.[15] Unemployment was also a major issue in the Labour Party campaign, especially in Newbridge.[16] Cumann na nGaedheal was not as prominent on the campaign trail as the other parties. Of the three candidates, George Wolfe excelled, and at one meeting was even introduced as a descendant of Wolfe Tone. He made no attempt to deny the family connections and turned the patriot's name to his political advantage, referring to Wolfe Tone as the man who bore the same name as his grandfather.[17] Conlon, the Farmers' and Ratepayers' candidate, undertook a vigorous canvass focusing on farming interests, falling agriculture prices and rates. He had the support and assistance of former Redmondites such as John Healy and unionists such as Bertram Barton.[18]

The turnout for the election in Kildare was a disappointing fifty-five per cent, a figure reduced further as 4.6 per cent of votes were spoiled.[19] That

Hugh Colohan topped the poll as sitting Labour TD was no surprise, but there was no second seat for Labour even though it polled well and obtained three times the national average. The biggest upsets were the return of John Conlon and, in particular, George Wolfe. The number of first preferences for Cumann na nGaedheal in Kildare was the lowest in any constituency in the country with the exception of the National University. Only Laois–Offaly, Longford–Westmeath, Wexford and Waterford demonstrated lower percentage support for the party.[20]

Unemployment in Newbridge and the Curragh areas, the base of the two Labour candidates, due to the departure of the British army was the principal reason for the significant Labour vote, which was well in excess of a quota. The support of former nationalists, particularly farmers, explains the performance of Conlon and Wolfe, who had only been associated with the government party for six weeks. For Conlon, who gained almost eighty per cent of a quota, it was a respectable vote for the Farmers' Party which obtained seven per cent more in Kildare than the national average. Although the result for Cumann na nGaedheal was disappointing, the party could derive some comfort from the fact that seventy-nine per cent of the Kildare electorate supported pro-Treaty candidates. Nationally, republicans achieved twenty-seven per cent, while in Kildare they obtained twenty-one per cent.[21] Nonetheless, the results in the county clearly showed that despite a crushing defeat in the Civil War, there was still strong republican support in the constituency. Even though large numbers were in prison and could not vote, the republican vote was within six per cent of that of Cumann na nGaedheal. In fact, it had increased by two per cent since the last election. This reflected a sympathy vote due to the executions. The most striking aspect of the election in Kildare was that in 1923 the successful candidates had never been members of SF or the IRA. The message from the voters was clear: be content with the level of independence obtained and deal with economic issues.

Politics in Kildare between September 1923 and July 1924 continued to be dominated by the political prisoner issue. Rows erupted over the dismissal by Ernest Blythe, minister for local government, of two imprisoned county council employees with suggestions that the dismissals were politically motivated. The county council denounced the dismissal of Patrick Carroll, a junior clerk and son of Mark Carroll, a Labour Party member of the county council.[22] A more serious clash between council and minister occurred when the government in October removed Art O'Connor as assistant county surveyor.[23] Councillors from all parties united in condemnation because it seemed that 'any employees of the council who are not Free Staters cannot work'. Referring to O'Connor's role as former minister for agriculture in the second Dáil, Michael Smyth claimed the present ministry was removing a colleague of their own, 'who did one man's part in putting them into the jobs they now hold'.[24] The council demanded O'Connor's unconditional release so that he could resume his duties.[25] In the event, both Carroll and O'Connor were reinstated in 1924.[26]

With unrest seemingly at an end in Kildare for the first time in years, in December 1923 another episode connected to the prison system in the county revealed that Civil War animosities lay barely below the surface. Colonel Michael Costello, National army director of intelligence, suspected that a mole in the army was in contact with Michael Carolan, the IRA director of intelligence in Dublin. An investigation was carried out by Captain Michael Murray, who suspected Joseph Bergin, a 23-year-old corporal from County Laois serving with the military police in the Curragh camp.[27] His friendship with Peggie Daly, a known republican, who was released from internment on 28 September, aroused suspicion.[28] On 13 December, Bergin was abducted on his way to the Curragh camp by three intelligence agents, taken to a hut at Guiderstown, close to Kildare, and subjected to gruesome violence before being shot six times. The following day his badly mutilated body was found in the canal at Milltown close to the Curragh.[29] This brutal act had similarities with the sadistic murder of Noel Lemass, a leading republican, some months previously. Notably, at the Lemass inquest in October 1923, evidence emerged linking Captain Murray with that killing.[30] A cover-up in the Bergin case was then attempted. Murray, the chief suspect, initially fled to Argentina, but was arrested following his return home and charged with Bergin's murder. At the trial in 1925, it was suggested that unofficial executions were accepted.[31] Murray, who claimed he was made a scapegoat for the Bergin killing and accused Costello of masterminding the crime, was convicted. A death sentence was later commuted to a life sentence.[32] The trial signified a return to some normality in the rule of law in spite of a common belief that some parties to the crime escaped justice. The Bergin murder was the last violent death connected with the Irish Revolution in Kildare. Despite brutal killings and numerous executions, the conflict was not as ruthless as civil conflicts in other countries such as that during the Finnish Civil War in 1918.[33]

As 1923 drew to a close, the gradual release of internees continued: Art O'Connor was freed on 24 December 1923 and Michael O'Kelly on 19 January 1924.[34] By the following May, 3,000 had been released with W.T. Cosgrave indicating in the Dáil on 21 May, that only 592 prisoners remained.[35] By mid-April only twenty from Kildare remained imprisoned.[36] Nonetheless, public bodies in Kildare kept up the pressure on the government, and Kildare County Council, impatient that resolutions were getting nowhere, organized a cross-party protest meeting in Newbridge on 4 May. Speakers included Hugh Colohan of Labour, Patrick Phelan of the Farmers' Party, and recently released internees such as Éamon Ó Modhráin. A motion calling for the unconditional release of all political prisoners was proposed by Michael Smyth and, notably, seconded by Nicholas Travers, a prominent pro-

Treaty supporter. This was adopted.[37] When Ua Buachalla returned to a county council meeting a week later he was unanimously offered his old role as chairman but he refused on the grounds of inability to attend meetings.[38] On 7 June the remaining imprisoned members of the Mullaney column were freed. As they were sentenced prisoners, their release was unexpected with local speculation suggesting that differences in government circles in the aftermath of the Army Mutiny may have been a factor.[39] On 5 July, Patrick Carroll, the last Kildare political prisoner, was freed eleven days before a general prisoner release was announced.[40] Pressure from Kildare County Council and the unity shown among members on the prisoner issue may have had a bearing on the timing of the government's decision to release the Mullaney column. That Carroll was the last released sent an unambiguous message of government disapproval of Kildare County Council's stance.

The 1926 census revealed that the population of County Kildare had fallen by 12.9 per cent since 1911. As one would expect, the Protestant population accounted for most of the decline. Whereas the Catholic population fell by 0.5 per cent, the Protestant population was reduced by 69.6 per cent. This was a far greater decrease than in any other county. The withdrawal of the British army is the chief explanation for the decline, which was especially evident in the garrison towns. The historian Andy Bielenberg regards Kildare and Fermoy as extreme examples with their Protestant populations declining by over 93 per cent between 1911 and 1926, followed by Tipperary and Newbridge, which registered a loss of almost 89 per cent.[41] Ballysax parish, which includes the Curragh camp, experienced a loss of 96 per cent and Naas, where Protestants constituted 9 per cent of the population in 1911, declined to 5.6 per cent in 1926.[42]

The Protestant population of Kildare in 1911 totalled 11,900. Of this figure, 5,000 were listed as serving members of the British army temporarily based in the county. In addition, a further unknown number were family members of the servicemen.[43] By 1926 the recorded Protestant population was 3,600.[44] In addition to the departure of British army personnel in 1922, there were a number of other factors behind Protestant decline, including low levels of births and marriages. However, intimidation played a big part.[45] Violence against Protestants in Kildare continued into the late 1920s. The rented house of Captain Henry Hosie at Castlereban was burned in February 1924. A boycott of this property was still in operation in 1928 with the freeholder, Henry Large, residing in an outhouse adjacent to the burnt-out house and unable to rent a house in the Athy area.[46] In addition to intimidation, the 1923 Land Act forced many more to sell up as the new Irish government accelerated the process of land reform.[47] In 1925 Charles Bury's estate at Downings, Prosperous, was acquired at a much reduced price by the Irish Land Commission for distribution among smallholders in the area. But favouritism was sometimes practised by the new government as Bury's house and 100 acres was allocated to a retired National army officer.[48] The same fate awaited many of the remaining demesne estates held by former southern unionists who were forced either by the land acts, rates or high running costs to dispose of their properties. Leonard Wilson-Wright, who left Ireland during the truce period, fared better than most, eventually returning home to manage his extensive farming interests. Protestants were significantly over-represented on larger farms, which made them the target of agrarian outrages. In some districts ethno-religious factors also entered into the equation and they suffered reprisals for Catholic expulsions from Belfast.[49] Despite this, Protestant intimidation in Kildare was not as severe as in other areas and the northern section of the county to some extent became a haven for loyalists fleeing from other counties. Henry Sampey, a substantial landowner who was boycotted and driven from his native Roscommon, moved to the Ballymore Eustace area.[50] Alexander Cornelius, who had provided accommodation for British troops on his farm in County Laois and as a result was boycotted, relocated thirty miles to a farm close to the Curragh where the family lived without interference.[51]

Although the population decline in the garrison towns was considerable, they did not become ghost towns. The Curragh camp, the largest urban area in the county in 1911, still maintained a sizeable population of 4,100 after a decline of 41 per cent. Similarly, the populations of Newbridge and Kildare fell by 34 and 11 per cent respectively with Naas falling by 11.6 per cent.[52] The replacement of British garrisons by National army troops eased the decline to some extent. However, in Naas where the army barracks was the smallest in the county, the population fall was only partially attributable to the departure of the British army with economic issues the major reason for the decline.

In the decades following the revolution, four of the Kildare activists successfully carved out political careers at a national level. The best known was Ua Buachalla who returned to the Dáil as a Fianna Fáil TD in 1927 and was appointed governor general by de Valera in 1932.[53] Thomas Harris distinguished himself by successfully contesting ten Dáil elections and serving as a TD from 1931 to 1957.[54] Michael Smyth, who continued his work as a Labour councillor for thirty-five years, briefly served as a senator in the 1950s. His Labour Party colleague, Frank Purcell, obtained the post of secretary general of the ITGWU and also served in the Upper House.[55]

Other figures from the revolution did not achieve the same level of success. Art O'Connor continually failed to regain a Dáil seat. Following the split in SF in 1926, he succeeded de Valera as party leader but subsequently departed politics to study law. In his new profession he was called to the bar and eventually appointed a circuit court judge.[56] Ted O'Kelly qualified as a doctor and emigrated to London where he operated a medical practice until his death in the London blitz in 1941.[57] Michael O'Kelly, who did much to promote the republican cause at the expense of his career as editor of the *Leinster Leader*, failed to obtain full-time employment following his release from prison. In total, he spent more than two years in jail. Although he served briefly as a member of Naas UDC in the 1920s he became disenchanted with politics and moved to Dublin.[58] Paddy Mullaney, the most successful Kildare militant of the revolution, returned to his native Mayo following his release and spent the remainder of his life working as a primary school teacher and engaged in GAA activity at county board level.[59] Pro-Treaty SF activists from Kildare faded almost completely from the scene playing no meaningful role in the politics in the IFS. Throughout the remainder of the 1920s the chairmanship of Kildare County Council was held by Michael Fitzsimons, the only Redmondite to retain his county council seat during the entire revolution.[60] Following George Wolfe's retirement from the Dáil in 1932, his seat was won by Sidney Minch, a former British army captain and son of a Redmondite MP.[61]

Politically, in 1923 Kildare was an example of a county that to a large extent returned to its Redmondite roots. This was reflected in the results of the election of August 1923 that saw the rejection at the polls of militant activists who had been prominent during the War of Independence and Civil War. Kildare was exceptional in that no Oireachtas member from the county had previously served in the IRA or Sinn Féin. Furthermore, local politicians of all persuasions demonstrated an unusual unity by acting independently of the government in opposing ministerial interference in local affairs and calling for the early release of prisoners when the conflict had ended. The Irish Revolution had left a legacy of bitterness and recriminations in Kildare as elsewhere in the country. While the conflict was not as intense as in Dublin or Cork, in many respects it was no different to events in other counties. However, in a comparative context, the extent to which the politics of the majority in Kildare reverted to a viewpoint held in the pre-revolutionary period was notable and exceptional.

# Notes

CHAPTER ONE *Kildare in 1912*

1 CI Kildare, Jan. 1912 (The National Archives (hereafter TNA), CO 904/86).
2 Con Costello, 'John O'Donovan's Curragh' in William Nolan and Thomas McGrath (eds), *Kildare: history and society: interdisciplinary essays on the history of an Irish county* (Dublin, 2006), p. 538.
3 Census of Ireland 1911, Leinster province, Kildare; Dublin City, p. 32.
4 Census of Ireland 1911, Leinster province, Kildare, District Electoral Division (DED) Ballysax East, Newbridge District, p. 36; Kilcullen District, p. 29. The census shows the DED of Ballysax which includes the Curragh camp had a population of 7,439; see also Con Costello, *A most delightful station: the British army on the Curragh of Kildare, Ireland, 1855–1922* (Cork, 1999), p. 343.
5 Census of Ireland 1911, Kildare, p. 74.          6 Ibid., p. 2.
7 Ibid.; *Irish Times* (hereafter *IT*), 24 Dec. 1921.
8 Census of Ireland 1911, Kildare, p. 2; Mark McLoughlin, *Kildare barracks: from the Royal Field Artillery to the Irish Artillery Corps* (Dublin, 2014), pp 1–142.
9 Census of Ireland 1911, Kildare, p. 2; Frank Taaffe, 'Eye on the past', *Kildare Nationalist*, 9 June 1995, 8 Aug. 1996.
10 *Thom's Directory 1913*, p. 1197; Mary Cullen, *Maynooth: a short historical guide* (Maynooth, 1979).
11 *Thom's Directory 1913*, p. 1197; Tony Doohan, *History of Celbridge* (Celbridge, 2011), pp 137–9.
12 *Thom's Directory 1913*, p. 1197; Con Costello, *Looking back: aspects of history, County Kildare* (Naas, 1988), pp 101, 121; Seamus Kelly, *A ramble in Rathangan* (Leixlip, 2005).
13 Census of Ireland 1911, Kildare, pp vii, 74–5.
14 Ibid., Dublin City, p. viii; *Thom's Directory 1913*, p. 1289.
15 Census of Ireland 1911, Kildare, p. 74.
16 *Irish Church Directory 1912–13*, pp 112–14.
17 Georgina Clinton and Bridget Hourican, 'Peacocke, Joseph Ferguson' in *Dictionary of Irish biography* (9 vols, Cambridge, 2009) (hereafter *DIB*).
18 Michael Comerford, *Collections relating to the dioceses of Kildare and Leighlin* (3 vols, Dublin, 1883), i, 71–3.
19 *Irish Catholic Directory 1913*, pp 182–4, 209–10. The breakdown of the figures for Catholic clergymen in County Kildare includes twelve parish priests and eighteen curates in the section of the county in the diocese of Kildare and nine parish priests and thirteen curates in the rest of the county which is part of the archdiocese of Dublin.
20 Thomas Morrissey, 'Walsh, William Joseph', *DIB*.
21 Bernard J. Canning, *Bishops of Ireland, 1870–1987* (Ballyshannon, 1987), pp 209–10.
22 James McConnel, *The Irish Parliamentary Party and the third home rule crisis* (Dublin, 2013), p. 54.
23 *Thom's Directory 1913*, p. 1197; *Constabulary Gazette (RIC)*, 14 Feb. 1912.
24 *Thom's Directory 1913*, p. 1200; Jim Herlihy, *Royal Irish Constabulary officers: a biographical dictionary and genealogical guide, 1816–1922* (Dublin, 2005), p. 355.
25 Michael Farry, *Sligo: the Irish Revolution, 1912–23* (Dublin, 2012), p. 7.
26 Kerry Supple (1862–1921) was CI for King's County in late 1909, see Herlihy, *Royal Irish Constabulary officers*, p. 295; *Kildare Observer* (hereafter *KO*), 20 Aug. 1921.

27 *Constabulary Gazette* (RIC), 20 Jan. 1912.

28 Census of Ireland 1911, Kildare, p. vi.

29 Ibid., p. 49; Meath, p. 55; King's County, p. 44; Queen's County, p. 45; Wicklow, p. 47.

30 *Report of the Department of Agriculture and Technical Instruction for Ireland on agricultural statistics of Ireland for the year ended 31 March 1913*, Cd. 6987, pp 57, 154–5.

31 Ibid., p. 132.      32 Ibid., p. 57.      33 Ibid., p. 56.

34 Ibid., pp 46, 56. The highest proportion of freeholders was in Longford (83 per cent) and the lowest was in Carlow (38 per cent).

35 F.S.L. Lyons, *Ireland since the famine* (London, 1973), pp 18–19; Terence Dooley, *The decline and fall of the dukes of Leinster, 1872–1948* (Dublin, 2014), pp 122–9.

36 Patrick J. Cosgrave, 'The sale of the Leinster estate under the Wyndham Land Act, 1903', *Journal of the Kildare Archaeological Society* (hereafter *JKAS*), 20:1 (2008–9), 9.

37 *Nationalist and Leinster Times* (hereafter *NLT*), 17 Oct. 1913; Paul Bew, *Conflict and conciliation in Ireland, 1890–1910: Parnellites and radical agrarians* (Oxford, 1987), pp 134–5.

38 *Freeman's Journal* (hereafter *FJ*), 25 Nov. 1903; 27 Nov. 1903; Cosgrave, 'The sale of the Leinster estate', 19–20.

39 Census of Ireland 1911, Kildare, p. vi.

40 'General monthly return of the regimental strength of the British army, January 1912', pp 91–6 (TNA, WO 73/94).

41 Ibid., p. 93.      42 Costello, *Delightful station*, p. 254.

43 *IT*, 7 June 1911.      44 Costello, *Delightful station*, p. 260.

45 Frank Porter, *Porter's post office guide and directory for the counties of Carlow and Kildare, 1910* (Dublin, 1910).

46 Con Costello, *Kildare: saints, soldiers and horses* (Naas, 1991), p. 142.

47 Trade analysis ledgers, 1900–1920 (Guinness Archive, Dublin, GOB/ PK04/0002; GOB/ PK04/0003).

48 Liam Clare, 'The rise and demise of the Dublin cattle market, 1863–1973' in Denis Cronin, Jim Gilligan and Karina Holton (eds), *Irish fairs and markets: studies in local history* (Dublin, 2001), p. 193.

49 *Thom's Directory 1914*, p. 1197.

50 Adam Pole, 'Kilbride, Denis', *DIB*.

51 Georgina Clinton and Owen McGee, 'O'Connor, John', *DIB*.

52 Barry O'Brien to John Redmond, 3 Mar. 1905 (NLI, John Redmond papers, MS 15,214/3).

53 *The Times*, 29 Oct. 1928, indicated that O'Connor was unmarried; *KO*, 12 Jan. 1929.

54 *Irish People*, 13 June, 21 Nov. 1908; *KO*, 5 Sept. 1908; McConnel, *Irish Parliamentary Party*, pp 71–2.

55 Liam Kenny, *Kildare County Council: 1899–1999: first election and first meeting* (Naas, 2001).

56 John J. Clancy, *A handbook of local government in Ireland* (Dublin, 1899), pp 12–40; Brian Donnelly, 'Local government in Kildare, 1920–70' in Nolan and McGrath (eds), *Kildare*, pp 673–4.

57 See Thomas Nelson, 'Kildare County Council and perceptions of the past' in Terence Dooley (ed.), *Ireland's polemical past: views of Irish history in honour of R.V. Comerford* (Dublin, 2010), pp 176–91.

58 Donnelly, 'Local government in Kildare', p. 673.

59 Laurence William White, 'Wolfe, George', *DIB*. George Wolfe (1860–1941) was a member of an old Anglo-Irish gentry family who supported home rule. From 1899 to 1920, he served as a nationalist councillor on Kildare County Council and between 1923 and 1931 served as a TD for the county.

60 Thomas P. Nelson, *Through peace and war: Kildare County Council in the years of revolution, 1899–1926* (Maynooth, 2015), pp 46–8.

61 *KO*, 17 June 1911; *Thom's Directory 1913*, p. 1200.

62 CI Kildare, Jan. 1912 (TNA, CO 904/86).

63 Donnelly, 'Local government in Kildare', p. 662.

64 Marie Coleman, *County Longford and the Irish Revolution, 1910–1923* (Dublin, 2006), pp 13–15.

65 Michael Wheatley, *Nationalism and the Irish Party: provincial Ireland, 1910–1916* (Oxford, 2005), pp 44–8.

66 *KO*, 10 Dec. 1910.

67 Alan O'Day, *Irish home rule, 1867–1921* (Manchester, 1998), pp 247–50; Alvin Jackson, *Home rule: an Irish history, 1800–2000* (London, 2003), pp 107–9.

68 Minutes, 3 June 1912 (Kildare County Archives (hereafter KCoA), County Council meetings).

69 *KO*, 31 Aug. 1912.

70 These were Helen and Marie Gordon: http://apps.proni.gov.uk/ulstercovenant/SearchResults.aspx (accessed 16 Dec. 2015).

71 For example, CI Kildare, Feb. 1912 (TNA, CO 904/86).

72 *KO*, 6 Jan. 1912; *Leinster Leader* (hereafter *LL*), 22 June 1912.

73 *KO*, 6 Apr. 1912.            74 *LL*, 22 June 1912.

75 Ibid., 29 June 1912; C.J. Woods, *Bodenstown revisited: the grave of Theobald Wolfe Tone, its monuments and its pilgrimages* (Dublin, 2018), p. 77.

76 CI Kildare, Mar. 1912 (TNA, CO 904/86), Oct. 1912 (TNA, CO 904/88).

77 A.C. Hepburn, *Catholic Belfast and nationalist Ireland in the era of Joseph Devlin, 1871–1934* (Oxford, 2008), pp 96, 131–3.

78 *KO*, 6 Apr. 1912.            79 *KO*, 10 Dec. 1910.            80 *LL*, 27 Apr. 1912.

81 *KO*, 6 Jan. 1912; on fears of Rome rule, see Daithí Ó Corráin, 'Resigned to take the bill with its defects: the Catholic Church and the third home rule crisis, 1912–14' in Gabriel Doherty (ed.), *The home rule crisis, 1912–14* (Cork, 2014), pp 189–97.

82 *KO*, 2 Mar. 1912.            83 Ibid., 4 Apr. 1908.

84 For details of Lord Mayo, see Patrick Maume, 'Bourke, Dermot Robert Wyndham', *DIB*; Con Costello, *A class apart: the gentry families of County Kildare* (Dublin, 2004), pp 74–6.

85 *KO*, 10 Feb. 1912.

86 *KO*, 2 Mar. 1912; Rachel E. Finley-Bowman, 'An ideal unionist: the political career of Marchioness Londonderry, 1911–1919', *Journal of International Women's Studies*, 4 (2003), 18; Diane Urquhart, *The ladies of Londonderry: women and political patronage, 1800–1959* (London, 2007), pp 102–5.

87 *KO*, 16 Mar. 1912.

88 'The voice of the Church of Ireland on Home Rule: Resolutions of the General Synod, special meeting 16th Apr. 1912' (Dublin, 1912), p. 18, online, digital.slv.vic.gov.au/dtl_publish/pdf/marc/11/2703855.html (accessed 11 Feb. 2015); Andrew Scholes, *The Church of Ireland and the third home rule bill* (Dublin, 2010), pp 32–3.

89 R.B. McDowell, *The Church of Ireland, 1869–1969* (London, 1975), p. 104.

90 *IT*, 7 Oct. 1912; Scholes, *Church of Ireland*, p. 44.

91 *IT*, 2, 22 Oct. 1913; Clinton and Hourican, 'Peacocke, Joseph Ferguson', *DIB*.

92 *KO*, 31 Aug. 1912.

93 Ibid., 19 Apr. 1913; Margaret Ward, *Hanna Sheehy-Skeffington: a life* (Dublin, 1997).

94 Dooley, *Dukes of Leinster*, pp 119, 197.            95 Woods, *Bodenstown*, p. 4.

96 Ibid., p. 78.            97 Patrick Colgan (BMH WS 850, p. 4).

98 Thomas Harris (BMH WS 320, pp 1–2); on the IRB, see Matthew Kelly, *The Fenian ideal and Irish nationalism, 1882–1916* (Woodbridge, 2006), pp 171–204.

99 Michael O'Kelly (BMH WS 1,155, pp 2–3).            100 *LL*, 21 Apr. 1917.

101 Domhnall Mac Carthaigh, 'A glance at the Irish language in Co. Kildare', *Leinster Leader*, centenary issue 1980.

102 *LL*, 11 Oct. 1913, 12 Jan. 1918.
103 Seán Ó Conaill, 'The Irish language and the Irish legal system – 1922 to present' (PhD, Cardiff University, 2013), p. 34; *KO*, 17 Feb. 1906; Ruth Dudley Edwards, *Patrick Pearse: the triumph of failure* (London, 1979), pp 79–81; Joost Augusteijn, *Patrick Pearse: the making of a revolutionary* (Basingstoke, 2010), pp 65–6.
104 Adhamhnán Ó Súilleabháin, *Domhnall Ua Buachalla: rebellious nationalist, reclusive governor* (Dublin, 2015), pp 29–35.
105 John Drennan, *Cannon balls and croziers* (Maynooth, 1994), p. 103.
106 Patrick Colgan (BMH WS 850, p. 2); Patrick Maume, 'O'Hickey, Michael (Ó Hiceadha Micheál)', *DIB*.
107 Kevin Collins, *Catholic churchmen and the Celtic revival in Ireland, 1848–1916* (Dublin, 2002), pp 52–5; Sean O'Casey, *Drums under the windows, the third volume of O'Casey's memoirs* (New York, 1950).
108 Eoghan Corry, *Kildare GAA: a centenary of history* (Clane, 1984), pp 74–7, 88–90, 95–111.
109 *LL*, 9 Aug. 1913. Fitzgerald was arrested in 1916 and 1920. He was a prominent Sinn Féin organizer in 1917 and a county councillor from 1920, see *LL*, 11 Feb. 1950.
110 Mike Cronin, William Murphy and Paul Rouse (eds), *The Gaelic Athletic Association, 1884–2009* (Dublin, 2009), p. 64.
111 Michael O'Kelly (BMH WS 1,155, pp 48–56); Liam Kenny, 'Leader editor termed a gentle giant'.

CHAPTER TWO *Redmondism and home rule, 1913–14*

1 CI Kildare, Oct. 1913 (TNA, CO 904/56).   2 *KO*, 14 June 1913.
3 *LL*, 27 Sept. 1913; McConnel, *IPP*, pp 271–3; Wheatley, *Nationalism and the Irish Party*, pp 167, 177–8.
4 Alan O'Day, 'The Ulster crisis; a conundrum' in D.G. Boyce and Alan O'Day (eds), *The Ulster crisis, 1885–1921* (Basingstoke, 2006), p. 19.   5 *KO*, 23 Oct. 1913.
6 O'Day, *Irish home rule*, pp 256–9; Jackson, *Home rule*, pp 114–15, 127.
7 *Irish Independent* (hereafter *II*), 4 Mar. 1914; McConnel, *IPP*, pp 280–4.
8 McConnel, *IPP*, pp 285–6.   9 *LL*, 4 Apr. 1914.
10 Ibid., 18 Apr. 1914.   11 *KO*, 14 Mar. 1914.
12 Jackson, *Home rule*, pp 122–4; R.B. McDowell, *Crisis and decline: the fate of the southern unionists* (Dublin, 1997), pp 50–2; Scholes, *Church of Ireland*, pp 82–3.
13 *LL*, 6 June 1914; *KO*, 6 June 1914. O'Connor was not related to John O'Connor, the local MP.
14 *KO*, 13 June 1914.   15 Nelson, *Through peace and war*, p. 435.
16 *LL*, 30 May 1914.   17 McDowell, *Crisis and decline*, p. 51.
18 *KO*, 11 July 1914; *Hansard (Lords)*, 9 July 1914, vol. 16, cols 1049–52.
19 *The Times*, 15 July 1913.   20 CI Kildare, Aug. 1913 (TNA, CO 904/ 55).
21 Padraig Yeates, *Lockout: Dublin 1913* (Dublin, 2000), p. 27.
22 John Colgan, *Leixlip County Kildare* (Leixlip, 2005), pp 112–13.
23 CI Dublin, Sept. 1913 (TNA, CO 904/ 56); R.M. Fox, *The history of the Irish Citizen Army* (Dublin, 1944), p. 52.
24 CI Dublin, Sept. 1913 (TNA, CO 904/ 56); *LL*, 25 Oct., 8 Nov. 1913; Colgan, *Leixlip*, p. 113.
25 Shackletons' Mills, Lucan (NAI, CSORP, 1913/21041, 1913/19650); *IT*, 27 Oct. 1913.
26 Strike at Wookey's, Leixlip (NAI, CSORP, 1913/16355, 1913/16668); Colgan, *Leixlip*, p 112.   27 Yeates, *Lockout*, p. 123.   28 *IT*, 12 Nov. 1913.
29 CI Kildare, Nov., Dec. 1913 (TNA, CO 904/91); CI Kildare, Jan. 1914 (TNA, CO 904/92); *KO*, 6 Dec. 1913; *IT*, 9 Feb. 1914.
30 Ann Matthews, *The Irish Citizen Army* (Cork, 2014), pp 22–6; Yeates, *Lockout*, p. 437.
31 Fox, *Citizen Army*, pp 52–3; Colgan, *Leixlip*, p. 113.

32  *KO*, 13, 20 Sept. 1913; http://www.lucannewsletter.ie/history/lockout.html (accessed 2 Apr. 2015). The Shackleton papers consulted by the author are not available at present.

33  Information from Ua Buachalla's papers in the possession of Adhamhnán Ó Súilleabháin, Dublin; *LL*, 22 Nov. 1913. On Shackleton and Sinn Féin, see Richard P. Davis, *Arthur Griffith and non-violent Sinn Féin* (Dublin, 1974), pp 141, 173–5.

34  Patrick Colgan (BMH WS 850, p. 6).                                 35  *KO*, 18 Apr. 1914.

36  *LL*, 25 Oct. 1913.                        37  *KO*, 9 Dec. 1913.

38  *Irish Citizen*, 6 Dec. 1913; *IT*, 3 May 1913; Yeates, *Lockout*, p. 286.

39  Doohan, *Celbridge*, p. 84.

40  Karen Hunt, 'Women, solidarity and the 1913 Dublin Lockout: Dora Montefiore and the save the kiddies scheme' in Francis Devine (ed.), *A capital in conflict: Dublin City and the 1913 lockout* (Dublin, 2013), pp 107–28.

41  Conor Kostick, *Revolution in Ireland: popular militancy, 1917 to 1923* (London, 1996), p. 18.

42  *Manchester Guardian*, 27 Oct. 1913.

43  *IT*, 28 Oct. 1913; Leah Levenson, *With wooden sword: a portrait of Francis Sheehy-Skeffington, militant and pacifist* (Dublin, 1983), p. 147.

44  Solicitors' accounts concerning costs incurred on behalf of ITGWU, 25 Oct. 1913 (NLI, ITGWU, MS 27,054 (ii)); Mary Lawless to Sheehy-Skeffington, 4 Oct. 1913 (NLI, Sheehy Skeffington papers, MS 33,611 (7)); *IT*, 28 Oct. 1913; *Evening Telegraph*, 5 Nov. 1913.

45  *LL*, 29 Nov. 1913; *KO*, 6 Dec. 1913.                            46  *IT*, 4 Oct. 1913.

47  *Monthly army list for March 1914* (London, 1914), p. 28. On Paget see Lawrence William White, 'Paget, Sir Arthur Henry Fitzroy', *DIB*.

48  *Monthly army list for March 1914*, p. 29; Ian W.F. Beckett, *The army and the Curragh incident, 1914* (London, 1986), p. 439; John Wheelar-Bennett (revised Roger T. Stearn), 'Fergusson, Sir Charles', *Oxford dictionary of national biography* (Oxford, 2004) (hereafter *ODNB*).

49  http://www.curragh.info/articles/mutiny.htm (accessed 10 Oct. 2014); Beckett, *Curragh incident*, p. 439. Marlborough barracks is now known as McKee barracks.

50  A.P. Ryan, *Mutiny at the Curragh* (London, 1956), p. 129; on Gough, see Simon J. Potter, 'Gough, Sir Hubert', *DIB*.

51  'General monthly return of the regimental strength of the British army for March 1914', pp 90–7 (TNA, WO 73/96).

52  RIC inspector general (IG) report, Mar. 1914 (TNA CO 904/57).

53  A.T.Q. Stewart, *The Ulster crisis: resistance to home rule, 1912–1914* (London, 1967), p. 78; Beckett, *Curragh incident*, p. 5.

54  Costello, *Delightful station*, p. 286; Beckett, *Curragh incident*, pp 439–40.

55  Seven barracks made up the Curragh camp prior to independence namely: army service corps barracks (now Clarke barracks); Beresford barracks (now Ceannt barracks); Engineer barracks (now MacDermott barracks); Gough barracks (now MacDonagh barracks); Keane barracks (now Pearse barracks); Ponsonby barracks (now Plunkett barracks) and Stewart barracks (now Connolly barracks). The 5th Lancers in Marlborough Barracks, Dublin completed the 3rd Cavalry Brigade.

56  Elizabeth Muenger, *The British military dilemma in Ireland* (Dublin, 1991), p. 177.

57  Cabinet papers relating to the military situation in Ulster, 18 Mar. 1914 (TNA, CAB 41/35/8); Richard Holmes, *The little field-marshal: Sir John French* (London, 2004), p. 174.

58  IG report, Mar. 1914 (TNA, CO 904/57).

59  Correspondence relating to recent events in the Irish Command (TNA, WO 35/60), pp 2–4; Holmes, *French*, pp 173–4; Beckett, *Curragh incident*, p. 8.

60  James Fergusson, *The Curragh incident* (London, 1964), pp 47, 69; Beckett, *Curragh incident*, pp 9, 61–2.

61  Correspondence relating to recent events in the Irish Command (TNA, WO 35/60), pp 12–15; Beckett, *Curragh incident*, pp 10–11; Fergusson, *Curragh incident*, pp 53–5.

62 Papers of Admiral Sir John de Robeck, correspondence, n.d. (Churchill College, Cambridge, DRBK 3/7).

63 Fergusson, *Curragh incident*, p. 67.

64 Correspondence relating to recent events in the Irish Command (TNA, WO 35/60), pp 15–16; Beckett, *Curragh incident*, pp 12, 132–5, 162; Fergusson, *Curragh incident*, pp 72–3.

65 Hubert Gough, *Soldiering on: being the memoirs of General Sir Hubert Gough* (London, 1954), p. 101.

66 D.S. Daniell, *4th Hussars: the story of a British cavalry regiment* (Aldershot, 1959), p. 239.

67 Correspondence relating to recent events in the Irish Command (TNA, WO 35/60), p. 7; Beckett, *Curragh incident*, pp 79–80; Fergusson, *Curragh incident*, pp 86–7.

68 Beckett, *Curragh incident*, p. 15.

69 Lord Derby to Bonar Law, 22 Mar. 1914 (Parliamentary Archives, Bonar Law papers, BL 32/1/43); Gough, *Soldiering on*, p. 104.

70 Fergusson, *Curragh incident*, p. 386; on Wilson see Keith Jeffery, *Field Marshal Sir Henry Wilson: a political soldier* (Oxford, 2006).

71 Beckett, *Curragh incident*, p. 183, citing Wilson's diary of 23 Mar. 1914.

72 Gough, *Soldiering on*, pp 105–6.

73 Correspondence relating to recent events in the Irish Command (TNA, WO 35/60), p. 11; Beckett, *Curragh incident*, pp 8–9; Holmes, *French*, pp 187–8.

74 Correspondence relating to recent events in the Irish Command (TNA, WO 35/60), p. 11; Homes, *French*, p. 188; Gough, *Soldiering on*, p. 109.

75 Goulding to Bonar Law, 21 Mar. 1914 (Parliamentary Archives, Bonar Law papers, BL 32/1/40); Pauric J. Dempsey and Shaun Boylan, 'Goulding, Sir William Joshua', *DIB*.

76 Derby to Bonar Law, 22 Mar. 1914 (Parliamentary Archives, Bonar Law papers, BL 32/1/43); on Greer, see Angela Murphy, 'Greer, Sir (Joseph) Henry', *DIB*.

77 Ryan, *Mutiny*, p. 157.    78 Beckett, *Curragh incident*, p. 156.

79 *KO*, 28 Mar. 1914.

80 Cabinet papers relating to the military situation in Ulster, 28 Mar. 1914 (TNA CAB, 41/35/10); Fergusson, *Curragh incident*, pp 158, 162–3; Beckett, *Curragh incident*, p. 193 quoting extracts from the diary from Sir John Spencer Ewart.

81 *Hansard 5 (Commons)*, 25 Mar. 1914, vol. 60, col. 420.    82 *FJ*, 26 Mar. 1914.

83 *LL*, 20 Apr. 1914.    84 *IT*, 26 Mar. 1914.    85 *LL*, 6 Dec. 1913.

86 IG report, Apr. 1914 (TNA, CO 904/57).

87 IG reports, Jan.–Apr. 1914 (TNA, CO 904/57); *Irish Volunteer*, 7 Feb.–9 May 1914.

88 *LL*, 2 May 1914.    89 IG report, Apr. 1914 (TNA, CO 904/57).

90 *LL*, 2 May 1914.

91 Wheatley, *Nationalism and the Irish Party*, p. 189.

92 Michael Tierney, *Eoin MacNeill: scholar and man of action, 1867–1945* (Oxford, 1980), p. 137.    93 Thomas Harris (BMH WS 320, p. 2).

94 *LL*, 16 May 1914.    95 Michael O'Kelly (BMH WS 1,155, p. 7).

96 *LL*, 16 May 1914; *Leinster Leader* Centenary Supplement, 1980.

97 CI Kildare, May 1914 (TNA, CO 904/57).

98 *KO*, 6 June 1914.    99 *LL*, 6 June 1914.

100 Ibid.; Patrick O'Keeffe, 'My reminiscences of 1914–1923', *Oughterany: Journal of the Donadea Local History Group*, 1:1 (1993), 42.

101 O'Keeffe, 'Reminiscences'; for details the massacre at the Gibbet Rath, see Mario Corrigan, *All that delirium of the brave – Kildare in 1798* (Naas, 1997), pp 59–61; Liam Chambers, *Rebellion in Kildare, 1790–1803* (Dublin, 1998), pp 83–4.

102 *LL*, 13 June 1914.

103 *FJ*, 10 June 1914; McConnel, *IPP*, p. 288; Tierney, *MacNeill*, p. 141.

104 *LL*, 20 June 1914.

105 J.J. Bergin to MacDonagh, 8 July 1914 (NLI, Thomas MacDonagh papers, MS 20,643/9); *Irish Volunteer*, 25 July 1914.
106 CI Kildare, July 1914 (TNA, CO 904/58).
107 CI King's County, July 1914; CI Queen's County, July 1914 (TNA, CO 904/58); *Thom's Directory 1913*, pp 1197, 1206, 1247, 1279.
108 Elizabeth Bloxham (BMH WS 632, p. 5); *Irish Volunteer*, 25 July 1914; Lil Conlon, *Cumann na mBan and the women of Ireland, 1913–1925* (Cork, 1968), pp 7–8; Cal McCarthy, *Cumann na mBan and the Irish Revolution* (Cork, 2007), p. 38; Ann Matthews, *Renegades: Irish republican women, 1900–1922* (Cork, 2010), pp 101–2.
109 *KO*, 1 Aug. 1914; *LL*, 29 Aug. 1914; *Irish Volunteer*, 25 July, 29 Aug. 1914.
110 *KO*, 1 Aug. 1914.  111 Padraig O'Connor (BMH, WS 813, pp 1–2).
112 O'Keeffe, 'Reminiscences', 42.  113 *LL*, 1 Aug. 1914; *KO*, 1 Aug. 1914.
114 *LL*, 1, 8 Aug. 1914.  115 CI Kildare, July 1914 (TNA, CO 904/58).

CHAPTER THREE *The impact of the First World War, August 1914–March 1916*

1 *KO*, 8 Aug. 1914
2 *Hansard 5 (Commons)*, 3 Aug. 1914, vol. 65, col. 1828; *FJ*, 4 Aug. 1014; *LL*, 8 Aug. 1914; *KO*, 8 Aug. 1914.
3 *LL*, 8 Aug. 1914; *KO*, 8 Aug. 1914; Minutes, 17 Aug. 1914 (KCoA, county council meetings).
4 CI, Kildare, Aug. 1914 (TNA, CO 904/94).
5 Redmond to Asquith, 22 Aug. 1914 (Bodleian Library, Asquith papers, MS Asquith, 36/79); *IT*, 16 Aug. 1914; David Miller, *Church, state and nation in Ireland, 1898–1921* (Dublin, 1973), p. 310.
6 Michael J. Curran (BMH WS 687, pp 1, 13); Daithí Ó Corráin, 'Archbishop William Joseph Walsh' in Eugenio Biagini and Daniel Mulhall (eds), *The shaping of modern Ireland: a centenary reassessment* (Sallins, 2016), p. 120; Curran served as Walsh's secretary.
7 *KO*, 31 Oct. 1914; Clinton and Hourican, 'Peacocke, Joseph Ferguson', *DIB*.
8 Alan Megahey, *The Irish Protestant Churches in the twentieth century* (London, 2000), p. 39; Pauric J. Dempsey, 'Bernard, John Henry', *DIB*.
9 Denis Gwynn, *The life of Redmond* (London, 1932), pp 348–9; Jackson, *Home rule*, p. 164.
10 *LL*, 8 Aug. 1914.  11 *KO*, 22 Aug. 1914.
12 O'Day, *Irish home rule*, p. 261; Gwynn, *Redmond*, p. 381.
13 *LL*, 26 Sept. 1914; *KO*, 26 Sept. 1914.
14 IG report, Sept. 1914 (TNA, CO 904/94); Breandán Mac Giolla Choille (ed.), *Intelligence notes, 1913–1916, preserved in the State Paper Office* (Dublin, 1966), p. 111.
15 *Cork Examiner*, 30 Sept. 1914.
16 O'Connor to Kitchener, 26 July 1915 (NLI Redmond papers, MS 15201/1); O'Connor to Gray, 26 July, 3 Sept. 1915 (NLI, Redmond papers, MS 15,214/3); copy O'Connor to Sir Edward Grey, 28 May 1915 (NLI, Moore papers, MS 10,544/2/69); James Connel, 'Après la guerre: John Redmond, the Irish Volunteers and the armed constitutionalism, 1913–1915', *English Historical Review*, 131:553 (Dec. 2016), 1445–70.
17 *FJ*, 21 Sept. 1914.
18 Ibid., 25 Sept. 1914; Dermot Meleady, *John Redmond: the national leader* (Dublin, 2014), p. 307.
19 IG report, Sept. 1914 (TNA, CO 904/94); IG report, Dec. 1914 (TNA, CO 904/95).
20 Éamon Ó Mordháin also known in documents as Éamon or Edward Moran.
21 *LL*, 10 Oct. 1914; *KO*, 10 Oct. 1914.  22 *LL*, 24 Oct. 1914.
23 *KO*, 10 Oct., 21 Nov. 1914; Padraig O'Connor (BMH, WS 813, p. 1). Hubert O'Connor, a prominent officer in the Celbridge Volunteers, enlisted and died in Flanders in 1915 – see obituary, *The Clongowian* (1917), pp 119–20 (Clongowes Wood College Archive).

24  Patrick Colgan (BMH, WS 850, p. 6); *KO*, 10 Oct. 1914.      25  *LL*, 7 Nov. 1914.
26  CI Kildare, Nov., Dec. 1914 (TNA, CO 940/95).
27  Michael O'Kelly (BMH, WS 1,155, p. 12); *LL*, 10 Oct. 1914.
28  CI Kildare, Sept. 1914 (TNA, CO 904/94).
29  CI Kildare, Oct. 1914 (TNA, CO 904/95); Michael O'Kelly (BMH, WS 1,155, p. 12); *LL*, 4 Oct. 1914.
30  *Northern Whig*, 5 Aug. 1914; *II*, 10 Aug. 1914; Thomas Hennessy, *Dividing Ireland: World War 1 and partition* (London, 1998), pp 61, 66.
31  *KO*, 22 Aug. 1914.         32  *LL*, 15 Aug. 1914; *KO*, 15 Aug. 1914.
33  *KO*, 7 Nov. 1914.          34  *LL*, 15 Aug. 1914.
35  Ibid., 8 Aug. 1914; *KO*, 8 Aug. 1914.
36  Catriona Pennell, 'Going to war' in John Horne (ed.), *Our war: Ireland and the Great War* (Dublin, 2008), p. 40.
37  *LL*, 12 Sept. 1914; *II*, 10 Oct. 1914; Costello, *Delightful station*, p. 281.
38  Costello, *Delightful station*, p. 284.
39  CI Kildare, Oct. 1914 (TNA, CO 904/95).               40  *KO*, 2 Jan. 1915.
41  CI Kildare, Oct. 1914 (TNA, CO 904/95).
42  Keith Jeffery, *Ireland and the Great War* (Cambridge, 2000), p. 39; Lady Fingall, *Seventy years young: memories of Elizabeth, countess of Fingall* (Dublin, 1991), p. 348. On Mayo and the Arts and Crafts Society of Ireland and guild of Irish Art-Workers, see *FJ*, 5 May 1915.
43  *II*, 9 Jan. 1915; *IT*, 9 Jan. 1915; *LL*, 16 Jan. 1915.
44  *Hansard (Lords)*, 8 Jan. 1915, vol. 18, cols 358–60; *II*, 9 Jan. 1915; *LL*, 16 Jan. 1915.
45  *FJ*, 12 Jan. 1915; *IT*, 12 Jan. 1915.               46  *FJ*, 14 Jan. 1915.
47  *LL*, 16 Jan. 1915; Minutes, 20 Jan. 1915 (KCoA, county council meetings).
48  *LL*, 8 Aug. 1914; *KO*, 8 Aug., 15 Aug. 1914.
49  *LL*, 8 Aug. 1914; Costello, *Delightful station*, p. 279.
50  *KO*, 22, 29 Aug. 1914.
51  *Agricultural Statistics, Ireland, 1917–18* (Cd. 8453), p. 10.      52  Ibid., p. 9.
53  *LL*, 8 Aug. 1914.          54  *Hansard 5 (Commons)*, 30 Mar. 1916, vol. 81, col. 905.
55  For details see Costello, *Delightful station*, p. 289.
56  *KO*, 22 Aug. 1914; Frank Taaffe, 'Athy and the Great War' in Nolan and McGrath (eds), *Kildare*, p. 589; Paul Fussell, *The Great War and modern memory* (Oxford, 2013), p. 343.
57  *KO*, 9 Oct. 1915.
58  Padraig Yeates, *City in wartime: Dublin, 1914–1918* (Dublin, 2011), p. 48; Pat McCarthy, *Waterford: the Irish Revolution, 1912–23* (Dublin, 2015), p. 32; Thomas P. Dooley, *Irishmen or English soldiers? The times and world of a southern Catholic Irishman (1876–1916) enlisting in the British army during the First World War* (Liverpool, 1995), pp 103–7.
59  *KO*, 4 Sept. 1915.
60  Holly Dunbar, 'Women and alcohol during the First World War in Ireland', *Women's History Review*, 27:3 (2018), 381, 392.
61  Costello, *Delightful station*, p. 296; James Durney, *In a time of war: Kildare, 1914–18* (Sallins, 2014), pp 120–4.
62  RDF website: http://www.dublin-fusiliers.com/Naas/naas.html (accessed 2 May 2016); *KO*, 24 Apr. 1915; *IT*, 7 Nov. 1914, 23 Oct. 1915.               63  *KO*, 31 Oct. 1914.
64  *KO*, 10 June 1916. On POW camps see Heather Jones, *Violence against prisoners of war in the First World War: Britain, France and Germany, 1914–1920* (Cambridge, 2011).
65  *LL*, 11 Sept. 1915.
66  Clare O'Neill, 'The Irish home front 1914–1918 with particular reference to the treatment of Belgian refugees, prisoners of war, enemy aliens and war casualties' (PhD, NUI Maynooth, 2006), pp 52–83; Fionnuala Walsh, 'The impact of the First World War on Celbridge, Co. Kildare', *JKAS*, 20:3 (2012–13), 295–7.

67 Belgian Refugee Committee minutes, 21 Oct. 1914, p. 7 (UCDA, Belgian Refugees' Committee, P105); *KO*, 24 Oct. 1915.

68 *LL*, 31 Oct. 1914, 17 Apr. 1915; *KO*, 16 Jan., 6 Mar. 1915.

69 Bishop Browne of Cloyne to Archbishop Walsh, 31 Dec. 1914 (Dublin Diocesan Archives, William Walsh papers, 384/4 Bishops 1914); *LL*, 21 Nov. 1914.

70 Belgian Refugee Committee minutes, 29 Apr. 1915, p. 80, 1 Sept. 1915, p. 117 (UCDA, P105).

71 *KO*, 3 Apr. 1915.          72 Ibid., 28 Nov. 1914.          73 Ibid., 17 Apr. 1915.

74 Belgian Refugee Committee minutes, 1 Sept. 1915, p. 117.

75 *LL*, 15 Aug. 1914; Donal Ó Drisceoil, 'Keeping disloyalty within bounds?: British media control in Ireland, 1914–19', *IHS*, 38:149 (2012), 52–69.

76 *KO*, 22, 29 May 1915.          77 *LL*, 2 Nov. 1915.

78 *KO*, 29 May 1915; *LL*, 5 June 1915.

79 *LL*, 8 May 1915. On Gallipoli, see Philip Orr, *Field of bones: an Irish division at Gallipoli* (Dublin, 2006); Tom Johnstone, *Orange, Green and Khaki: the story of the Irish regiments in the Great War, 1914–18* (London, 1992), pp 104–5, 152; R.R. James, *Gallipoli* (London, 2004), p. 348; Durney, *Time of war*, p. 60.

80 *KO*, 8, 22 May 1915.          81 *KO*, 10 July 1915.

82 *LL*, 7 Aug. 1915.          83 *KO*, 23 Oct. 1915.

84 Terence Denman, *Ireland's unknown soldiers: the 16th (Irish) Division in the Great War, 1914–1918* (Dublin, 1992), pp 131–2.

85 *Statement giving particulars regarding men of military age in Ireland, 1916* (Cd. 8390), vol. xvii, p. 3; see also David Fitzpatrick, 'Militarism in Ireland, 1900–1922' in Thomas Bartlett and Keith Jeffrey (eds), *A military history of Ireland* (Cambridge, 1996), p. 388.

86 Mac Giolla Choille (ed.), *Intelligence notes*, pp 142, 146, 181–2; Walsh, 'Impact of the First World War on Celbridge', 290; Durney, *Time of war*, p. 55.

87 *KO*, 5 June, 11 Sept., 23 Oct. 1915; Walsh, 'Impact of the First World War on Celbridge', 290.

88 Durney, *Time of war*, p. 197.

89 Patrick Callan, 'Recruiting for the British army in Ireland during the First World War', *Irish Sword*, 17 (1987–90), 42.

90 *KO*, 17 Apr. 1915.

91 Minutes, 31 May 1915 (KCoA, county council meetings); *KO*, 5 June 1915; *LL*, 5 June 1915.          92 *KO*, 29 May 1915.

93 On IPP MPs and enlistment, see James McConnel, 'Recruiting sergeants for John Bull? Irish Nationalist MPs and enlistment during the early months of the Great War', *War in History*, 14:4 (2007), 408–28.

94 *KO*, 7 Aug. 1915.          95 *LL*, 27 Nov. 1915.          96 *KO*, 7 Aug 1915.

97 *Irish Catholic*, 6 Nov. 1915; Miller, *Church, state and nation in Ireland*, pp 313–14.

98 *FJ*, 16 Nov. 1915.

99 *LL*, 27 Nov. 1915; see also Jérôme aan de Wiel, 'Mgr O'Riordan, Bishop Dwyer and the shaping of new relations between nationalist Ireland and the Vatican during World War One' http://www.limerickcity.ie/media/o%27dwyer,%20edward%20thomas%2019.pdf (accessed 24 Apr. 2016).

100 *Munster News*, 10 Nov. 1915; *KO*, 20 Nov. 1915; Thomas J. Morrissey, *Bishop Edward Thomas O'Dwyer of Limerick, 1842–1917* (Dublin, 2003), pp 368–9.

101 *LL*, 27 Nov. 1915.

102 *KO*, 4 Dec. 1915.

103 Sworn statement by Michael Cosgrove, 13 Mar. 1937 (IMA, MSPC, WMSP34REF4156).

104 *KO*, 29 Jan. 1915.

105 David Synnott, 'Diary of a recruiting drive for the British armed forces undertaken by Barbara Synnott, Co. Kildare, 24 January to 2 February 1916', *JKAS*, 19:3 (2004–5), 549–58.

106 Ibid., 533, 545.                    107 *LL*, 13 Nov. 1915.
108 *KO*, 18 Nov. 1916.                  109 *LL*, 27 Nov. 1915.

CHAPTER FOUR *Rebellion and its aftermath: Kildare in 1916*

1 Patrick Colgan, 'The Maynooth Volunteers in 1916', *An tÓglach*, 8 May 1926, 3–5.
2 *Royal Commission on the Rebellion in Ireland: report of commission (June 1916)*, Cd. 8279, p. 26.
3 Domhnall Ó Buachalla (BMH WS 194, pp 1–2); Patrick Colgan (BMH WS 850, p. 6).
4 Michael O'Kelly (BMH WS 1,155, p. 9); Michael Smyth (BMH WS 1,531, pp 1–2); Thomas Harris (BMH WS 320, p. 3).
5 Reports of attendance varied. The CI suggested 1,500, CI Kildare, July 1915 (TNA, CO 904/97); 2,000 according to *II*, 21 June 1915; and 9,000 according to the *LL*, 26 June 1915.
6 Thomas Pugh (BMH WS 397, p. 22); *FJ*, 21 June 1915.
7 *LL*, 26 June 1915; *KO*, 26 June 1915.
8 *FJ*, 21 June 1915; on Clarke, see Gerard MacAtasney, *Tom Clarke: life, liberty, revolution* (Sallins, 2013); Michael T. Foy, *Tom Clarke: the true leader of the Easter Rising* (Dublin, 2014).
9 *LL*, 26 June 1915.          10 CI Kildare, June 1915 (TNA, CO 904/97).
11 CI Kildare, Aug. 1915 (ibid.).
12 O'Keeffe family papers, Thomas O'Keeffe, Kilcock, handwritten account of Patrick O'Keeffe's reminiscences of 1914–23.
13 Daithí Ó Corráin, 'A most public spirited and unselfish man: the career and contribution of Colonel Maurice Moore, 1854–1939', *Studia Hibernica*, 40 (2014) 104; *LL*, 26 June 1915; James Dunne (BMH WS 1,571, p. 1).
14 Michael Smyth (BMH WS 1,531, p.1).
15 *LL*, 27 Nov. 1915; O'Keeffe, 'Reminiscences', 42.
16 Sworn statement by Edward O'Kelly, 27 Apr. 1935 (IMA, MSPC, WMSP34REF4176); Daithí Ó Corráin, 'J.J. O'Connell's memoir of the Irish Volunteers, 1914–16, 1917', *Analecta Hibernica*, 47 (2016), 15–16, 84.
17 CI Kildare, Sept. 1915 (TNA, CO 904/98).
18 Michael O'Kelly (BMH WS 1,155, pp 2, 13–14); Michael Smyth (BMH WS 1,531, p. 2).
19 *FJ*, 24 Sept. 1915; Michael Smyth (BMH WS 1,531, p. 2).
20 Michael Smyth (BMH WS 1,531, p. 3); *Gaelic American*, 23 Jan. 1925; John Devoy, *Recollections of an Irish rebel* (Shannon, 1969), pp 403–4.
21 On Devoy see Terry Golway, *Irish rebel: John Devoy and America's fight for Ireland's freedom* (New York, 2008) and Robert Schmuhl, *Ireland's exiled children: America and the Easter Rising* (Oxford, 2016), pp 24–37.
22 Patrick Colgan (BMH WS 850, p. 3).          23 Devoy, *Recollections*, p. 477.
24 John Kenny, 'John Kenny's trip to Germany with plea to Kaiser', *Gaelic American*, 26 Apr. 1924; Frances Christ, 'John Kenny, 1847–1924', *JKAS*, 20:4 (2014–15), 183–206. Kenny was born in Kilcock in 1847. After emigrating to New York he became a leading figure in Clan na Gael.
25 Michael Smyth (BMH WS 1,531, p. 3).
26 CI Kildare; Meath; Wicklow; Carlow; King's County; Queen's County, Mar. 1916 (TNA, CO 904/99).
27 Thomas Byrne (BMH WS 564, pp 3–16). Byrne was born in Carrickmacross in 1877 and emigrated to Johannesburg 1896. In South Africa he joined McBride's Irish Brigade when the Boer War began in 1899. After the war he settled in America, subsequently returned to Ireland and joined the Volunteers in 1913.
28 Patrick Colgan (BMH WS 850, p. 7).
29 Thomas Byrne (BMH WS 564, pp 17–18).

30  Thomas Harris (BMH WS 320, p. 7).
31  Michael Smyth (BMH WS 1,531, pp 5–6).
32  Patrick Colgan (BMH WS 850, pp 7–9).
33  Thomas Harris (BMH WS 320, pp 5–6); Thomas Byrne (BMH WS 564, p. 16).
34  Sworn statement by Edward O'Kelly, 27 Apr. 1935 (IMA, MSPC, WMSP34REF4176).
35  Michael Smyth (BMH WS 1,531, p. 6); Thomas Harris (BMH WS 320, pp 6–7).
36  Éamon Fleming statement (IMA, MSPC, WMSP34REF21802); Michael Gray (BMH WS 489, p. 4); CI Kildare, Apr. 1916 (TNA, CO 904/99).
37  'Details of finding explosives in Sherlockstown' (NAI, CSORP, 1916/18311); CI Kildare, Oct. 1916 (TNA, CO 904/101).
38  Thomas Byrne (BMH WS 564, p. 18).
39  Service time tables 1911–, Trains Dept., Easter Monday, 24 Apr. 1916, details also on a handwritten note written on the blank page opposite, p. 7. (Irish Railway Records Society Archives, Heuston station, Dublin).
40  'Details of finding explosives in Sherlockstown' (NAI, CSORP, 1916/18311); Thomas Byrne (BMH WS 564, p. 18).
41  Michael O'Kelly (BMH WS 1,155, p. 16); *An tÓglach*, 22 May 1926, 5.
42  Domhnall Ó Buachalla (BMH WS 194, p. 2).
43  Patrick Colgan (BMH WS 850, pp 8–10).
44  Domhnall Ó Buachalla (BMH WS 194, p. 3); Patrick Colgan (BMH WS 850, pp 9–11).
45  Patrick Colgan (BMH WS 850, pp 10, 12); Thomas Byrne (BMH WS 564, pp 19–20).
46  Sworn statement by James O'Neill, 22 July 1935 (IMA, MSPC, WMSP34REF8368).
47  Feargus de Búrca (BMH WS 694); Sworn statement by Frank Burke, 10 May 1935 (IMA, MSPC, WMSP34REF1124); Gerry Cummins and Éanna de Búrca, *The Frank Burke story: patriot, scholar, GAA dual-star, guardian of Pearse's vision and legacy* (Naas, 2016).
48  Sworn statement by Aoife de Búrca, 8 Feb. 1938 (IMI, MSPC, WMSP34REF53445). Personal communication with Éanna de Búrca. Mr de Búrca is son of Frank Burke. Jimmy Wren, *The GPO garrison: a biographical dictionary* (Dublin, 2015), p. 17.
49  See the following pension files: Sworn statement by Mark Wilson, 16 Feb. 1926 (IMA, MSPC, 24SP9687); Sworn statement by Michael Cosgrove, 13 Mar. 1937 (IMA, MSPC, WMSP34REF4156); Sworn statement by Catherine Beattie, 8 Feb. 1938 (IMA, MSPC, WMSP34REF40382); Sworn statement by Patrick Brennan, 7 July 1937 (IMS, MSPC, WMSP34REF1513); Sworn statement by Seán McGlynn, 21 June 1938 (IMA, MSPC, WMSP34REF22827). For details of Patrick Brennan from Monasterevin, see *LL*, 14 Jan. 1967.
50  Sworn statement by Catherine Beattie, 8 Feb. 1938 (IMA, MSPC, WMSP34REF40382). Katie was also known as Dolly. For details of the activity of women activists, see Senia Pašeta, *Irish nationalist women, 1900–1918* (Cambridge, 2013), pp 170–81. For details of women activists attached to the Four Courts garrison see Mary McAuliffe and Liz Gillis, *We were there: 77 women of the Easter Rising* (Dublin, 2016), pp 46–53.
51  R. Henderson (BMH WS 1,686, p. 22); Identity statement for Republican soldiers, 1916 (UCDA, Republican Soldiers Casualty Committee, P156/61); *1916 Sinn Féin Rebellion handbook* (Dublin, 1917), p. 264; James Durney, *On the one road: political unrest in Kildare, 1913–1994* (Naas, 2001), p. 25; http://www.nga.ie/1916–George_Geoghegan.php (accessed 23 July 2016).
52  George Geoghegan, death certificate, General Register Office (GRO), Dublin.
53  Thomas Harris (BMH WS 320, p. 11).
54  Sworn statement by Edward O'Kelly, 27 Apr. 1935 (IMA, MSPC, WMSP34REF4176); Patrick Colgan (BMH WS 850, pp 29–31).
55  Sworn statement by Catherine Beattie, 8 Feb. 1938 (IMA, MSPC, WMSP34REF40382).
56  Tom Byrne (BMH WS 564, pp 23–7).

57 Michael Kavanagh, death certificate, GRO, Dublin; *LL*, 27 May 1916; James Stephens, *The insurrection in Dublin* (New York, 1916), pp 21–4.

58 http://source.southdublinlibraries.ie/bitstream/10599/11507/5/Fragment1916.pdf, pp 12–3.

59 http://www.glasnevintrust.ie/visit-glasnevin/news/edward-murphy-1874-1916 (accessed 24 July 2016); *II*, 26 Oct. 2015.

60 Geoffrey Sloan, 'The British state and the Irish Rebellion of 1916: an intelligence failure or a failure of response?', *Intelligence and National Security*, 28:4 (2013), 453–94.

61 *Royal Commission on the Rebellion in Ireland: minutes of evidence and appendix of documents* (1916), Cd. 8311, p. 7; *Royal Commission on the Rebellion in Ireland: report of commission* (June 1916), Cd. 8279, p. 158.

62 Ibid., p. 166.                    63 Ibid., p. 177.

64 *Irish Mirror*, 29 Apr. 2013; *IT*, 4 May 2013; http://www.mullocksauctions.co.uk/lot-60736-ireland_easter_rising_diary.html?p=10 (accessed 15 Aug. 2016). Sir Bertram Portal (1866–1949) was commissioned in 1885 and fought in the Boer War before retiring in 1907. When the First World War broke out in 1914 he re-enlisted. In 1917 he was honoured by King George with a CB, for his services in Ireland. Later appointed commander of a cavalry brigade serving in France until 1918, he was promoted brigadier general in 1919. Following his retirement he served as a county councillor in Hampshire, see details http://thepeerage.com/p43338.htm (accessed 30 July 2016).

65 *II*, 23 June, 27 Sept. 1915; *FJ*, 25 Oct. 1915, 8 Feb. 1916; Costello, *Delightful station*, pp 295–6.

66 http://www.irishmirror.ie/news/irish-news/british-colonels-diary-suggests-top-1860268 (accessed 15 Aug. 2016); Charles Townshend, *Easter Rising 1916: the Irish Rebellion* (London, 2005), p. 143.

67 *1916 Rebellion handbook*, p. 172; Michael Foy and Brian Barton, *The Easter Rising* (Stroud, 2004), p. 79.

68 Army field message book of H. de Courcy-Wheeler, 29 Apr.–1 May 1916 (NLI, de Courcy-Wheeler papers, n.5670, p.5892); Alex Findlater, *1916 surrenders: Captain H.E. de Courcy-Wheelers eyewitness account* (Dublin, 2016).

69 Trains Dept., Easter Monday, 24 Apr. 1916, also manuscript notes (Irish Railway Records Society Archives).

70 *1916 Rebellion handbook*, p. 93.

71 Orders from General Lowe to Portal to maintain a cordon, 27 Apr. 1916 (NLI, de Courcy-Wheelers papers, MS 15,000/7/8–9).

72 Army field message book of H. de Courcy-Wheeler, 29 Apr.–1 May 1916 (NLI, de Courcy-Wheeler papers, n.5670, p.5892); http://www.irishmirror.ie/news/irish-news/british-colonels-diary-suggests-top-1860268' (accessed 15 Aug. 2016).

73 Townshend mentions Portal in a minor role following the surrender: Townshend, *Easter Rising*, p. 272; Foy and Barton only acknowledge Portal's role in establishing a line of posts from Kingsbridge to Trinity College, see Foy and Barton, *The Easter Rising*, p. 336.

74 Alex Findlater, *Findlaters: the story of a Dublin merchant family, 1774–2001* (Dublin, 2001), pp 281–2 (Alex Findlater is a grandson of de Courcy-Wheeler); Anne Haverty, *Constance Markievicz: Irish revolutionary* (Dublin, 2016), pp 174–5.

75 For details of arresting leading rebels and giving evidence at court-martials, see Army field message book of H. de Courcy-Wheeler, 29 Apr.–1 May 1916 (NLI, de Courcy-Wheeler papers, n.5670, p.5892).

76 Findlater, *Findlaters*, p. 287; *Burkes Irish family records* (London, 1976), p. 1204.

77 *KO*, 6 May 1916; Volunteer, 'South Dublin Union area', *Capuchin Annual* (1966), 206–7, 209; Stannus Geoghegan, *The campaigns and history of the Royal Irish Regiment: vol. II from 1900 to 1922* (Edinburgh, 1927), p. 159; Costello, *Delightful station*, p. 294.

78  James Durney, *Foremost and ready: Kildare and the 1916 Rising* (Naas, 2015), p. 181; Mary Gallagher, *16 lives: Eamon Ceannt* (Dublin, 2014), pp 246–8.

79  *KO*, 13 May 1916, 14 Apr. 1917.

80  Michael O'Kelly (BMH WS 1,155, p. 17); Alphonsus Sweeney (BMH WS 1,147, p. 2).

81  Michael Smyth (BMH WS 1,531, p. 6); Michael O'Kelly (BMH WS 1,155, p. 17). For details of numbers arrested nationally, see William Murphy, *Political imprisonment and the Irish, 1912–21* (Oxford, 2014), p. 54.

82  CI Kildare, Apr. 1916 (TNA, CO 904/99).

83  Michael O'Kelly (BMH WS 1,155, p. 19).

84  Michael Smyth (BMH WS 1,531, pp 3, 6).

85  Sworn statement by Patrick Brennan, 7 July 1937 (IMS, MSPC, WMSP34REF1513); Patrick Colgan (BMH WS 850, p. 42); Thomas Harris (BMH WS 320, p. 12); *KO*, 13, 20 May 1916; *LL*, 20 May 1916; *1916 Rebellion handbook*, pp 70–81. Graves, Ledwith and Weafer, participants in Dublin, were arrested in Kildare.

86  *1916 Rebellion handbook*, p. 75; Durney, *Foremost and ready*, pp 178–9.

87  Michael O'Kelly (BMH WS 1,155, p. 17); Michael Smyth (BMH WS, 1,531, p. 6); *LL*, 20 May, 24 June 1916; *1916 Rebellion handbook*, pp 82–91; Durney, *Foremost and ready*, pp 119, 179.

88  *LL*, 27 May 1916.                    89  *KO*, 3 June 1916.

90  Fr Pat Conlon to Maisy O'Kelly, Apr. 1940, Ted O'Kelly papers, Edward O'Kelly, London; Josephine Clarke (BMH WS 699, pp 2–3).

91  Michael Laffan, *The resurrection of Ireland: the Sinn Féin Party, 1916–1923* (Cambridge, 1999), p. 53.

92  Ailbe Ó Monacháin (BMH WS 298, p. 45); Durney, *On the one road*, p. 33.

93  Thomas Morrissey, *William J. Walsh, archbishop of Dublin, 1841–1921: no uncertain voice* (Dublin, 2000), pp 294–5.

94  *LL*, 13, 27 May 1916; *KO*, 13 May 1916.

95  *IT*, 8 May 1916; *LL*, 13 May 1916.

96  Goulding to Bonar Law, 4 May 1916 (Parliamentary Archives, Bonar Law papers, BL 53/2/5). Goulding was subsequently chairman of the Property Losses (Ireland) Committee.

97  *IT*, 11 Aug. 1916.                    98  *KO*, 13 May 1916.

99  Patrick Maume, *The long gestation: Irish nationalist life, 1891–1918* (Dublin, 1999), pp 182–4; F.S.L. Lyons, *John Dillon: a biography* (London, 1968), pp 285–6.

100 Minutes, 14 July 1916 (KCoA, county council meetings).

101 *Headings of a settlement as to the Government of Ireland (1916)*, Cd. 8310; O'Day, *Irish home rule*, p. 274.                    102 *KO*, 12 Aug. 1916.

103 *Irish Examiner*, 1 July 2016; James E. Edmonds, *Military operations France and Belgium, 1916: Sir Douglas Haig's command to the 1st July: Battle of the Somme, vol. 1* (London, 1993), p. 483.

104 Durney, *Time of war*, pp 75, 197.

105 Callan, 'Recruiting for the British army', 44.                    106 *KO*, 26 Aug. 1916.

107 CI Kildare, May, June 1916 (TNA, CO 904/100).

108 *KO*, 4 Nov. 1916; Costello, *Delightful station*, p. 297.

109 Michael O'Kelly (BMH WS 1,155, pp 28–9); *KO*, 2 Dec. 1916.

110 Caoimhe Nic Dháibhéid, 'The Irish National Aid Association and the radicalization of public opinion in Ireland, 1916–1918', *Historical Journal*, 55:3 (2012), 706–7; Murphy, *Political imprisonment*, pp 71–5.

111 Townshend, *Easter Rising*, p. 316.        112 Laffan, *Resurrection*, p. 66.

113 Kathleen Clarke, *Revolutionary woman: my fight for Ireland's freedom* (Dublin, 1991), pp 127, 137.

114 M.J. Curran (BMH WS 687, p. 97, 101); Morrissey, *William J. Walsh*, pp 289, 293.

115 Correspondence suggesting cooperation between the Irish National Aid Association and the Volunteer Dependents' Fund, letter of 6 July 1916 and 12 July 1916 (NLI, Irish National Aid Association papers, MS 24,345); IG report, Aug. 1916 (TNA, CO 904/100); M.J. Curran (BMH WS 687, p. 102); *II*, 12 Aug. 1916; *Evening Herald* (hereafter *EH*), 19 Aug. 1916.

116 List of parishes with accounts collected in each on behalf of the I.N.A.V.D.F., 1916–1917 (NLI, Irish National Aid Association and Volunteer Dependents Fund papers, MS 24,381).

117 Michael Smyth (BMH WS 1,531, p. 19).

118 List of parishes with accounts collected in each on behalf of the I.N.A.V.D.F., 1916–1917 (NLI, Irish National Aid Association and Volunteer Dependents Fund papers, MS 24,381); *Leinster Express*, 8 July 1916.

119 'Irish National Aid Association meeting, Naas' (NAI, CSORP, 1916/16,257); List of parishes with accounts collected in each on behalf of the I.N.A.V.D.F., 1916–1917 (NLI, Irish National Aid Association and Volunteer Dependents' Fund papers, MS 24,381).

120 Reports on the state of public feeling in Ireland, July 1916 (NLI, Joseph Brennan papers, MS 26,182); IG report, Aug. 1916 (TNA, CO 904/100). On advanced nationalist control, see Murphy, *Political imprisonment*, pp 73–4.

121 *KO*, 29 July 1916.

122 'List of prisoners detained Oct. 1916' (NAI, CSORP, 1916/18970; 1916/17714).

123 Townshend, *Easter Rising*, pp 326–7.

124 Ó Súilleabháin, *Ua Buachalla*, p. 88; *LL*, 6 Jan. 1917.

CHAPTER FIVE *The emergence of a new political order, 1917–18*

1 Laffan, *Resurrection*, p. 76.

2 CI Clare, Feb. 1917 (CO 904/102); Laffan, *Resurrection*, p. 77.

3 Personal communication Éanna de Búrca, 2 Aug. 2015; Cummins and de Búrca, *The Frank Burke story*, p. 103.

4 *EH*, 4 Apr. 1918; *FJ*, 8 Apr. 1918.

5 Patrick Colgan (BMH WS 850, pp 53, 55).

6 Ibid., pp 48, 58; James Dunne (BMH WS 1,571, p. 2).

7 Sworn statement by Donal Buckley, 22 Dec. 1941 (IMA, MSPC, WSP34REF8261).

8 CI Kildare, May, June 1917 (TNA, CO 904/103).

9 Patrick Colgan (BMH WS 850, pp 58–9); Smyth (BMH WS 1,531, p. 7).

10 Seán Boylan (BMH WS 1,715, p. 2).

11 Pádraig Ó Catháin (Patrick Kane) (BMH WS 1572, p. 3); William Nolan, 'Events in Carlow, 1920–1921', *Capuchin Annual* (1970), 582, 584; Patrick Long, 'O'Sullivan, Gearóid', *DIB*.

12 Patrick Doyle (BMH WS 807, p. 6); Pádraig Ó Catháin (Patrick Kane) (BMH WS 1,572, pp 3, 4).

13 Michael Smyth, 'Kildare battalions', *Capuchin Annual* (1970), 570.

14 *LL*, 5, 12 May 1917.     15 Townshend, *Easter Rising*, p. 327.

16 Laffan, *Resurrection*, p. 82.     17 Ibid., pp 90–3.

18 *KO*, 24 Mar., 7 Apr. 1917; Nelson, *Through peace and war*, pp 183–4.

19 *KO*, 7 Apr. 1917     20 *LL*, 21 Apr. 1917.

21 See Laffan, *Resurrection*, pp 94–6.     22 *LL*, 12 May 1917.

23 Ó Corráin, 'Archbishop William Joseph Walsh', p. 120.

24 Michael O'Kelly (BMH, WS 1,155, pp 31–2).     25 *KO*, 9 June 1917.

26 *LL*, 23 June 1918.

27 For named councillors supporting SF, see *LL*, 2 June–28 July 1917.

28 CI Kildare, July 1917; CI King's County, July 1917; CI Queen's County, July 1917 (TNA, CO 904/103); David Fitzpatrick, *Politics and Irish life, 1913–1921* (2nd ed., Cork, 1998), p. 120.

29 For details of the Irish Convention see R.B. McDowell, *The Irish Convention, 1917–18* (London, 1970); Alvin Jackson, *Home rule*, p. 177; Nicholas Mansergh, *The unresolved question: the Anglo-Irish settlement and its undoing, 1912–72* (London, 1991), pp 103–7.

30 *LL*, 16 June 1917.              31 *KO*, 14 July 1917.              32 Ibid., 11 Aug. 1917.

33 CI Kildare, June 1917 (TNA, CO 904/103).

34 CI Kildare, July 1917 (ibid.).                                    35 *KO*, 1 Sept. 1917.

36 *Hansard 5 (Commons)*, 18 Oct. 1917, vol. 98, col. 313.

37 Ibid., 5 Dec. 1917, vol. 100, col. 536; *LL*, 24 Nov. 1917.       38 *KO*, 6 Oct. 1917.

39 Ibid., 11 Aug. 1917; *LL*, 29 Sept. 1917.                         40 *LL*, 20 Oct. 1917.

41 Ibid., 6 Oct. 1917.            42 McDowell, *Irish Convention*, pp 151, 221, 224–5.

43 O'Day, *Irish home rule*, p. 283; Robert H. Murray, *Archbishop Bernard: professor, prelate and provost* (Dublin, 1931), pp 315–27.

44 Jackson, *Home rule*, p. 181; Hennessy, *Dividing Ireland*, pp 206–12.

45 Durney, *Time of war*, p. 197; http://www.kildare.ie/Library/KildareCollectionsandResearch Services/World-War-One/Kildare-Casualties-World-War-1.asp (accessed 1 Nov. 2016).

46 Callan, 'Recruiting for the British army', 42, 44. According to Callan, no separate figures for regimental recruiting centres were given after mid-1917, subsequently only a total of the entire country was given.

47 CI Kildare, Mar., May 1917 (TNA, CO 904/102 and 103).

48 Michael O'Kelly (BMH WS 1,155, p. 35); *KO*, 11 Aug. 1917.

49 *LL*, 29 Sept., 6 Oct. 1917; CI Kildare, Sept. 1917 (TNA, CO 904/104).

50 *KO*, 29 Sept. 1917; *LL*, 29 Sept. 1917.                         51 *KO*, 6 Oct. 1917.

52 *II*, 5 Nov. 1917; *NLT*, 10 Nov. 1917.                           53 *FJ*, 5 Nov. 1917.

54 Ibid.; CI Kildare, Nov. 1917 (TNA, CO 904/104).                   55 *FJ*, 5 Nov. 1917.

56 CI Kildare, Nov. 1917 (TNA, CO 904/104).

57 *FJ*, 5 Nov. 1917; *LL*, 10 Nov. 1917.       58 *LL*, 10, 17 Nov. 1917.

59 Ibid., 8, 15 Dec. 1917.

60 Patrick Colgan (BMH WS 850, p. 62); *LL*, 27 Oct. 1917.

61 Sworn statement by Éamon Price, 21 Jan. 1925 (IMA, MSPC, 24SP5655).

62 Pádraig Ó Catháin (Kane) (BMH WS 1572, p. 5).

63 CI Kildare, Nov. 1917 (TNA, CO 904/104).

64 Details of illegal drilling in Castledermot, 23 Nov. 1917 (TNA, CO 904/122, file no. 17346/S); *NLT*, 1 Dec. 1917.

65 Fergus Campbell, *Land and revolution: nationalist politics in the west of Ireland, 1891–1921* (Oxford, 2005), pp 242–3; Paul Bew, 'Sinn Féin, agrarian radicalism and the war of independence, 1919–1921' in D.G. Boyce (ed.), *The Revolution in Ireland, 1879–1923* (Basingstoke, 1988), pp 221–2.

66 Campbell, *Land and revolution*, p. 243.

67 *LL*, 5 Jan. 1918; *KO*, 12 Jan. 1918.

68 'Kill district cattle drives' (NAI, CSORP/1918/1784); CI Kildare, Jan. 1918 (TNA, CO 904/105).

69 *KO*, 26 Jan. 1918.            70 *LL*, 9, 16 Feb. 1918.            71 Ibid., 19 Jan. 1918.

72 *FJ*, 25 Feb. 1918; *NLT*, 9, 23 Mar. 1918; Campbell, *Land and revolution*, pp 240–6.

73 Mary Ryan, *The Clongory evictions* (Naas, 2001).                 74 *LL*, 23 Mar. 1918.

75 *KO*, 2 Mar. 1918.            76 Ibid., 30 Mar. 1918.

77 'Colonel Burn to Mr Samuels' (NAI, CSORP/1918/16903); *Hansard 5 (Commons)*, 20 Mar. 1918, 104, col. 1012. On Ginnell's support for land radicalism see Wheatley, *Nationalism and the Irish Party*, p. 120.

78 Johnston, *Orange, Green and Khaki*, p. 390.  79 Ibid., p. 371.
80 *The Times*, 20 Mar. 1963; Potter, 'Gough, Sir Hubert de le Poer'; Robin Prior and Trevor Wilson, 'War in the west, 1917–18' in John Horne (ed.), *A companion to World War I* (Chichester, 2012), pp 132–3.
81 *II*, 10 Apr. 1918.
82 McDowell, *Irish Convention*, pp 180–4; Jackson, *Home rule*, p. 185.
83 Pádraig Yeates, *A city in turmoil: Dublin, 1919–1921* (Dublin, 2012), pp 8–9; Patrick Maume, 'Brodrick, William St John Fremantle (Earl of Midleton)', *DIB*.
84 *Sunday Independent*, 26 Jan. 1919; Alvin Jackson, *The two unions: Ireland, Scotland, and the survival of the United Kingdom, 1707–2007* (Oxford, 2012), p. 309; R.B. McDowell, *Crisis and decline: the fate of southern unionists* (Dublin, 1997), pp 65–6.
85 *II*, 25 Jan. 1919.
86 Ibid., 29 Jan., 12 Feb. 1919, 23 Mar. 1920.
87 CI Kildare, Apr. 1918 (TNA, CO 904/105).  88 *KO*, 13 Apr. 1918.
89 Ibid., 20 Apr. 1918.
90 See *II*, 19 Apr. 1918; Thomas J. Morrissey, *Laurence O'Neill, 1864–1943: lord mayor of Dublin 1917–1924: patriot and man of peace* (Dublin, 2014); Miller, *Church, state and nation*, pp 404–5; Jérôme aan de Wiel, *The Catholic Church in Ireland, 1914–1918, war and politics* (Dublin, 2013), pp 217–9; John Privilege, *Michael Logue and the Catholic Church in Ireland, 1879–1925* (Manchester, 2009), pp 122–4.
91 Morrissey, *William J. Walsh*, p. 309.
92 For a profile of Assistant Commissioner Quinn, see Gregory Allen, 'The police and the workers revolt', p. 3 in http://www.garda.ie/Documents/User/The%20Workers%20Revolt%20-%20Greg%20Allen.pdf (accessed 1 Oct. 2018).
93 *IT*, 18, 26 Apr. 1918.  94 *NLT*, 27 Apr. 1918.
95 *KO*, 27 Apr. 1918; *LL*, 27 Apr. 1918.  96 *FJ*, 24 Apr. 1918.
97 *KO*, 27 Apr. 1918.
98 *LL*, 4 May 1918; Carmel Doyle, 'O'Brien, Ellen Lucy (Nelly)', *DIB*.
99 Pauric Travers, 'The priest in politics: the case of conscription' in Oliver MacDonagh, W.F. Mandle and Pauric Travers (eds), *Irish culture and nationalism, 1750–1950* (London, 1983), pp 173–4.
100 Michael O'Kelly (BMH WS 1,155, pp 32–3); C. Desmond Greaves, *The Irish Transport and General Workers' Union: the formative years, 1919–1923* (Dublin, 1982), p. 193.
101 *LL*, 23, 30 Mar. 1918.
102 For details of the strike regionally see Kostick, *Revolution in Ireland*, pp 36–7; Arthur Mitchell, *Labour in Irish politics, 1890–1930: the Irish Labour movement in the age of revolution* (Dublin, 1974), pp 88–9; Greaves, *ITGWU*, p. 201.
103 *FJ*, 24 Apr. 1918; *Belfast Newsletter*, 24 Apr. 1918; *KO*, 27 Apr. 1918.
104 *KO*, 27 Apr. 1918; *NLT*, 24 Apr. 1918; Frank Taaffe, 'Athy and the Great War', p. 610.
105 *KO*, 4 May 1916.  106 *LL*, 4 May 1918.  107 *KO*, 27 Apr. 1918.
108 *LL*, 18 May 1918; *KO*, 18 May 1918. For details of the conscription fund, see Laffan, *Resurrection*, pp 140–1.
109 Charles Townshend, *The Republic: the fight for Irish independence, 1918–1923* (London, 2013), p. 15.
110 Personal communication with Deirdre Lawlor, daughter of Alphonsus Sweeney, January 2017; Michael O'Kelly (BMH WS 1155, pp 43–4); *KO*, 1 June 1918; James Durney with Liam Kenny, *A rebel's desk: Seumas and Michael O'Kelly, Leinster Leader editors in a revolutionary time* (Naas, 2016), p. 23.
111 *LL*, 1 June 1918.
112 Michael O'Kelly (BMH, WS 1155, pp 45–6); James Dunne (BMH WS 1571, p. 3); *KO*, 1 June 1918.

113 O'Kelly (BMH WS 1155, p. 46); *LL*, 24 Aug. 1918.

114 *LL*, 1 June 1918.                         115 Ibid., 22 June 1918.

116 See McCarthy, *Cumann na mBan*, pp 94–6.                         117 *LL*, 15 June 1918.

118 *FJ*, 5 July 1918; *II*, 5 July 1918.                         119 *KO*, 6 July 1918.

120 *LL*, 13, 20 July 1918; *KO*, 13 July 1918.

121 *LL*, 10 Aug. 1918; Richard McElligott, '1916 and the radicalization of the GAA', *Éire-Ireland*, 48:1 & 2 (2013), 109. For details of Gaelic Sunday in Kildare see Corry, *Kildare GAA*, p. 114.

122 *LL*, 10 Aug. 1918; *KO*, 10 Aug. 1918.

123 Piaras Béaslaí, *Michael Collins and the making of a new Ireland* (2 vols, Dublin, 1926), i, 224–5.

124 *KO*, 24 Aug. 1918; *LL*, 24 Aug. 1918.                         125 *LL*, 28 Sept. 1918.

126 Request for ameliorations, Oct. 1918 (NAI, GPB Dora Box 7, 1917–20/6290); *LL*, 12 Oct. 1918.

127 *KO*, 9 Nov. 1918.

128 Ida Milne, *Stacking the coffins: influenza, war and revolution in Ireland, 1918–19* (Manchester, 2018), p. 63.

129 Ida Milne, 'The 1918–19 influenza pandemic: a Kildare perspective of a global disaster', *JKAS*, 20:3 (2012–13), 304–7.

130 For details of County Kildare casualties see http://www.kildare.ie/library/kildarecollectionsandresearchservices/World-war-One/Kildare-Casualties-World-War-1.asp (accessed 24 Sept. 2016); Taaffe, 'Athy and the Great War', p. 615; Durney, *Time of war*, pp 196–7.

131 *FJ*, 15 Nov. 1918.

132 John Coakley, 'The impact of the 1918 Reform Act in Ireland', *Parliamentary History*, 37:1 (2018), 116–32.

133 *KO*, 19 Oct. 1918; Mitchell, *Labour in Irish politics*, p. 97.

134 Patrick Colgan (BMH WS 850, p.62); Michael Smyth (BMH WS 1531, p. 8); *LL*, 14 Sept. 1918.

135 Patrick Colgan (BMH, WS 850, p. 62); *LL*, 14 Sept. 1918.

136 *LL*, 21 Sept. 1918; *KO*, 23 Nov. 1918; Colgan (BMH WS 850, p. 62).

137 *KO*, 30 Nov. 1918; *LL*, 30 Nov. 1918.                         138 *LL*, 30 Nov. 1918.

139 *Hansard 5 (Commons)*, 26 July 1916, vol. 84, col. 1799; *LL*, 23 Nov. 1918.

140 M.J. Curran, BMH WS 687, pp 318–19; *II*, 21, 26 Nov. 1918; Morrissey, *William J. Walsh*, pp 316–7.

141 Ó Corráin, 'Archbishop William Joseph Walsh', pp 119–21.

142 M.J. Curran (BMH WS 687, pp 319–21); *FJ*, 28 Nov 1918.

143 *KO*, 7 Dec. 1918.

144 *LL*, 14 Dec. 1918. Miss Ryan's forename has not been identified. She may have been either Bridget or Mary Ryan from Main Street, Naas who were among the nominators for Ua Buachalla.

145 J.J. Lee, *The modernization of Irish society, 1848–1918* (Dublin, 2008 [1973]), p. 164.

146 Brian Walker, *Parliamentary election results in Ireland, 1801–1922* (Dublin, 1978), pp 355–6.

147 *LL*, 23, 30 Nov. 1918.                         148 *II*, 3 Dec. 1918; *KO*, 7 Dec. 1918.

149 Patrick Maume, 'O'Flanagan, Michael', *DIB*.                         150 *KO*, 7 Dec. 1918.

151 *II*, 2 Dec. 1918; *KO*, 7 Dec. 1918.                         152 *KO*, 7 Dec. 1918.

153 *LL*, 30 Nov. 1918.                         154 Ibid., 7 Dec. 1918.

155 CI Kildare, Dec. 1918 (TNA, CO 904/107).

156 McCarthy, *Waterford*, pp 56–7.

157 Michael Smyth (BMH WS 1531, p. 9); *KO*, 21 Dec. 1918.

158 *KO*, 4 Jan. 1919.                         159 *LL*, 4 Jan. 1919.                         160 *KO*, 30 Nov. 1918.

161 William Murphy, 'How Ireland was lost in the 1918 conscription crisis', *Sunday Business Post*, 15 Apr. 2018.

162 Joost Augusteijn, *From public defiance to guerrilla warfare: the experience of ordinary volunteers in the Irish War of Independence, 1916–1921* (Dublin, 1996), pp 71–3, 340–1.

CHAPTER SIX *War of Independence, 1919–21*

1 Peter Hart, 'The geography of revolution in Ireland, 1917–23', *Past and Present*, 155:1 (May 1997), 147.

2 Tom Garvin, *The evolution of Irish nationalist politics* (Dublin, 1981), p. 123; Michael Hopkinson, *The Irish War of Independence* (Dublin, 2002), p. 145.

3 *LL*, 11 Jan. 1919.      4 *KO*, 1 Mar. 1919.

5 *LL*, 10 Nov. 1917; *NLT*, 10 Nov. 1917; William Murphy, 'Sport in time of revolution: Sinn Féin and the hunt in Ireland, 1919', *Éire-Ireland* (Spring 2013), 112–47.

6 CI Kildare, Jan. 1919 (TNA, CO 904/108).      7 *KO*, 8 Feb. 1919.

8 Murphy, 'Sport in time of revolution', 125, 132.

9 *LL*, 15 Feb. 1919; CI Kildare, Feb. 1919 (TNA, CO 904/108).

10 *KO*, 8, 15 Mar. 1919.      11 *LL*, 8 Mar. 1919; *KO*, 22 Mar. 1919.

12 *EH*, 6 Mar. 1919; *Nenagh Guardian*, 8 Mar. 1919.      13 *EH*, 11 Mar. 1919.

14 *NLT*, 12 Apr. 1919.      15 CI Kildare, Apr. 1919 (TNA, CO 904/108).

16 On the boycott see Fitzpatrick, *Politics and Irish life*, pp 10–11.

17 *KO*, 7 June 1919; *LL*, 7 June 1919.

18 CI Kildare, June 1919 (TNA, CO 904/109); *NLT*, 14 June 1919.

19 *LL*, 26 July 1919.

20 Ibid., 7 June 1919; *NLT*, 7 June, 12 July 1919.

21 CI Kildare, July 1919 (TNA, CO 904/109); *NLT*, 26 July, 2 Aug. 1919.

22 *NLT*, 26 July 1919; Frank Taaffe, *Athy Urban District Council: a brief overview of its first 100 years* (Athy, 2001), pp 68–9.

23 CI Kildare, July 1919 (TNA, CO 904/109).      24 *NLT*, 2 Aug. 1919.

25 *KO*, 26 July 1919; Costello, *Delightful station*, pp 311–12.

26 *NLT*, 9 Aug. 1919.

27 *KO*, 5, 12, July 1919; Nelson, *Through peace and war*, p. 214; Kostick, *Revolution in Ireland*, p. 111.

28 *KO*, 26 July 1919; Dan Bradley, *Farm labourers: Irish struggle, 1900–1976* (Belfast, 1988), p. 45.

29 *KO*, 5 July 1919; *LL*, 19 July 1919.      30 Patrick Colgan (BMH WS 850, p. 66).

31 *KO*, 19 July 1919; *II*, 22 July 1919.      32 *KO*, 23 Aug. 1919.

33 Ibid., 12 July, 2 Aug. 1919.      34 Ibid., 16 Aug. 1919.

35 Ibid., 30 Aug. 1919; Nelson, *Through peace and war*, p. 216.

36 *KO*, 19 Apr. 1919; Laffan, *Resurrection*, p. 324.

37 Laffan, *Resurrection*, p. 326.      38 *KO*, 10 Jan. 1920.      39 Ibid., 17 Jan. 1920.

40 *NLT*, 24 Jan. 1920; *KO*, 17, 24 Jan. 1920.      41 *KO*, 17 Jan. 1920.

42 CI Kildare, Jan. 1920 (TNA, CO 904/111).

43 *KO*, 24 Jan. 1920; *LL*, 24 Jan. 1920; *Watchword of Labour*, 31 Jan. 1920.

44 *LL*, 31 Jan. 1920; for details of the career of William Cummins, later a senator, see ibid., 31 July 1943.

45 Hugh Martin, *Ireland in insurrection: an Englishman's record of fact* (London, 1921), p. 217; Richard Sinnott, *Irish voters decide: voting behaviour in elections and referendums since 1918* (Manchester, 1995), p. 28.

46 *LL*, 12 June 1920; Nelson, *Through peace and war*, p. 229.

47 Minutes, 25 May 1920 (KCoA, county council meetings); *KO*, 29 May 1920; *NLT*, 5 June 1920; Nelson, *Through peace and war*, p. 226.

48  *LL*, 12 June 1920; *KO*, 12 June 1920. For examples of workers flying red flags, see Kostick, *Revolution in Ireland*, pp 70, 115, 164.

49  *KO*, 12 June 1920; Liam Kenny, 'Kildare County Council, 1919–1921' in Nolan and McGrath (eds), *Kildare*, p. 662.                      50  *LL*, 23 Aug. 1919.

51  *NLT*, 19 June 1920; *KO*, 19 June 1920.                      52  *KO*, 26 June 1920.

53  Minutes, 29 May 1916 (KCoA, county council meetings); Nelson, *Through peace and war*, p. 232.

54  Nelson, *Through peace and war*, pp 234–8.   55  *II*, 28 June 1919.

56  *IT*, 25 Aug. 1920; *FJ*, 25 Aug. 1920; McDowell, *Crisis and decline*, p. 106.

57  *KO*, 25 Sept. 1920.

58  Paddy Mullaney interview (UCDA, O'Malley notebooks, P17b/106,110).

59  Dominion of Ireland Bill, *Hansard (Lords)*, 1 July 1920, vol. 40, col. 1157.

60  *IT*, 29 May, 21 Aug. 1920.

61  *Hansard (Lords)*, 24 Nov. 1920, vol. 42, cols 592–600; *IT*, 25 Nov. 1920.

62  McDowell, *Crisis and decline*, pp 74–7.

63  C.M. Byrne to Dulcibella Barton, 1 May 1921 (NLI, Dulcibella Barton papers, MS 8786). Dulcibella Barton was a sister of Robert Barton.

64  *LL*, 21 May 1921. For profiles of the Wicklow based nominees see Pauric Dempsey and Shaun Boylan, 'Barton, Robert Childers', *DIB*; Michael Hopkinson 'Childers (Robert) Erskine', *DIB*; Emmet O'Byrne, 'Byrne was a devoted local figure: Wicklow history: respected Ashford politician C.M Byrne' in *Wicklow People*, 4 May 2011.

65  Laffan, *Resurrection*, p. 341.

66  Patrick Colgan (BMH WS 850, p. 73); James Dunne (BMH WS 1,571, pp 2, 6).

67  Patrick Colgan (BMH WS 850, pp 63, 67).

68  Alphonsus Sweeney (BMH WS 1,147, pp 3–4); James Dunne (BMH WS, 1,571, p. 2).

69  Patrick Colgan (BMH WS 850, pp 64–5).

70  Alphonsus Sweeney (BMH WS 1,147, p. 5).

71  Patrick Colgan (BMH WS, 850, pp 71–2).

72  Seán Kavanagh (BMH WS, 524, p. 5).

73  Seán Kavanagh, 'The Irish Volunteers' intelligence organization', *Capuchin Annual* (1969), 360. This replicates his statement to the BMH.

74  Patrick Doyle (BMH WS, 807, p. 25).

75  Hugh Jeudwine, 'History of the 5th Division in Ireland, November 1919–March 1922', p. 143 (Imperial War Museum (IWM) London, Jeudwine papers, 72/82/2); Seán Kavanagh (BMH WS, 524, p. 3).

76  Seán Kavanagh (BMH WS 524, p. 3).                      77  *LL*, 11 Sept. 1920.

78  Ibid., 25 Sept. 1920. Kavanagh, 'Irish Volunteers' intelligence', 359–60; Maher later became the first Garda Síochána chief superintendent in charge of Kildare and Carlow and was based in Naas barracks where he had previously served.

79  Seán Kavanagh (BMH WS, 524, pp 4–5); Michael Smyth (BMH WS 1,531, p. 11).

80  *LL*, Jan. 1921; CI Kildare, Jan. 1921 (TNA, CO 904/114).

81  *LL*, 5 Mar. 1921; Seán Kavanagh (BMH WS, 524, p. 5). Casey later joined the Gardaí where he obtained the rank of superintendent.

82  *An tÓglach*, 31 Jan. 1919.                      83  Laffan, *Resurrection*, pp 75–6.

84  Seán Boylan, 'Meath – 1920', *Capuchin Annual* (1970), 540.

85  *LL*, 8 Nov. 1920.

86  IG report, Nov. 1919 (TNA, CO 904/110). On the difficulties experienced by police see Joost Augusteijn (ed.), *The memoirs of John Regan: a Catholic officer in the RIC and RUC, 1909–1948* (Dublin, 2007), pp 113–75.

87  CI Kildare, Nov. 1919 (TNA, CO 904/110); Michael O'Kelly (BMH WS 1,155, p. 60); *KO*, 29 Nov. 1919.

88 CI Kildare, Dec. 1919 (TNA, CO 904/110).

89 Brigade activity reports, 7th Bde. 1st Eastern Division (IMA/MSPC/A/62(1)); CI Kildare, Jan. 1920 (TNA, CO 904/111).

90 *LL*, 31 Jan. 1920; Smyth, 'Kildare battalions', 570; Kevin Cullen, 'The RIC and the IRA in Wicklow's War of Independence', *West Wicklow Historical Journal*, 7 (2013), 66–7.

91 *II*, 23 Feb. 1920.  92 *LL*, 6, 13 Mar. 1920.

93 Patrick Colgan (BMH WS 850, pp 69–70).

94 *LL*, 13 Mar. 1920; Terence Dooley, 'IRA activity in Kildare during the War of Independence' in William Nolan and Thomas McGrath (eds), *Kildare: history and society: interdisciplinary essays on the history of an Irish county* (Dublin, 2006), p. 629; W.J. Lowe, 'The war against the RIC, 1919–1921', *Éire-Ireland*, 37:3 & 4 (Autumn/Winter 2002), 107–13.

95 *KO*, 24 Apr. 1920.  96 *LL*, 23 Mar. 1920; *KO*, 23 Mar. 1920.

97 *LL*, 3 Apr. 1920.

98 Charles Townshend, *The British campaign in Ireland, 1919–1921: the development of political and military policies* (Oxford, 1975), p. 65.

99 *LL*, 10 Apr. 1920; *KO*, 10 Apr. 1920.

100 Personal communication, Tony Maher, Celbridge, 2010. For details of compensation claimed by Sergeant Lane see Compensation Ireland Commission, County Kildare, 1919–1922 (TNA, CO 905/7/307).

101 Michael Smyth (BMH WS 1,531, p. 10); Dooley, 'IRA activity in Kildare', p. 629.

102 Smyth, 'Kildare battalions', 570.  103 *LL*, 22 May 1920.

104 Stephen O'Reilly (BMH WS 1,761, pp 3–4).

105 Patrick McCrea (BMH WS 413, p. 40).

106 Compensation Ireland Commission, County Kildare, 1919–1922 (CO 905/7/277); *KO*, 14 Aug. 1920; Patrick Colgan (BMH WS 850, p. 67).

107 Compensation Irish Grants Committee claim of Henry Hendy, 12 Feb. 1929 (TNA, Irish Grants Committee, CO 762/197/4); author's observation of Hendy gravestone in Timolin churchyard.

108 Jeudwine, '5th Division', p. 35; Richard Bennet, *Black and Tans* (New York, 1995), p. 77; Lowe, 'The war against the RIC', 107–13.

109 Jeudwine, '5th Division', p. 25; for details of the Auxiliaries, see A.D. Harvey, 'Who were the Auxiliaries?', *Historical Journal*, 35:3 (1992), 665–9.

110 The constructive work of Dáil Éireann, no. 1, 6 (NAI, decree no. 8 Session 4 1919); Arthur Mitchell, *Revolutionary government in Ireland: Dáil Éireann, 1919–1922* (Dublin, 1995), pp 138–9.

111 Rules and forms of parish and district courts (NAI, Dept. of Justice files H 140/5 also 47/17); Seán O'Duffy (BMH WS 619, p. 3); Mary Kotsonouris, *Retreat from revolution: the Dáil courts, 1920–24* (Dublin, 1994); Francis J. Costello, 'The republican courts and the decline of British rule in Ireland, 1919–1921', *Éire-Ireland*, 25:2 (1990), 36–55.

112 *FJ*, 4 June 1920; *KO*, 5 June 1920.

113 *IT*, 31 May 1920; Francis Costello, *The Irish Revolution and its aftermath, 1916–1923: years of revolt* (Dublin, 2003), pp 198–9.

114 Simon Donnelly (BMH WS 481, pp 35–8); Mitchell, *Revolutionary government*, p. 151.

115 CI Kildare, July 1920 (TNA, CO 904/112).

116 *KO*, 24 July 1920.  117 Ibid., 17 July 1920.

118 CI Kildare, Aug. 1920 (TNA, CO 904/112); *KO*, 7 Aug. 1920.

119 *KO*, 20 Nov. 1920.  120 Murphy, *Political imprisonment*, p. 157.

121 O'Kelly to Max Green, 2 Oct. 1919 (NAI, General Prisons Board – Hunger strikers 1915–1920 (hereafter, GPBHS), 1919/8622); *EH*, 7 Oct. 1919; Murphy, *Political imprisonment*, p. 158. O'Kelly now used Éamon as his forename.

122 Munro to Green, 11–14 Oct. 1919 (NAI, GPBHS/1919/7213–7282); *II*, 20 Oct. 1919;
     Frank Gallagher, *Four glorious years* (Dublin, 2005 [1953]), pp 143–6; Murphy, *Political
     imprisonment*, p. 159.
123 CI Kildare, Sept. 1919 (TNA, CO 904/110); CI Kildare, Dec. 1919 (TNA, CO 904/113);
     *LL*, 20 Sept., 25 Oct., 8 Nov. 1919.
124 Pauric J. Dempsey, 'Clancy, Peadar', *DIB*; Gallagher, *Four glorious years*, p. 162.
125 *LL*, 10, 24 Apr. 1920.
126 *II*, 10 Apr. 1920; Murphy, *Political imprisonment*, p. 165; Townshend, *Republic*, pp 142–3.
127 Nevil Macready, *Annals of an active life* (2 vols, London, 1924), ii, 445; Murphy, *Political
     imprisonment*, p. 165.
128 Miller, *Church, state and nation*, p. 483; Morrissey, *William J. Walsh*, p. 347.
129 Murphy, *Political imprisonment*, p. 165; *Irish Bulletin*, 15 Apr. 1920; Mitchell, *Labour in Irish
     politics*, pp 119–20.
130 *LL*, 31 Jan. 1920, 17 Apr. 1920.
131 T. Foran to William O'Brien, 15 Apr. 1920 (NLI, William O'Brien papers MS 15,670).
132 *KO*, 17 Apr. 1920.
133 T. Foran to O'Brien, 15 Apr. 1920 (NLI, O'Brien papers MS 15,670).
134 *LL*, 24 Apr. 1920.              135 Ibid., 15 May 1920.
136 Kostick, *Revolution in Ireland*, p. 128.
137 Townshend, *Republic*, pp 143–4; Keith Jeffery, 'Macready, Sir (Cecil Frederick) Nevil',
     *ODNB*.
138 *Hansard 5 (Commons)*, 15 Apr. 1920, vol. 127, cols 1810–12; Seán McConville, *Irish politi-
     cal prisoners, 1848–1922: theatres of war* (London, 2003), p. 721.
139 Dublin district historical record, Apr. 1920 (TNA, WO 141/93).
140 *LL*, 24 Apr., 8 May 1920; *NLT*, 8 May 1920.
141 Kostick, *Revolution in Ireland*, p. 127.
142 Jeudwine, '5th Division', p. 143.
143 Murphy, *Political imprisonment*, p. 167.
144 *KO*, 3 July 1920; see Charles Townshend, 'The Irish railway strike of 1920: industrial action
     and civil resistance in the struggle for independence', *IHS*, 21:83 (1979), 265–82.
145 Jeudwine, '5th Division', p. 50; Cases of refusal by railway employees to operate trains car-
     rying troops or military stores, July–Dec. 1920 (TNA, CO 904/157/2).
146 Laffan, *Resurrection*, p. 286.              147 Jeudwine, '5th Division', p. 15.
148 Brigade activity reports, 7th Bde. 1st Eastern Division (IMA/MSPC/A/62(1)); James
     Dunne (BMH WS 1,571, pp 6–7); *LL*, 28 Aug. 1920; *KO*, 28 Aug. 1920; James Durney,
     *War of Independence in Kildare* (Cork, 2013), pp 110–13.
149 *FJ*, 25 Aug. 1920; *KO*, 28 Aug. 1920; James Dunne (BMH WS 1,571, pp 5, 6).
150 CI Kildare, Aug. 1920 (TNA, CO 904/112); *LL*, 28 Aug., 4 Sept. 1920; Richard Abbott,
     *Police casualties Ireland, 1919–1922* (Cork, 2000), p. 112. Prior to his posting to Kill, he was
     in charge of Clane barracks.
151 *LL*, 28 Aug. 1920. Bishop Foley's letter was published in *KO*, 4 Sept. 1920.
152 Compensation Ireland Commission, County Kildare, 1919–1922 (TNA, CO 905/7/207);
     *LL*, 28 Aug. 1920; *II*, 28 Aug. 1920.
153 *LL*, 28 Aug. 1920; *KO*, 28 Aug. 1920; *NLT*, 4 Sept. 1920.
154 *KO*, 4 Sept. 1920; CI Kildare, Aug. 1920 (TNA, CO 904/112).
155 Compensation Ireland Commission, County Kildare, 1919–1922 (TNA, CO 905/7/198);
     Patrick Colgan (BMH WS 850, p. 70); *KO*, 7 Aug. 1920; *LL*, 4 Sept. 1920.
156 *LL*, 4 Sept. 1920; *KO*, 4 Sept. 1920.
157 Fitzpatrick, *Politics and Irish life*, p. 35; Dooley, 'IRA activity in Kildare', p. 629.
158 *KO*, 11 Sept. 1920.

159 *LL*, 25 Sept. 1920; Sworn statement by Christopher Murphy, 9 Mar. 1937 (IMA, MSPC, WMSP34REF15040).

160 Smyth, 'Kildare battalions', pp 564–5.

161 Patrick Colgan (BMH WS 850, p. 71); Michael Smyth (BMH WS 1,531, p. 9).

162 CI Kildare, Oct. 1920 (TNA, CO 904/113); *KO*, 16 Oct. 1920; Smyth, 'Kildare battalions', 573.

163 *IT*, 1 Nov. 2013.

164 Smyth, 'Kildare battalions', 566; *LL*, 20 Nov. 1920; *KO*, 27 Nov. 1920.

165 Patrick Colgan (BMH WS 850, p. 75); *KO*, 6 Nov. 1920.

166 Michael Smyth (BMH WS 1,531, p. 11); Frank Purcell was a member of Celbridge Guardians. Subsequently, he served as secretary general of the ITGWU and a member of the Senate in the 1950s. See his obituary in *LL*, 9 Apr. 1960.

167 Lists of prisoners in Rath camp, Curragh, 1921 (TNA, WO 35/140/1; WO 35/141/1; WO 35/143).

168 *KO*, 4 Sept. 1920; *LL*, 18 Sept. 1920.

169 CI Kildare, Oct. 1920 (TNA, CO 904/113).    170 *LL*, 25 Sept. 1920.

171 CI Kildare, May and June 1921 (TNA, CO 904/115); *LL*, 28 May, 18 June 1921; *KO*, 18 June 1921.

172 Compensation Ireland Commission, County Kildare, 1919–1922 (CO 905/7/101); *LL*, 13, 21 May 1921.

173 CI Kildare, Apr. 1920 (TNA, CO 904/114).

174 Dáil Éireann Department of Labour report, May 1921 (UCDA, Mulcahy papers, P7/A/63).

175 Compensation Ireland (Shaw) Commission, County Kildare, 1919–1922 (CO 905/7/24); CI Kildare, Mar. 1921 (TNA, CO 904/114); David Johnson, 'The Belfast boycott 1920–1922' in J.M. Goldstrom and L.A. Clarkson (eds), *Irish population, economy, and society* (Oxford, 1981), p. 299.

176 Jeudwine, '5th Division', p. 68; Townshend, *British campaign*, p. 146.

177 Jeudwine, '5th Division', appendix viii; Colm Campbell, *Emergency law in Ireland, 1918–1925* (Oxford, 2005), pp 9–38; Keith Jeffery, 'The British army and internal security 1919–1939', *Historical Journal*, 24:2 (1981), 377–97.

178 Jeudwine, '5th Division', pp 25, 26, 86.    179 Ibid., appendix xviii.

180 Ibid., p. 44.

181 Returns of outrages, daily summeries, Jan.–Mar. 1921 (TNA, CO 904/144).

182 CI Kildare, Feb. 1921 (TNA, CO 904/114).

183 *EH*, 22 Feb. 1921; *II*, 23, 25, 26 Feb. 1921; *FJ*, 22, 23 Feb. 1921; *LL*, 26 Feb. 1921; Abbott, *Police casualties*, p. 200.

184 Paddy Mullaney interview (UCDA, O'Malley notebooks, P17b/106,110); Brigade activity reports, 1st Meath Bde. 1st Eastern Division (IMA/MSPC/A/57(2)).

185 For details see Anne Dolan, 'The British culture of paramilitary violence in the Irish War of Independence' in Robert Gerwarth and John Horne (eds), *War in peace: paramilitary violence in Europe after the Great War* (Oxford, 2012), pp 206–7.

186 Anne Dolan, 'The shadow of a great fear: terror and revolutionary Ireland' in David Fitzpatrick (ed.), *Terror in Ireland, 1916–1923* (Dublin, 2012), p. 35.

187 *Leinster Express*, 26 Feb. 1921; *LL*, 2 Apr. 1921; Abbott, *Police casualties*, p. 315.

188 Inquest on the death of Harold Stiff, 7 Mar. 1921 (TNA, WO/159B/14); *LL*, 12 Mar. 1921.

189 Dolan, 'The shadow of a great fear', pp 29–30.

190 Seamus Finn (BMH WS 1,060, p. 52).

191 'General monthly return of the regimental strength of the British army, May 1921', pp 105, 108–9 (TNA, WO 73/114); Jeffery, 'The British army and internal security', 377–97.

192 'General monthly return of the regimental strength of the British army, January 1921', pp 104–9 (TNA, WO 73/114).

193 Report No. 2 Batt Kildare to GHQ, 22 Apr. 1921 (UCDA, Mulcahy papers, P7/A/39); Brigade activity reports, 7th Bde. 1st Eastern Division (IMA/MSPC/A/62(1)); CI Kildare, Mar. 1921 (TNA, CO 904/114).

194 Report No. 2 Batt Kildare to GHQ, 22 Apr. 1921 (UCDA, Mulcahy papers, P7/A/39); Michael Smyth (BMH WS 1,531, p. 13).

195 CI Kildare, May 1921 (TNA, CO 904/115); *KO*, 28 May 1921.

196 Seán Boylan (BMH WS 1,715, p. 37); see also Seamus Cullen, 'Attempted ambush and escape from Stacumny, 2 July 1921', *Irish Sword*, 29:115 (Summer 2013), 62–77.

197 Paddy Mullaney interview (UCDA, O'Malley notebooks, p17B/106); Seamus Finn (BMH WS 1,060, pp 52–6).

198 Brigade activity reports, 1st Meath Bde. 1st Eastern Division (IMA/MSPC/A/57(2)); Paddy Mullaney interview (UCDA, O'Malley notebooks, p17B/106); Seán Boylan (BMH WS 1,715, p. 38); Matthew Barry (BMH WS 932, pp 9–19); John Gaynor (BMH WS 1,447, pp 28–32); Seamus Finn (BMH WS 1060, pp 52–7); *KO*, 9 July 1921.

199 Jeudwine, '5th Division', p. 54.

200 Smyth, 'Kildare battalions', 568.

201 MA-MSPC-CMB-144/146.pdf (accessed 7 May 2017).

202 Durney, *War of Independence*, p. 148.

203 http://www.leinsterleader.ie/news/news/205008/Naas-woman-Daisy-s-daring-deeds.html (accessed 7 May 2017).

204 MA-MSPC-CMB-144.Pdf; MA-MSPC-CMB-146.Pdf (accessed 7 May 2017); Smyth, 'Kildare battalions', 571.

205 Sworn statement by Kathleen Browne, 19 Jan. 1956 (IMA, MSPC, WMSP34REF14843).

206 McCarthy, *Cumann na mBan*, p. 130.

207 Brighid O'Mullane (BMH WS 450, pp 21–4); Smyth, 'Kildare battalions', 571; Anne Dolan, 'Spies and informers beware …' in Diarmaid Ferriter and Susannah Riordan (eds), *Years of turbulence: the Irish Revolution and its aftermath: in honour of Michael Laffan* (Dublin, 2015), p. 159.

208 Brighid O'Mullane (BMH WS 450, pp 23–5).

209 CI Kildare, Apr. 1921 (TNA, CO 904/114); *LL*, 16 Apr. 1921.

210 Jeudwine, '5th Division', p. 50.

211 http://mspcsearch.militaryarchives.ie/docs/files//Pdf_Membership/10/MA-MSPC-FE-37.pdf.

212 Census of Ireland 1911 / Kildare / Newbridge Urban-Rural & Morristownbiller.

213 CI Kildare, Dec. 1920 (TNA, CO 904/113).

214 Ibid., Mar. 1921 (TNA, CO 904/114).

215 CI King's County, May 1921 (TNA, CO 904/115); Keith Jeffery, *The British army and the crisis of empire, 1918–22* (Manchester, 1984), pp 88–90; W.H. Kautt, *Ambushes and amour: the Irish Rebellion, 1919–1921* (Dublin, 2010), p. 160.

216 Jeudwine, '5th Division', appendix XV & XV (b).

217 Sworn statement of Michael O'Kelly (IMA, MSPC, WMSP34REF9986).

218 Report No. 2 Batt. Kildare to GHQ, 22 Apr. 1921 (UCDA, Mulcahy papers, P7/A/39).

219 Jeudwine, '5th Division', pp 66, 90.          220 Ibid., pp 29, 91.

221 Alex Finlater, *Findlaters*, pp 295–6. Dorothea Findlater was Ireland's oldest woman when she died in Nov. 2017 aged 107, see *IT*, 25 Nov. 2017.

222 CI Kildare, July 1921 (TNA, CO 904/116).

223 For a chart detailing civilian spies and informers killed by the IRA, by county, 1920–1 see Eunan O'Halpin, 'Problematic killing during the War of Independence and its aftermath:

civilian spies and informers' in James Kelly and Mary Ann Lyons (eds), *Death and dying for Ireland, Britain and Europe: historical perspectives* (Sallins, 2013), pp 328–9.

224 CI Kildare, June 1921 (TNA, CO 904/115); *KO*, 25 June 1921; Smyth, 'Kildare battalions', 568.

225 Compensation Ireland Commission, County Kildare, 1919–1922 (TNA, CO 905/7/70); CI Kildare, June 1921 (TNA, CO 904/115); *KO*, 18 June 1921; Smyth, 'Kildare battalions', 571.

226 *LL*, 9 Apr. 1921; Dooley, 'IRA activity in Kildare', pp 628–9. For details of the punishment of alleged spies and informers in Cork, see Peter Hart, *The IRA and its enemies: violence and community in Cork, 1916–1923* (Oxford, 1998), pp 293–315. For a chart showing the extent of IRA violence in various counties, see Peter Hart, *The IRA at war, 1916–1923* (Oxford, 2003), p. 36.

227 Lists of enemy agents forwarded to GHQ from Brigade No. 6, Edenderry, July 1921; Report from Brigade No. 7 Naas, Sept. 1921 [but dating from pre-truce period] (UCDA, Mulcahy papers, P7a/6).

228 Dooley, 'IRA activity in Kildare', p. 637.

229 Detail of three samples from the Irish Grants Committee see claim of Pim Goodbody, James Bedford and Frank Latimer (TNA, CO 762/85/1; CO 762/84/8; CO 762/38/15).

230 Irish Grants Committee claim of Paul Goodwin, 5 Jan. 1929 (TNA, CO 762/193/7).

231 Hart, *The IRA at war*, pp 75–6.      232 *KO*, 15 Feb. 1919.

233 Brigade activity reports, 7th Bde. 1st Eastern Division (IMA/MSPC/A/62(1)); Compensation Ireland Commission, County Kildare, 1919–1922 (TNA, CO 905/7/66 and 68); *FJ*, 8 July 1921.

234 Liam Ó Duibhir, *Prisoners of war: Ballykinlar internment camp, 1920–21* (Cork, 2013), pp 91–3.

CHAPTER SEVEN *From truce to Civil War, July 1921–June 1922*

1 Michael Gallagher, 'The pact general election of 1922', *IHS*, 21:84 (1981), 414.

2 Jeudwine, '5th Division', p. 110; Paul McMahon, 'British intelligence and the Anglo-Irish truce, 1921', *IHS*, 35:140 (2007), 529.

3 CI King's County, July 1921 (TNA, CO 904/116).

4 *LL*, 16, 23 July 1921; *KO*, 23 July 1921.

5 Breaches of the truce, July–Nov. 1921 (TNA, CO 904/153).

6 Pádraig Ó Ruairc, 'The Anglo-Irish truce: an analysis of its immediate military impact, 8–11 July 1921' (PhD, University of Limerick, 2014), pp 229–30.

7 CI Kildare, July 1921 (TNA, CO 904/116).

8 Jeudwine, '5th Division', p. 110; see also McMahon, 'British intelligence and the Anglo-Irish truce', 526–7.

9 Jeudwine, '5th Division', appendix xxi.

10 Ibid., p. 110; *KO*, 16 July 1921.

11 See Brian Hughes, 'Loyalists and loyalism in a southern Irish community, 1921–1922', *Historical Journal*, 59:4 (2016), 1075–1105; Andy Bielenberg, 'Exodus: the emigration of southern Irish Protestants during the Irish War of Independence and the Civil War', *Past and Present*, 218 (2013), 206–9.

12 Irish Grants Committee claim of L.A.W. Wright, 31 Jan. 1927 (TNA, CO 762/117/16).

13 CI Kildare, July 1921 (TNA, CO 904/116).

14 Jeudwine, '5th Division', p. 112.

15 CI Kildare, Aug. 1921 (TNA, CO 904/116); for details of RIC dealings with liaison officers, see Augusteijn (ed.), *The memoirs of John M. Regan*, pp 176–8.

16  CI Meath, Aug. 1921 (TNA, CO 904/116).

17  Irish Grants Committee claim of Pim Goodbody, 30 Dec. 1926 (TNA, CO 762/85/1); CI Kildare, Sept. 1921 (TNA, CO 904/116).

18  Membership 3rd Batt., 1st Meath Bde (IMA, MSPC, RO/482); *KO*, 15 Oct. 1921; Breaches of the truce, July–Nov. 1921 (TNA, CO 904/153).

19  For details, see CI Carlow, Sept. 1921 (TNA, CO 904/116); Brian Hughes, *Defying the IRA: intimidation, coercion and communities during the Irish Revolution* (Liverpool, 2016), pp 91–6.

20  CI Kildare, Sept. 1921 (TNA, CO 904/116); Jeudwine, '5th Division', p. 118.

21  Jeudwine, '5th Division', p. 116.

22  CI Carlow, Oct. 1921 (TNA, CO 904/116).                       23  *KO*, 29 Oct. 1921.

24  Breaches of the truce, July–Nov. 1921 (TNA, CO 904/153); *LL*, 29 Oct. 1921.

25  Jeudwine, '5th Division', p. 122; Macready, *Annals*, ii, 602–6; S.M. Lawlor, 'Ireland from truce to Treaty: war or peace? July to October 1921', *IHS*, 22:85 (1980–1), 49–64. See also Michael Hopkinson (ed.), *The last days of Dublin Castle: the Mark Sturgis diaries* (Dublin, 1999), pp 213–14.

26  Murphy, *Political imprisonment*, p. 238.

27  Jeudwine, '5th Division', appendix xvi; *LL*, 17 Sept. 1921. For a full account of the escape see James Durney, 'The Curragh internees', *JKAS*, 20:3 (2010–11), 14.

28  *Manchester Guardian*, 10 Oct. 1921; Murphy, *Political imprisonment*, p. 221.

29  *LL*, 12, 26 Nov., 3 Dec. 1921.

30  CI Kildare, Oct. 1921 (TNA, CO 904/116).                      31  *LL*, 10 Sept. 1921.

32  *LL*, 10 Dec. 1921.                                           33  *NLT*, 10 Dec. 1921.

34  Jeudwine, '5th Division', appendix xvi.

35  *NLT*, 31 Dec. 1921; *LL*, 31 Dec. 1921, 7 Jan. 1922.

36  *LL*, 7 Jan. 1922; *KO*, 7 Jan. 1922; Nelson, *Through peace and war*, pp 254–7.

37  *LL*, 7 Jan. 1922; *KO*, 7 Jan. 1922.

38  http://oireachtasdebates.oireachtas.ie/debates, vol. T, no. 10, 3 Jan. 1922 (accessed 2 Aug. 2017); *FJ*, 4 Jan. 1922.

39  http://oireachtasdebates.oireachtas.ie/debates, vol. T, no. 11, 4 Jan. 1922 (accessed 2 Aug. 2017); *FJ*, 5 Jan. 1922; Ó Súilleabháin, *Ua Buachalla*, pp 148–50.

40  *LL*, 21 Jan. 1922; *NLT*, 28 Jan. 1922.                      41  *LL*, 4 Feb. 1922.

42  Ibid., 28 Jan. 1922.          43  *KO*, 4 Feb. 1922.           44  *LL*, 4 Feb. 1922.

45  Laffan, *Resurrection*, p. 370.  46  *KO*, 18 Mar. 1922.

47  *LL*, 1 Apr. 1922; *NLT*, 1 Apr. 1922.

48  *LL*, 15 Apr. 1922; *NLT*, 15 Apr. 1922.                      49  *II*, 17 Apr. 1922.

50  *KO*, 15 Apr. 1922; *II*, 4 May 1922; *LL*, 6 May 1922.

51  See *KO*, 27 May 1922; Gallagher, 'The pact general election', 404–21.

52  Townshend, *Republic*, p. 398.

53  *II*, 15 June 1922; *KO*, 17 June 1922.

54  *II*, 15 June 1922; Garvin, *Irish nationalist politics*, p. 133; Gallagher, 'The pact general election', 412.

55  *LL*, 1 Apr. 1922; *KO*, 1 Apr. 1922.                         56  *LL*, 15 Apr. 1922.

57  See Niamh Puirséil, *The Irish Labour party, 1922–73* (Dublin, 2007), pp 11–12.

58  *LL*, 27 May 1922.            59  *KO*, 27 May 1922.

60  See *Irish Farmer*, 26 Mar., 14 May 1921; see also Raymond Ryan, 'Farmers, agriculture and politics in the IFS area, 1919–1936' (PhD, UCD, 2005), p. 43 . For a comparative view of the activities of the Ratepayers' Association in Sligo, see Farry, *Sligo*, pp 74–5, 114.

61  *KO*, 27 May, 3 June 1922.                                    62  *IT*, 17 Jan. 1922.

63  *II*, 20 Jan. 1922; *KO*, 21 Jan. 1922.                       64  *IT*, 28 Jan. 1922.

65  Macready to Jeudwine, 2 May 1922 (IWM, Jeudwine papers, 72/82/2); Hart, *The IRA and its enemies*, pp 273–92.
66  *IT*, 13 May 1922; *II*, 13 May 1922.
67  Irish Grants Committee claim of Esmee Lascelles and Doreen Buchanan, 15 Jan. 1929 (TNA, CO 762/199/5).
68  *IT*, 13 May 1922.
69  Éamon Kane, 'The Civil War in Castledermot and Graney', *JKAS*, 21:1 (2016–17), 221–4.
70  *KO*, 24 June 1922; http://www.electionsireland.org/result.cfm?election=1922 (accessed 10 Aug. 2017).
71  For details of Labour's success nationally see Emmet O'Connor, *A labour history of Ireland, 1824–2000* (Dublin, 2011), p. 125; Francis Devine, *Organising history: a century of SIPTU, 1909–2009* (Dublin, 2009), p. 128.
72  http://www.electionsireland.org/result.cfm?election=1922 (accessed 10 Aug. 2017). For details of the success nationally of the Farmers' Party see 'Farmers' Union report for the year 1922', 15 Mar. 1923 (NLI, Irish Farmers' Union papers, MS 43,567/1).
73  Gallagher, 'The pact general election', 414.
74  Jeudwine, '5th Division', p. 112.
75  Properties handed over to the Provisional government by 18 May 1922 (IMA, Liaison and evacuation papers, LE/14/2); Anthony Kinsella, 'The British military evacuation', *Irish Sword*, 20:82 (Winter 1997), 277; Michael C. O'Malley, *Military aviation in Ireland, 1921–45* (Dublin, 2010), p. 9.
76  Kinsella, 'British military evacuation', 275.
77  Evacuation of the Curragh camp, 1 Apr.–31 May 1922 (TNA, WO 35/182A).
78  *LL*, 4 Feb. 1922.
79  Jeudwine, '5th Division', p. 132; 'General monthly returns of the army, Jan. to June 1922', p. 93, Jan. 1922 figures (TNA, WO 73/116).
80  Properties handed over to the Provisional government by 18 May 1922 (IMA, Liaison and evacuation papers, LE 14/2); 'General monthly returns of the army, Jan. to June 1922', p. 94 (TNA, WO 73/116); John Duggan, *A history of the Irish army* (Dublin, 1991), p. 76.
81  Kinsella, 'British military evacuation', 281.
82  Emmet Dalton to J.J. O'Connell, 28 Feb. 1922 (NLI, J.J. O'Connell papers, MS 22126).
83  *LL*, May 1920; Townshend, *Republic*, p. 393.
84  Jeudwine, '5th Division', p. 119; *LL*, 4 Feb. 1922.
85  Officers service papers, Lt John Wogan-Browne, 1914–1923 (TNA, WO 339/43238). The killing of Wogan-Browne features in many accounts of the Irish Revolution in Kildare, see Costello, *Kildare: saints, soldiers and horses*, pp 92–4; James Durney, *The Civil War in Kildare* (Cork, 2011), pp 37–43; Mark McLoughlin, 'The killing of Lt John Wogan Browne on 10 February 1922: a test of Anglo-Irish relations', *JKAS*, 20:3 (2012–13), 9–25.
86  Report by Seán Kavanagh to Chief Liaison Officer, 13 Feb. 1922 (IMA, Liaison and evacuation papers, LE/4/14).
87  Evacuation of the Curragh camp, 1 Apr.–31 May 1922 (TNA, WO 35/182A); Jeudwine, '5th Division', p. 128.
88  *IT*, 14, 15 Feb. 1922; *Hansard 5 (Commons)*, 14 Feb. 1922, vol. 150, col. 807.
89  Jeudwine, '5th Division', p. 128.
90  Report by Seán Kavanagh to Chief Liaison Officer, 29 Mar. 1922 (IMA, Liaison and evacuation papers, LE/4/14); McLoughlin, 'Wogan Browne', 22.
91  *KO*, 28 Jan. 1922.        92  *FJ*, 4 Feb. 1922; *KO*, 4, 25 Feb., 4 Mar. 1922
93  Jeudwine, '5th Division', p. 129; Visit of Mulcahy to the Curragh, 23 Feb. 1922 (IMA, Liaison and evacuation papers, LE 14/2).
94  Evacuation of the Curragh camp, 1 Apr.–31 May 1922 (TNA, WO 35/182A).

95  Irish Grants Committee claim of Ernest Northern, 26 Oct. 1926 (TNA, CO 762/143/1); *LL*, 1 Apr. 1922; McLoughlin, *Kildare barracks*, p. 141.

96  Emmet Dalton to the Adjutant General, 12 Apr. 1922; *LL*, 22 Apr. 1922 (IMA, Liaison and evacuation papers, LE 14/2).

97  Movement and evacuations of British army personnel and units, Jan.–May 1922 (IMA, Liaison and evacuation papers, LE 14); Evacuation of the Curragh camp, 1 Apr.–31 May 1922 (TNA, WO 35/182A).

98  Properties handed over to the Provisional government by 18 May 1922 (IMA, Liaison and evacuation papers LE 14/2); Macready to Jeudwine, 2 May 1922 (IWM, Jeudwine papers, 72/82/2).

99  Evacuation of the Curragh camp, 1 Apr.–31 May 1922 (TNA, WO 35/182A).

100 *KO*, 20 May 1922.

101 Evacuation of the Curragh camp, 1 Apr.–31 May 1922 (WO 35/182A).

102 Niall Brannigan, 'Changing of the guard: Curragh evacuation seventy years on', *An Cosantóir: the Irish Defence Journal*, 52:12 (Dec. 1992), 30.

103 Desmond Swan, 'The Curragh of Kildare', *An Cosantóir: the Irish Defence Journal*, 32:5 (May 1972), 67; *LL*, 20 May 1922. Both McNally and Prendergast were officers in the Monasterevin IRA Company.

104 *LL*, 20 May 1922.

105 Evacuation of the Curragh camp, 1 Apr.–31 May 1922 (TNA, WO 35/182A).

106 *IT*, 20 May 1922; Brannigan, 'Changing of the guard', 30.   107  *FJ*, 17 May 1922.

108 *IT*, 20 May 1922.         109  Swan, 'The Curragh of Kildare', 67–8.

110 *IT*, 20 May 1922; *LL*, 20 May 1922.

111 Evacuation of the Curragh camp, 1 Apr.–31 May 1922 (TNA, WO 35/182A).

112 *LL*, 20 May 1922. Captain J. Rowan was appointed in charge of the Newbridge police district following the departure of the RIC.

113 *LL*, 20 May 1922; *KO*, 20 May 1922.

114 Costello, *Delightful station*, p. 340.

115 'Average prices of agricultural products sold at fairs and markets in Ireland, May 1922' in *Monthly statistical statement, issued by Department of Agriculture, 1921–1923* (Dublin, n.d.), p. 16.

116 Memo detailing a meeting between members of the Provisional government and a deputation from the Curragh area, undated (NAI, Department of Justice, H/99/10); *LL*, 11 Feb. 1922.

117 Jim Smith, *The Curragh camp pre-1922: through the eyes of a young boy Jim Smith* in http://www.curragh.info/articles/smith.htm (accessed 23 Oct. 2017).

118 *IT*, 24 Dec. 1921.

119 Evacuation of the Curragh camp, 1 Apr.–31 May 1922 (TNA, WO 35/182A); Memo detailing a meeting between members of the Provisional government and a deputation from the Curragh area, undated (NAI, Department of Justice, H/99/10); *LL*, 11 Feb. 1922.

120 Costello, *Delightful station*, p. 345.

121 Duggan, *Irish army*, p. 75; Eoin Neeson, *The Civil War, 1922–23* (Dublin, 1969), p. 89.

122 Diarmuid O'Connor and Frank Connolly, *Sleep soldier sleep: the life and times of Pádraig O'Connor* (Dublin, 2011), p. 67.

123 *IT*, 2 Feb. 1922; *An tÓglach*, 7 Apr. 1923, 14–15; O'Connor and Connolly, *Sleep soldier sleep*, p. 67.

124 *LL*, 15 Apr. 1922.                   125 Ibid., 11 Feb. 1922.

126 James Dunne (BMH WS 1,571, p. 9).

127 *NLT*, 18 Mar. 1922; *LL*, 1, 8 Apr. 1922; *KO*, 8 Apr. 1922.

128 *LL*, 1 Apr. 1922.

129 *LL*, 1 Apr. 1922; Neeson, *Civil War*, p. 96; Patrick Taaffe, 'Richard Mulcahy and the genesis of the Civil War', *Irish Sword*, 29:118 (Winter 2014), 452.

130 *LL*, 8, 15 Apr. 1922.

131 Michael McEvilly, *A splendid resistance: the life of IRA chief of staff, Dr Andy Cooney* (Dublin, 2011), pp 72–3; *Meath Chronicle*, 15 Apr. 1922; *Drogheda Independent*, 15 Apr. 1922.

132 James Dunne (BMH WS 1,571, pp 9–10); *KO*, 15 Apr. 1922.

133 Michael Hopkinson, *Green against green: the Irish Civil War* (Dublin, 1988), pp 43–4.

134 Sworn statement by Thomas McHugh, 10 Mar. 1936 (IMA, MSPC, WMSP34REF15403); James Dunne (BMH WS 1,571, p. 10).

135 *An tÓglach*, 25 Apr. 1922.

136 Paddy Mullaney interview, p. 27 (UCDA, O'Malley notebooks, P17/b/106); Sworn statement by Thomas Mangan, 5 Jan. 1937 (IMA, MSPC, WMSP34REF10614); Sworn statement by Tim Tyrrell, 5 Jan. 1937 (IMA, MSPC, WMSP34REF10613).

137 Duggan, *Irish army*, pp 76, 330–1.

138 Patrick Kane (BMH WS 1,572, pp 22–23).

139 Michael O'Kelly (BMH WS 1,155, p. 68).

140 Report by Seán Kavanagh to Chief Liaison Officer, 17 Mar. 1922 (IMA, Liaison and evacuation papers, LE/4/14); *KO*, 11 Mar., 22 Apr., 20 May 1922; *LL*, 22 Apr. 1922.

141 *KO*, 20 May 1922.                    142 *LL*, 13 May 1922.

143 James Dunne (BMH WS 1,571, p. 10); *LL*, 6, 20 May 1922.

144 Hart, *IRA and its enemies*, pp 273–92; Hughes, 'Loyalists and loyalism', 1075–1105.

145 *KO*, 1 Apr. 1922.

146 Details of the various houses burned acquired from: Irish Grants Committee claim of Ernest Northern, 26 Oct. 1926 (TNA, CO 762/143/1); *NLT*, 15 Apr. 1922; *LL*, 29 Apr. 1922.

147 *II*, 15 June 1922; *KO*, 17 June 1922; *LL*, 17 June 1922.

148 Irish Grants Committee claim of Sarah Giltrap, 29 Jan. 1927 (TNA, CO 762/147/12). Kilbride camp is situated four miles north-east of Blessington.

149 Irish Grants Committee claim of Anna Glynn, 23 Nov. 1926 (TNA, CO 762/79/16).

150 Irish Grants Committee claim of Robert Eccles, 14 Nov. 1928 (TNA, CO 762/189/3).

151 Compensation claims of Loyalists, Harry Andree, 28 Oct. 1922 (NAI, Department of Finance 1922–1924, FIN 1/1084 303/31); Irish Grants Committee claim of Harry Andree, 28 Oct. 1926 (TNA, CO 762/59/11).

152 *KO*, 20 May 1922.

153 Provisional government minutes, 31 Jan. 1922 (NAI, TSCH/1/1/1); Report of the commission of inquiry into the Civic Guard mutiny, 17 Aug. 1922 (NAI, TAO/ S 9048); Brian McCarthy, *The Civic Guard mutiny* (Cork, 2012), p. 54.

154 McCarthy, *Civic Guard mutiny*, p. 55.

155 Conor Brady, *Guardians of the peace* (Dublin, 1974), p. 54.

156 Evidence of J.A. O'Connell, 15 July [1922], Civic Guard mutiny inquiry, 1922 (NAI, JUS/ H 235/329).

157 Gregory Allen, *The Garda Síochána: policing independent Ireland, 1922–82* (Dublin, 1999), pp 33–6; McCarthy, *Civic Guard mutiny*, pp 92–7.

158 Brady, *Guardians*, pp 58–9.

159 Ibid., pp 60–1; Liam McNiffe, *A history of the Garda Síochána: a social history of the force, 1922–52 with an overview of the years 1952–97* (Dublin, 1997), p. 21.

160 http://oireachtasdebates.oireachtas.ie/debates, vol. 1, no. 2, col. 72, 11 Sept. 1922 (accessed 20 Oct. 2017).

161 Report of the commission of inquiry into the Civic Guard mutiny, 17 Aug. 1922 (NAI, DT S 9048); Ernie O'Malley, *The singing flame* (Dublin, 1978), pp 106–8; McCarthy, *Civic Guard mutiny*, pp 124–8.

162 McCarthy, *Civic Guard mutiny*, pp 131–3; Allen, *Garda Síochána*, pp 65–6.
163 On O'Shiel see Eda Sagarra, *Kevin O'Shiel: Tyrone nationalist and Irish state-builder* (Dublin, 2013), pp 174–8.
164 Report of the commission of inquiry into the Civic Guard mutiny, 17 Aug. 1922 (NAI, DT S 9048).
165 McCarthy, *Civic Guard mutiny*, p. 187; Fearghal McGarry, *Eoin O'Duffy: a self-made hero* (Oxford, 2005), p. 113.

CHAPTER EIGHT *Unpopular militancy, Kildare during the Civil War 1922–3*

1 *KO*, 1 July 1922.
2 Paddy Mullaney interview, p. 26 (UCDA, O'Malley notebooks, P17/b/106); Mick O'Neill interview, p. 47 (UCDA, O'Malley notebooks, P17/b/107); *LL*, 22 July 1922; O'Keeffe, 'Reminiscences', 45; Ó Súilleabháin, *Ua Buachalla*, p. 169.
3 Hegarty to minister for defence detailing a report from Patrick Colgan, 5 July 1922 (UCDA, Mulcahy papers, P7/B/106/157).                              4 *LL*, 1 July 1922.
5 Sworn statement by Thomas McHugh, 10 Mar. 1936 (IMA, MSPC WMSP34REF15403); *LL*, 1 July 1922; *KO*, 15 July 1922.
6 James Dunne (MA, BMH WS 1,571, pp 11–2); *FJ*, 11 July 1922; *Southern Star*, 15 July 1922.                              7 Neeson, *Civil War*, p. 125.
8 O'Malley to chief of staff, 12 July 1922 (UCDA, Moss Twomey papers, P69/38/66); James Dunne (BMH WS 1571, p. 12).
9 Sworn statement by Laurence O'Brien, 24 May 1935 (IMA, MSPC, WMSP34REF1336); O'Malley to chief of staff, 12 July 1922 (UCDA, Twomey papers, P69/38/66); *NLT*, 8 July 1922.
10 O'Malley to chief of staff, 12 July 1922 (UCDA, Twomey papers, P69/38/ 66); O'Malley, *Singing flame*, p. 129; David Fitzpatrick, *Harry Boland's Irish Revolution* (Cork, 2003), p. 310.
11 O'Donovan to O/C Batt., 4 July 1922 (UCDA, Mulcahy papers, P 7/B/106/347); Duggan, *Irish army*, p. 86.
12 O'Donovan to O/C, 4 July 1922 (UCDA, Mulcahy papers, P 7/B/106/351); *KO*, 8 July 1922.
13 O'Malley to chief of staff, 12 July 1922 (UCDA, Twomey papers, P69/38/76); *LL*, 8 July 1922.
14 *II*, 10 July 1922.                    15 *LL*, 15 July 1922.
16 Fitzpatrick, *Boland*, p. 331.
17 Military situation, R. Harris to O/C Barracks, 8 July 1922 (UCDA, Mulcahy papers, P7/B/60/219); Fitzpatrick, *Boland*, p. 312.
18 O'Malley to chief of staff, 12 July 1922 (UCDA, Twomey papers, P69/38/78); *II*, 8, 10 July 1922.
19 Seán Boylan report, 11 July 1922 (UCDA, Mulcahy papers, P7/B/60/218).
20 Interview of Thomas McHugh by Seamus Cullen and Des O'Leary, Oct. 1992; Report to HQ Trim, 20 July 1922 (UCDA, Mulcahy papers, P7/B/107/110); *KO*, 29 July 1922.
21 Emmet Dalton report, 17 July 1922 (UCDA, Mulcahy papers, P7/B/107/77); *NLT*, 22 July 1922.
22 Military report to A/G GHQ, 11 July 1922 (UCDA, Mulcahy papers, P7/B/106/407).
23 Sworn statement by Christopher Murphy, 9 Mar. 1937 (IMA, MSPC, WMSP34REF 15040).                    24 *NLT*, 8 July 1922.
25 Sworn statement by Peter Lambe, 14 June 1937 (IMA MSPC WMSP34REF38425); Handwritten material submitted to the advisory committee by Patrick Shepherd, 29 Dec. 1933 (IMA, MSPC DP6497).

26  *NLT*, 8 July 1922; *LL*, 15 July 1922.
27  National army (hereafter NA) military situation, 9 July 1922 (UCDA, Mulcahy papers, P/B/60/220).
28  Civil War prisoner ledgers (IMA, CW/P, digitized collection). This collection includes CW/P/01/01 together with several other ledgers.
29  *MC*, 8, 15 July 1922.
30  Report by Price to O'Malley, 5 Aug. 1922 (MA, S/12006/6).
31  ATIRA report, 6 Aug. 1922 (IMA, S/12008/6).
32  Memo relating to 7th Kildare Brigade, 5 Aug. 1922 (IMA, CW/CAPT/001/2/04); James Dunne (BMH WS 1,571, p. 13), *KO*, 5 Aug 1922.
33  Report by Gallivan, 13 Aug. 1922 (IMA, S/12006/6).
34  Sworn statement by Thomas Mangan, 5 Jan. 1937 (IMA, MSPC, WMSP34REF10614).
35  Report by Gallivan, 13 Aug. 1922 (IMA, S/12006/6); Ernie O'Malley papers, interview with Gallagher, 1 July 1922 (IMA, CW/CAP/001/2/03).
36  ATIRA report, 27 Aug. 1922 (IMA, S/12008); NA military situation Eastern Command, 25 Aug. 1922 (UCDA, Mulcahy papers, 7/B/60/99); *KO*, 2 Sept. 1922.
37  Military situation, 1st Eastern Division, 10 Sept. 1922 (UCDA, Mulcahy papers, P/7/B/60/81); *EH*, 9 Sept. 1922.
38  Memorandum from Gallivan to O'Malley, 22 Aug. 1922 (UCDA, Mulcahy papers, P17A/61); Cormac O'Malley and Anne Dolan, *'No surrender here': the Civil War papers of Ernie O'Malley, 1922–1924* (Dublin, 2007), p. 125.
39  Memorandum from O'Malley to Price, 7 Sept. 1922 (UCDA, Mulcahy papers, P17A/56 & 61); Civil War prisoner ledgers (IMA, CW/P, digitized collection).
40  *Poblacht na h-Éireann, War News*, 25 July 1922; *NLT*, 13 Sept. 1958.
41  *II*, 22 Sept. 1922; NAI, Census of Ireland, 1911/Kildare/Grangbeg/Gilltown; Census of Ireland, 1911/Kildare/Ballymore Eustace town/Ballymore Eustace. The newspaper account incorrectly detailed that Smith was fourteen and Driver was sixteen. An examination of census figures indicates the reverse was the case.
42  *II*, 22 Sept. 1922; *LL*, 30 Sept. 1922; Durney, 'Curragh internees', *JKAS*, 20:3 (2010–11), 17–8.
43  *KO*, 9 Sept. 1922, for report on the Curragh shooting; *LL*, 9 Sept. 1922, for report on the Portlaoise shooting.
44  *LL*, 9 Sept. 1922.
45  Military Governor Newbridge internment camp: Instructions to sentries around prisoners' compound, 3 Sept. 1922 (IMA, CW/P/02/01/06A); Anne-Marie McInerney, 'Internment of the anti-Treaty IRA in the Free State, 1922–4' (PhD, TCD, 2015), p. 122.
46  Dundalk jail register, transcript of rescued prisoners, 14 Aug. 1922, https://www.louth-coco.ie/.../PP00011–Transcript-of-Released-Prisoners-from-Dundalk (accessed 25 Jan. 2018). Prisoners numbered between 196 and 198. For details of the capture of Dundalk, see Donal Hall, *Louth: the Irish Revolution, 1912–23* (Dublin, 2019), pp 108–9.
47  Mick O'Neill interview, p. 47 (UCDA, O'Malley notebooks, P17/b/107).
48  James Dunne (BMH WS 1,571, pp 13–14).
49  Report by General McSweeney, 15 Aug. 1922 (UCDA, Mulcahy papers, P7/B/107/314 & 331).
50  James Dunne (BMH WS 1,571, pp 13–14).
51  Mick O'Neill interview, p. 48 (UCDA, O'Malley notebooks, P17/b/107).
52  NA report, 14 July 1922 (UCDA, Mulcahy papers, P17A/61 & P7/B/59/97); *MC*, 19 Aug. 1922.
53  *II*, 16 Aug. 1922.
54  NA report, 14 July 1922 (UCDA, Mulcahy papers, P7/B/59/97); *FJ*, 17 Aug. 1922.
55  James Dunne (BMH WS 1,571, p. 14).          56  *II*, 17 Aug. 1922.

57 James Dunne (BMH WS 1,571, p. 13); Mick O'Neill interview, p. 48 (UCDA, O'Malley notebooks, P17/b/107).

58 Mick O'Neill interview, p. 48 (UCDA, O'Malley notebooks, P17/b/107); Ó Súilleabháin, *Ua Buachalla*, pp 173–5.

59 Paddy Mullaney interview, pp 26–7 (UCDA, O'Malley notebooks, P17/b/106); Neeson, *Civil War*, p. 189.

60 Sworn statement by Michael O'Kelly, 3 Feb. 1938 (IMA, MSPC, WMSP34REF9986).

61 O'Keeffe, 'Reminiscences'. The *Arvonia* was used as a troop carrier to transport the NA to Cork and elsewhere earlier in the conflict before its use as a prison ship. See *LL*, 31 Dec. 1927.

62 *LL*, 16 Sept. 1922.          63 Ibid., 31 Dec. 1927.          64 Ibid.

65 *II*, 17, 18 Oct. 1922.

66 Civil War prisoner ledgers (IMA, CW/P/01/01); Newbridge numerical list of prisoners, 06/1922–01/1924 (IMA, CW/P/10/15); Newbridge Roll Book, 30/8/1922–09/03/1923, escaped prisoners named (IMA, CW/P/10/16).

67 Dundalk jail register; Civil War prisoner ledgers (IMA, CW/P/01/01).

68 Report by Price to O'Malley, 5 Aug. 1922 (IMA, S/12008/6).

69 Ibid., 20 Aug. 1922 (ibid.).

70 O'Malley & Dolan, *No surrender here*, p. 555; O'Malley, *Singing flame*, p. 202.

71 O'Malley & Dolan, *No surrender here*, pp 219, 222.

72 Memo by Price, 27 Sept. 1922 (IMA, S/12008); Captured document, 16 Nov. 1922 (IMA, S/12008); James Dunne (BMH WS 1571, p. 16). Dunne incorrectly referred to the trainer as Ted O'Kelly.

73 Price to O'Malley, 6 Oct. 1922 (IMA, CW/CAPT/001/2/14).

74 Sworn statement by Thomas McHugh, 10 Mar. 1936 (IMA, MSPC, WMSP34REF15403); NA operations report, 13 Sept. 1922 (IMA, CW/OPS/07/01).

75 ATIRA memo, 17 Oct. 1922 (IMA, CAP, Lot 25, No 66); James Dunne (BMH WS 1571, p. 17).

76 Post-truce claims, Costello, Dublin, 21 Oct. 1922 (NAI, FIN/COMP/2/9/328).

77 ATIRA report, 14 Oct. 1922 (IMA, S/12008/6); NA report, 12 Oct. 1922 (IMA, CW/OPS/07/01).

78 ATIRA reports, 24, 28 Oct. 1922 (IMA, S/12008/6).

79 NA operations report, 28 Nov. 1922 (IMA, CW/OPS/07/01).

80 James Dunne (BMH WS 1,571, pp 18–19).

81 NA report, Nov. 1922–Jan. 1923 (UCDA, Mulcahy papers, P/7/B/111/8); *LL*, 23 Dec. 1922.

82 Civil War prisoner ledgers (IMA, CW/P, digitized collection).

83 James Dunne (BMH WS 1,571, p. 15); *II*, 4 Nov. 1922.

84 Operation reports, Eastern Command, 3 Nov. 1922 (IMA, CW/OPS/07/01).

85 James Dunne (BMH WS 1,571, pp 19–20); NA operations report, 17 Nov. 1922 (IMA, CW/OPS/07/25).

86 Sworn statement by Thomas Harris, 9 Mar. 1936 (IMA, MSPC, WMSP34REF16113); James Dunne (BMH WS 1571, p. 19).

87 NA report, 25 Oct. 1922 (UCDA, Mulcahy papers, P7/B/109/4); NA operations report, 2 Dec. 1922 (IMA, CW/OPS/07/01). For details of the death of James Hunt, see *NLT*, 4 Nov. 1922; https://www.facebook.com/Coolkennohistory/posts/1560717730892254 (accessed 20 Feb. 2018).

88 NA operations report, 25 Oct. 1922 (MIA, CW/OPS/07/01). For details of local tradition relating to the ambush, see Paul Gorry, *Baltinglass chronicles, 1851–2001* (Dublin, 2006), p. 194; Éamon Kane, 'The Civil War in Castledermot and Graney', *JKAS*, 21:1 (2016–17), 232.

89 Operation reports, Eastern Command, 30 Oct. 1922 (IMA, CW/OPS/07/01).

90 Ibid., 4 Nov. 1922 (ibid.); *NLT*, 11 Nov., 2 Dec. 1922.

91 NA operations report, 7 Dec. 1922 (IMA, CW/OPS/07/01); Handwritten material submitted to the advisory committee by Michael O'Toole, 15 July 1933 (IMA, MSPC, 2RB385); *NLT*, 9, 16 Dec. 1922.

92 Submission to the advisory committee by Mary Lillis, 30 Jan. 1933 (IMA, MSPC, DP5395).

93 Seamus Cummins, 'A shout in the night: the rise and fall of the Leixlip Irregulars, July– Dec. 1922' [unpublished]; Durney, *Civil War in Kildare*, pp 101–7; Neeson, *Civil War*, pp 188–90.

94 Paddy Mullaney interview, p. 27 (UCDA, O'Malley notebooks, P17/b/106).

95 ATIRA memo, Price to O'Malley, 6 Oct. 1922 (IMA, CW/CAPT/001/2/14); ATIRA report from Mullaney, 4 Oct. 1922 (IMA, S/12008/6); Cummins, 'A shout in the night', p. 11.

96 C.S. Andrews, *Dublin made me: an autobiography* (Cork, 1979), pp 237–9; Durney, *Civil War in Kildare*, pp 101–2; Hopkinson, *Green against green*, p. 146.

97 Mary Flannery Wood (BMH WS 624, pp 3–4); Andrews, *Dublin made me*, p. 238.

98 NA operations report, 11 Oct. 1922 (IMA, CW/OPS/07/01); ATIRA report, 14 Oct. 1922 (IMA, S/12008/6); Sworn statement by William Wyse, 9 Dec. 1938 (IMA MSPC WMSP34REF15040) in author's possession.

99 ATIRA reports, 24, 26, 28 Oct. 1922 (IMA, S/12008/6).

100 ATIRA report, 24 Oct. 1922 (IMA, S/12008/6); NA operations report, 14 Oct. 1922 (IMA, CW/OPS/07/01); *KO*, 21 Oct. 1922.

101 ATIRA report, 28 Oct. 1922 (IMA, S/12008/6).

102 ATIRA report by Mullaney, 28 Oct. 1922 (IMA, S/12008/6); *KO*, 28 Oct. 1922.

103 Post-truce claims, Minister for Local Government (NAI,FIN/COMP/2/9/314); Cummins, 'A shout in the night', p. 12.

104 Operation reports, Eastern Command, 9 Nov. 1922 (IMA, CW/OPS/07/01).

105 Cummins, 'A shout in the night', p. 14.

106 ATIRA report, 30 Nov. 1922 (IMA, S/12008/6); Mick O'Neill interview, p. 48 (UCDA, O'Malley notebooks, P17/b/107).

107 NA operations report, 2 Dec. 1922 (IMA, CW/OPS/07/01).

108 Mick O'Neill interview, p. 53 (UCDA, O'Malley notebooks, P17/b/107); *IT*, 2 Dec. 1922.

109 NA operations report, 2 Dec. 1922 (IMA, CW/OPS/07/01); Paddy Mullaney interview, p. 38 (UCDA, O'Malley notebooks, P17/b/106); *KO*, 16 Dec. 1922.

110 NA operations report, 2 Dec. 1922 (IMA, CW/OPS/07/01); Mick O'Neill interview, p. 52 (UCDA, O'Malley notebooks, P17/b/107); *IT*, 2 Dec. 1922.

111 Paddy Mullaney interview, p. 38 (UCDA, O'Malley notebooks, P17/b/106); *IT*, 2 Dec. 1922; Christopher Lee, *A damn good clean fight: the last stand of the Leixlip Flying Column*, http://www.theirishstory.com/2015/01/08/a-damn-good-clean-fight-the-last-stand-of-the-leixlip-flying-column (accessed 20 Feb. 2018).

112 *IT*, 16 Aug. 1922.

113 O'Connor letter, Aug. 1922 (MA, Erskine Childers collection, BMH-CD-006-40-01(a)); *FJ*, 11 Sept. 1922; Thomas J. Morrissey, *Edward J. Byrne, 1872–1941: the forgotten archbishop of Dublin* (Dublin, 2010), p. 90.

114 http://oireachtasdebates.oireachtas.ie, 9 Sept. 1922, vol. 1. no. 1. (7) (accessed 28 Feb. 2018).

115 Campbell, *Emergency law*, p. 196; Hopkinson, *Green against green*, p. 181.

116 http://oireachtasdebates.oireachtas.ie, 27 Sept. 1922, vol. 1, no. 13 (accessed 28 Feb. 2018).

117 Ibid., 28 Sept. 1922, vol. 1, no. 13 (accessed 28 Feb. 2018); Timothy Murphy Breen, 'The government's execution policy during the Civil War, 1922–1923' (PhD, NUI Maynooth, 2010), pp 73–87.

118 Patrick Murray, *Oracles of God: the Roman Catholic Church and Irish politics, 1922–37* (Dublin, 2006), p. 72.

119 *IT*, 11 Oct. 1922; for an analysis, see Margaret O'Callaghan, 'Religion and identity: the Church and Irish independence', *The Crane Bag*, 7:2 (1983), 66–71.

120 Hopkinson, *Green against green*, p. 221.

121 *LL*, 2 Dec. 1922; *KO*, 2 Dec. 1922; Nelson, *Through peace and war*, pp 270–1.

122 *LL*, 23 Dec. 1922; NA report, Eastern Command, 15 Dec. 1922 (UCDA, Mulcahy papers, P7/B/111/8). This report indicated that 10 men were arrested.

123 *Éire: the Irish nation*, 31 Mar. 1923; Adrian Mullowney, *Civil War executions, December 19th, 1922* in http://www.curragh.info/articles/executions.htm (accessed 16 Feb. 2018); Durney, *Civil War in Kildare*, pp 124–7.

124 Captured note, undated (IMA, CAP, Lot 2, 4/a); Murphy, 'Execution policy', p. 175.

125 *LL*, 23 Dec. 1922.

126 Material submitted to the advisory committee by Mary Moore, 9 Mar. 1933 (IMA, MSPC, DP 7504); Material submitted to the advisory committee by Michael White, 23 May 1933 (IMA, MSPC, DP 6027).

127 *Éire: the Irish nation*, 31 Mar. 1923.  128 *LL*, 23 Dec. 1922.

129 *II*, 31 Oct. 1924; *KO*, 1 Nov. 1924.

130 Mick O'Neill interview, p. 53 (UCDA, O'Malley notebooks, P17/b/106).

131 Paddy Mullaney interview, p. 38 (ibid.).

132 Mick O'Neill interview, p. 53 (ibid.).

133 Gordon file, IRA Court of Enquiry, evidence of Patrick Mullaney, 12 Mar. 1925 (IMA, CAP, Lot. 214, IV (2/2)).

134 *II*, 9 Jan. 1923; *KO*, 13 Jan. 1923; *MC*, 13 Jan. 1923.

135 Mick O'Neill interview, p. 53 (UCDA, O'Malley notebooks, P17/b/106).

136 *LL*, 1 Nov. 1924.

137 Mick O'Neill interview, p. 44 (UCDA, O'Malley notebooks, P17/b/106).

138 Gordon file, IRA Court of Enquiry, evidence of Patrick Mullaney, 12 Mar. 1925 (IMA, CAP, Lot, 214, IV (2/2)).

139 Liam Deasy, *Brother against brother* (Cork, 1982); Seán Kearns, 'Deasy, Liam', *DIB*; Dorothy Macardle, *The Irish Republic: a documented chronicle of the Anglo-Irish conflict and the partitioning of Ireland with a detailed account of the period, 1916–1923* (London, 1937; 4th ed., Dublin, 1951), pp 833–4. Deasy, a moderate on ATIRA side, commanded the 1st Southern Division during the Civil War until his arrest in January 1923.

140 Gordon file, IRA Court of Enquiry, evidence of Patrick Mullaney, 12 Mar. 1925 (IMA, CAP, Lot, 214, IV (2/2)).

141 Handwritten material submitted to the advisory committee by Mary Lillis, 30 Jan. 1933 (IMA, MSPC, DP5395).

142 Martin O'Dwyer, *Seventy-seven of mine* (Cork, 2006), p. 203.

143 Murphy, 'Execution policy', p. 301.  144 Ibid., pp 299–301, 313.

145 Ibid., p. 313.  146 Murray, *Oracles of God*, p. 84.

147 Morrissey, *Edward J. Byrne*, pp 98–9.  148 Murray, *Oracles of God*, p. 85.

149 Lawrence William White, 'De Brún, Pádraig (Browne, Patrick)', *DIB*.

150 Morrissey, *Edward J. Byrne*, pp 89, 104; M.P. McCabe, *For God and Ireland: the fight for moral superiority in Ireland, 1922–1932* (Dublin, 2013), p. 154.

151 McCabe, *For God and Ireland*, p. 154.

152 In memory of Rory O'Connor, Liam Mellows, Joseph McKelvey, Richard Barrett, 1922 (NLI, MS 41,987/3); White, 'De Brún, Pádraig'.

153 Guiomar González Corona, *The Catholic Church in the Irish Civil War* (Cultivalibros, 2008), p. 51.

154 Civil War prisoner ledgers (IMA, CW/P, digitized collection).

155 http://oireachtasdebates.oireachtas.ie/debates, *Seanad debates*, vol. 1, no. 1, 11 Dec. 1922; vol. 1, no. 2, 13 Dec. 1922 (accessed 1 May 2018); Donal O'Sullivan, *The Irish Free State and its Senate: a study in contemporary politics* (London, 1940), pp 90–1.

156 http://oireachtasdebates.oireachtas.ie/debates, *Seanad debates*, vol. 1, no. 12, 21 Feb. 1923 (accessed 1 May 2018).

157 For details of victimization in Cork see Peter Hart, *The IRA & its enemies*, pp 273–92; in Cavan see Brian Hughes, 'Loyalists and loyalism in a southern Irish community, 1921–1922', *Historical Journal*, 59:4 (2016), 1075–1105.

158 Irish Grants files indicates that a total of forty-eight with County Kildare addresses claimed compensation, although, a small number of claimants had lived outside the county at the time of their distress (TNA, CO 762).

159 Irish Grants Committee claim of Cecil Johnson, 20 Jan. 1929 (TNA, CO 762/193/21).

160 Irish Grants Committee claim of Pim Goodbody, 30 Dec. 1926 (TNA, CO 762/85/1).

161 Irish Grants Committee claim of Esmee Lascelles and Doreen Buchanan, 15 Jan. 1929 (TNA, CO 762/199/5).

162 Analysis based on a survey of the entire Irish Grants files for County Kildare.

163 *KO*, 23 Sept., 23 Dec. 1922; 28 Apr. 1923; Bielenberg, 'Exodus', p. 208.

164 Hopkinson, *Green against green*, p. 195; Terence Dooley, *Decline of the big house in Ireland* (Dublin, 2001), p. 287.

165 Order from ATIRA chief of staff, 26 Jan. 1923 (UCDA, Twomey papers, P69/2 pp 18–20); O'Malley and Dolan, *No surrender here*, p. 533.

166 Irish Grants Commission claim of Countess Mayo, 18 Dec. 1926 (TNA, CO /762/133/1); *II*, 31 Jan. 1923; *KO*, 3 Feb. 1923.

167 *KO*, 12 Dec. 1925; James Dunne (BMH WS 1571, p. 15).

168 Irish Grants Committee claim of General Bryan Mahon, 13 Dec. 1928 (TNA, CO/762/97/15); *KO*, 24 Feb. 1923; O'Malley and Dolan, *No surrender here*, p. 533.

169 *KO*, 24 Feb. 1923.      170 *KO*, 19 May 1923.

171 Interview of John Wilson-Wright by Des O'Leary and Seamus Cullen, Apr. 1993.

172 Irish Grants Committee claim of Cecil Johnston, 20 Jan. 1929 (TNA, CO 762/193/21).

173 Gemma Clark, *Everyday violence in the Irish Civil War* (Cambridge, 2014), pp 69–85, 96–7.

174 *KO*, 28 Apr. 1923; James Dunne (BMH WS 1571, pp 16–17).

175 *LL*, 5 May 1923.

176 Hunger strike report, 1923, table showing approximate figure in respect of gaols etc. where strikes began, 14–24 Oct. 1923 (NAI, DT S 1369/10). For July figures see *IT*, 21 Nov. 1923; McCabe, *For god and Ireland*, p. 184.

177 Hunger strike report, 1923 (NAI, DT S 1369/10); *Éire: the Irish Nation*, 3 Nov. 1923, put the number at 7,800.

178 Hunger strike report 1923 (NAI, DT S 1369/10); for instance, Hopkinson, *Green against green*, pp 268–71; James Healy, 'The Civil War hunger strike – October 1923', *Studies: an Irish Quarterly Review*, 71 (1982), 213–26; Macardle, *Irish Republic*, p. 876.

179 *Daily Sheet*, 26 Oct. 1923; *Éire*, 3 Nov. 1923.

180 *Daily Sheet*, 17, 19 Nov. 1923.

181 Hunger strike report, 1923 (NAI, DT S 1369/10).

182 List of prisoners who are not on strike in Tintown A, 2 Nov. 1923 (IMA, CW/P/02/02/20).

183 Hunger strike figures for jails and camps, 3 Nov. 1923 (NAI, DT, S 1369/10).

184 List of prisoners who signed the Undertaking Form, 5 Nov. 1923 (IMA, CW/P/02/02/13).

185 Denis Barry, *The unknown commandant: the life and times of Denis Barry, 1883–1923* (Cork, 2010), p. 113; Andrews, *Dublin made me*, p. 302.

186 *IT*, 27 Nov. 1923; Barry, *Unknown commandant*, pp 110–11.
187 *LL*, 1 Dec. 1923.
188 *Irish Catholic Directory 1924*, p. 600.
189 Charlotte Fallon, 'Civil War hunger strikers: women and men', *Éire-Ireland*, 22:3 (1987), 88–9; Healy, 'The Civil War hunger strike', pp 221–2; Macardle, *Irish Republic*, p. 867.

CHAPTER NINE *A return to its Redmondite roots: Kildare in 1923*

1 http://www.irishstatutebook.ie/eli/1922, article 14, accessed 20 Apr. 2018; *KO*, 25 Aug. 1923.
2 *KO*, 9 June 1923.          3 Ibid., 21 July 1923.          4 Ibid., 4 Aug. 1923.
5 Ibid., 9 June 1923; *LL*, 9 June, 4 Aug. 1923.          6 *LL*, 11 Aug. 1923.
7 Ibid., 11, 18 Aug. 1923.          8 *KO*, 4 Aug. 1923.          9 *LL*, 25 Aug. 1923.
10 Ibid., 11 Aug. 1923.          11 *NLT*, 22 June 1935.          12 *LL*, 25 Aug. 1923.
13 Ibid., 11, 25 Aug. 1923.
14 Mick O'Neill interview, p. 48 (UCDA, O'Malley notebooks, P17/b/107); Ó Súilleabháin, *Ua Buachalla*, pp 188–9.
15 *LL*, 18, 25 Aug., 1 Sept. 1923; *KO*, 1 Sept. 1923; Anne Dolan, 'MacSwiney, Muriel Frances', *DIB*.
16 *LL*, 25 Aug. 1923.
17 Ibid., 18 Aug. 1923. George Wolfe's grandfather was named Theobald Wolfe see, George Wolfe, 'The Wolfe family of County Kildare', *JKAS*, 3:6 (1902), 361–7.
18 *LL*, 25 Aug. 1923.          19 *KO*, 1 Sept. 1923.
20 John Regan, *The Irish counter revolution, 1921–1936: treatyite politics and settlement in Independent Ireland* (Dublin, 1999), p. 205; Brian Walker, *Parliamentary election results in Ireland, 1918–92: Irish elections to parliaments and parliamentary assemblies at Westminster, Belfast, Dublin* (Dublin, 1992), pp 108–15.
21 For election results see, http://irelandelection.com/elections (accessed 30 Apr. 2018).
22 *LL*, 4 Aug., 1 Dec. 1923; Civil War prisoner ledgers (IMA, CW/P, digitized collection).
23 Nelson, *Through peace and war*, p. 286. The dismissal order was signed by E. Blythe, minister for local government.
24 *LL*, 20 Oct. 1923.
25 *Éire: the Irish Nation*, 3 Nov. 1923; *KO*, 20 Oct. 1923.
26 Nelson, *Through peace and war*, pp 285–9.
27 M. Burke, 'Shooting the messenger: Col. Costello and the Murray case', *Tipperary Historical Journal* (1997), 46. For Carolan as director of intelligence, IRA see J. Anthony Gaughan, *Memoirs of Senator Joseph Connolly (1885–1961): a founder of modern Ireland* (Dublin, 1996), p. 84.
28 *IT*, 10 June 1925; Civil War prisoner ledgers (IMA, CW/P, digitized collection); Burke, 'Shooting the messenger', 46–7.
29 *IT*, 10 June 1925; *Sunday Independent*, 16 Dec. 1922; *KO*, 22 Dec. 1922; *LL*, 17, 29 Dec. 1922.
30 Anne Dolan, 'Lemass, Noel Denis Joseph', *DIB*; Inquest on death of Noel Lemass, p. 39, Oct. 1923 (NAI, 1B-93-11A).
31 *II*, 10–13 June 1925; Burke, 'Shooting the messenger', p. 52.
32 *II*, 10–13 June 1925; *IT*, 13 June 1925; Burke, 'Shooting the messenger', 53.
33 See Perrtii Haapala and Marko Tikka, 'Revolution, Civil War and terror in Finland in 1918' in Robert Gerwarth and John Horne (eds), *War in peace: paramilitary violence in Europe after the Great War* (Oxford, 2012).
34 Civil War prisoner ledgers (IMA, CW/P, digitized collection).

35 *Dáil debates*, 21 May 1924, vol. 7, no. 11, www.oireachtas.ie/en/debates/debate/dail/1924–05–21 (accessed 30 Apr. 2018); Campbell, *Emergency law*, p. 241.

36 *KO*, 19 Apr. 1924.      37 Ibid., 10 May 1924.      38 Ibid., 24 May 1924.

39 *LL*, 14 June 1924; for divisions in Cumann na nGaedheal see, Regan, *Irish counter revolution*, pp 207–8. Details of the army mutiny see, Maryann Gialanella Valiulis, *Almost a rebellion: the Irish army mutiny of 1924* (Cork, 1985); Duggan, *History of the Irish army*, pp 129–37.

40 *II*, 17 July 1924; *II*, 18 July 1924; Returns of prisoners in military custody, 2 June to 21 July 1924 (NAI, SI369/4 SPO).

41 Bielenberg, 'Exodus', 202.

42 Irish Free State census, 1926, https://www.cso.ie/en/media/csoie/census/census1926 results/volume3/C_15_1926_V3_T12.pdf, pp 37–8.

43 Census of Ireland, 1911, province of Leinster, Kildare, religious professions of the people, pp 74–5.

44 Irish Free State Census, 1926, https://www.cso.ie/en/media/csoie/census/ census1926 results/volume3/C_12_1926_V3_T9.pdf, p. 13.

45 David Fitzpatrick, *Descendancy: Irish Protestant histories since 1795* (Cambridge, 2014), pp 159–240.

46 Irish Grants Committee claim of Henry Hosie, 27 Nov. 1927 (TNA, CO 762/153/4) & Henry Large, 28 Jan. 1927 (TNA, CO 762/139/2).

47 Bielenberg, 'Exodus', 206.

48 *Dáil Éireann debates*, 11 Mar. 1925, vol. 10, no. 11; Andrew Rynne, *The vasectomy doctor: a memoir* (Cork, 2005), p. 24.

49 Irish Grants Committee claim of Peter Kidd, 10 Nov. 1926 (TNA, CO 762,112/4); Andy Bielenberg, 'Exodus', pp 204–13; Hart, *The IRA at war*, pp 232–9.

50 Irish Grants Committee claim of Henry Sampey, 5 Dec. 1928 (TNA, CO 762/189/2).

51 Irish Grants Committee claim of Emmie Cornelius, 5 Apr. 1929 (TNA, CO 762/198/7).

52 Data acquired from a study of census of Ireland, 1911, province of Leinster, Kildare, pp 2, 4, and https://www.cso.ie/en/media/csoie/census/census1926results/volume1/C_1926_ V1_T8.pdf., p. 16.

53 Ó Súilleabháin, *Ua Buachalla*, pp 219, 230, 259.

54 *Irish Press*, 20 Feb. 1974.

55 For Smyth, see *LL*, 24 Nov. 1973; for Purcell, see *II*, 2 Apr. 1960.

56 William Murphy, 'O'Connor, Arthur James Kickham (Art)', *DIB*.

57 *LL*, 26 Apr. 1941.

58 Sworn statement by Michael O'Kelly, 3 Feb. 1938 (IMA, MSPC, WMSP34REF9986).

59 *Connaught Telegraph*, 22 Aug. 1974.

60 Fitzsimons elected chairman of KCC following the 1925 and 1928 elections, Nelson, *Through peace and war*, p. 306; *KO*, 14 July 1928.

61 On Minch's election see *II*, 19 Feb. 1932.

# Select bibliography

## PRIMARY SOURCES

### A. MANUSCRIPTS

*Cambridge*
**Churchill College**
John De Robeck papers.

*Clane*
**Clongowes Wood College Archive**
*The Clongowian* (1927).

*Dublin*
**Dublin Diocesan Archives**
Archbishop William J. Walsh papers.

**General Registration Office**
Register of births, deaths and marriages.

**Guinness Archive**
Trade analysis ledgers, 1900–20.

**Irish Railway Record Society Archives**
Special, weekly circulars 1 Jan.–31 Dec. 1916.
Service timetables, 1911–16, trains department.

**Military Archives**
Bureau of Military History, witness statements.
Civil War captured documents.
Civil War internment collection.
Civil War operations and intelligence reports.
Erskine Childers collection.
IRA membership series.
Irish army census records, 1922.
Military Service Pensions Collection.
Truce liaison and evacuation papers.

**National Archives of Ireland**
Chief Secretary's Office Registered Papers.
Dáil Éireann records.
Department of Finance.
Department of Justice.

Department of the Taoiseach.
General prison board papers.

**National Library of Ireland**
Dulcibella Barton papers.
Joseph Brennan papers.
Pádraig de Brún poem in memory of Rory O'Connor, Liam Mellows, Joseph
    McKelvey, Richard Barrett, 1922.
Henry de Courcy-Wheeler papers.
Irish Farmers' Union papers.
Irish National Aid Association and Volunteer Dependants' Fund papers.
Irish Transport and General Workers' Union papers.
Thomas MacDonagh papers.
Maurice Moore papers.
J.J. O'Connell papers.
William O'Brien papers.
John Redmond papers.
Francis Sheehy Skeffington papers.
United Irish League, minute book of the National Directory.

**University College Dublin Archives**
Belgian Refugees' Committee minutes (P105).
Richard Mulcahy papers (P7).
Ernie O'Malley papers & notebooks (P17).
Records of the Sinn Féin party (P163).
Republican Soldiers' Casualty Committee (P156).
Maurice Twomey papers (P69).

*London*
**Imperial War Museum**
Hugh Jeudwine papers.
F.H. Vinden papers.

**Parliamentary Archives**
Bonar Law papers.

**The National Archives**
Cabinet papers.
Colonial Office records.
Irish Grants Committee files.
Home Office records.
War Office records.

*Louth*
**Louth County Library, Dundalk**
Dundalk jail register, list of rescued prisoners, 14 August 1922.

*Newbridge*
**Kildare County Library**
Minutes of Kildare County Council meetings, 1899–1925.

*Oxford*
**Bodleian Library**
H.H. Asquith papers.

*Privately held collections*
Civil War prisoner detail, Fergus White, Maynooth.
Domhnall Ua Buachalla papers, Adhamhnán Ó Súilleabháin, Dublin.
Patrick O'Keeffe hand-written essay, Thomas O'Keeffe, Kilcock.
Ted O'Kelly papers, Edward O'Kelly, London.

B. OFFICAL RECORDS

*Census of Ireland 1901, 1911, 1926.*
*Dáil Éireann parliamentary debates.*
*Hansard 5 (Commons)* parliamentary debates.
*Hansard 5 (Lords)* parliamentary debates.
*Irish Statute Book.*
*Monthly statistical statement, issued by the Department of Agriculture, 1921–1923, relating to average prices of agricultural products sold at fairs and markets in Ireland, May 1922.*
*Report of the Department of Agriculture and Technical Instruction for Ireland on agricultural statistics, 31 March 1913,* Cd. 6987.
*Report of the Department of Agriculture and Technical Instruction for Ireland on agricultural statistics, 1917–18,* Cd. 8453.
*Royal Commission on the Rebellion in Ireland, 1916: report of commission* (June 1916), Cd.8279.
*Royal Commission on the Rebellion in Ireland, minutes of evidence and appendix of documents* (1916), Cd. 8311.
*Seanad Éireann debates.*
*Settlement as to the Government of Ireland* (1916), Cd. 8310.
*Statement giving particulars regarding men of military age in Ireland* (1916), Cd. 8390.

C. NEWSPAPERS AND PERIODICALS

*Éire: the Irish nation*
*Freeman's Journal*
*Gaelic American*
*Irish Catholic Directory*
*Irish Independent*
*Irish Times*
*Irish Volunteer*
*Kildare Nationalist*
*Kildare Observer*
*Leinster Express*
*Leinster Leader*
*Manchester Guardian*
*Meath Chronicle*
*Nationalist and Leinster Times (Carlow Nationalist)*
*Sunday Independent*
*Thom's Directory*
*The Times*

D. PRINTED PRIMARY MATERIAL

*1916 Sinn Féin Rebellion handbook* (Dublin, 1917).

Comerford, Michael, *Collections, diocese of Kildare and Leighlin, vol. i* (Dublin, 1883).

Gough, Hubert, *Soldiering on: being the memoirs of General Sir Hubert Gough* (London, 1954).

Macready, Nevil, *Annals of an active life, vol. ii* (2 vols, London, 1924).

Mac Giolla Choille, Breandán (ed.), *Intelligence notes, 1913–16, preserved in the State Paper Office* (Dublin, 1966).

Martin, Hugh, *Ireland in insurrection: an Englishman's record of fact* (London, 1921).

O'Hegarty, P.S., *The victory of Sinn Féin: how it won it and how it used it* (Dublin, 1924).

Stephens, James, *The insurrection in Dublin* (New York, 1916).


SECONDARY SOURCES

E. PUBLISHED WORKS

ann de Wiel, Jérôme, *The Catholic Church in Ireland, 1914–1918: war and politics* (Dublin, 2003).

Abbott, Richard, *Police casualties in Ireland, 1919–1922* (Cork, 2000).

Andrews, C.S., *Dublin made me: an autobiography, C.S. Andrews* (Cork, 1979).

Augusteijn, Joost, *Patrick Pearse: the making of a revolutionary* (Basingstoke, 2010).

——, *From public defiance to guerrilla warfare: the experience of ordinary volunteers in the Irish War of Independence, 1916–1921* (Dublin, 1996)

Beckett, Ian W.F., *The army and the Curragh incident, 1914* (London, 1986).

Bew, Paul, *Conflict and conciliation in Ireland, 1890–1910: Parnellites and radical agrarians* (Oxford, 1987).

Bielenberg, Andy, 'Exodus: the emigration of southern Irish Protestants during the Irish War of Independence and Civil War', *Past & Present*, 18 (2013), 199–233.

Brannigan, Niall, 'Changing of the guard: Curragh evacuation seventy years on', *An Cosantóir, the Irish Defence Journal*, 52:12 (Dec. 1992), 29–30.

Burke, M., 'Shooting the messenger: Col. Costello and the Murray case', *Tipperary Historical Journal* (1997), 42–59.

Callan, Patrick, 'Recruiting for the British army in Ireland during the First World War', *Irish Sword*, 17 (1987–8), 42–56.

Campbell, Colin, *Emergency law in Ireland, 1918–1925* (Oxford, 2004).

Campbell, Fergus, *Land and revolution: nationalist politics in the west of Ireland, 1891–1921* (Oxford, 1994).

Clark, Gemma, *Everyday violence in the Irish Civil War* (Cambridge, 2014).

Coleman, Marie, *County Longford and the Irish Revolution, 1910–1923* (Dublin, 2006).

Costello, Con, *A class apart: the gentry families of County Kildare* (Dublin, 2004).

——, *A most delightful station: the British Army on the Curragh of Kildare, Ireland, 1855–1922* (Cork, 1999).

Costello, Francis, *The Irish Revolution and its aftermath, 1916–1923: years of revolution: years of revolt* (Dublin, 2003).

——, 'The Republican Courts and the decline of British rule in Ireland, 1919–1921',
*Éire-Ireland*, 25:2 (1990), 36–55.

Cullen, Seamus, 'Attempted ambush and escape from Stacumny, 2 July 1921', *Irish
Sword*, 29:115 (Summer 2013), 62–77.

Cummins, Gerry and Éanna de Búrca, *The Frank Burke story: patriot, scholar, GAA
dual-star, guardian of Pearse's vision and legacy* (Naas, 2016).

Dolan, Anne, 'Spies and informers beware ...' in Diarmaid Ferriter and Susannah
Riordan (eds), *Years of turbulence: the Irish Revoloution and its aftermath: in honour
of Michael Laffan* (Dublin, 2015), pp 157–71.

——, 'The British culture of paramilitary violence in the Irish War of Independence'
in Robert Gerwarth and John Horne (eds), *War in peace: paramilitary violence in
Europe after the Great War* (Oxford, 2012), pp 200–15.

Donnelly, Brian, 'Local government in Kildare, 1920–1970' in William Nolan and
Thomas McGrath (eds), *Kildare: history and society* (Dublin, 2006), pp 673–712.

Dooley, Terence, *The decline of the dukes of Leinster, 1872–1948* (Dublin, 2014).

——, 'IRA activity in Kildare during the War of Independence' in William Nolan
and Thomas McGrath (eds), *Kildare: history and society*, pp 625–56.

Duggan, John, *A history of the Irish army* (Dublin, 1991).

Durney, James, *Foremost and ready: Kildare and the 1916 Rising* (Naas, 2015).

——, *In a time of war: Kildare, 1914–1918* (Sallins, 2014).

——, *The War of Independence in Kildare* (Cork, 2013).

——, *The Civil War in Kildare* (Cork, 2011).

——, 'The Curragh internees, 1921–24: from defiance to defeat', *JKAS*, 20:2 (2010–
11), 8–15.

——, *On the one road: political unrest in Kildare, 1913–1994* (Naas, 2001).

Durney, James with Liam Kenny, *A rebel's desk: Seumas and Michael O'Kelly,
Leinister Leader editors in a revolutionary time* (Naas, 2016).

Fanning, Ronan, *Éamon de Valera: a will to power* (London, 2015).

——, *Fatal path: British government and Irish revolution, 1910–1922* (London, 2013).

Fergusson, James, *The Curragh incident* (London, 1964).

Findlater, Alex, *1916 surrenders: Captain H.E. de Courcy-Wheeler's eyewitness account*
(Dublin, 2016).

Fitzpatrick, David, *Descendancy: Irish Protestant histories since 1795* (Cambridge,
2014).

——, *Harry Boland's Irish Revolution* (Cork, 2003).

——, *Politics and Irish life, 1913–1921: provincial experience of war and revolution*
(Cork, 1998 [1977]).

——, 'Militarism in Ireland, 1900–1922' in Thomas Bartlett and Keith Jeffrey (eds),
*A military history of Ireland* (Cambridge, 1996), pp 379–406.

Fox, R.M., *The history of the Irish Citizen Army* (Dublin, 1944).

Foy, Michael T. and Brian Barton, *The Easter Rising* (Stroud, 2004).

Fussell, Paul, *The Great War and modern memory* (Oxford, 2013).

Gallagher, Frank, *Four glorious years* (Dublin, 2005 [1953]).

Gallagher, Michael, 'The pact general election of 1922', *IHS*, 21:84 (1979), 404–21.

Garvin, Tom, *Nationalist revolutionaries in Ireland, 1858–1928* (Oxford, 1987).

——, *The evolution of Irish nationalist politics* (Dublin, 1981).

Greaves, C. Desmond, *The Irish Transport and General Workers' Union: the formative years, 1909–23* (Dublin, 1982).

Hart, Peter, *The IRA at war, 1916–1923* (Oxford, 2003).

——, *The IRA and its enemies: violence and community in Cork, 1916–1923* (Oxford, 1998).

——, 'The geography of revolution in Ireland, 1917–1923', *Past & Present*, 155 (1997), 142–76.

Harvey, A.D., 'Who were the Auxiliaries?', *Historical Journal*, 35:3 (1992), 665–9.

Healy, James, 'The Civil War hunger strike – October 1923', *Studies: an Irish Quarterly Review*, 71 (1982), 221–6.

Hennessy, Thomas, *Dividing Ireland: World War I and partition* (London, 1998).

Herlihy, Jim, *Royal Irish Constabulary officers: a biographical dictionary and genealogical guide, 1816–1922* (Dublin, 2005).

Holmes, Richard, *The little field-marshal: Sir John French* (London, 2004).

Hopkinson, Michael, *The Irish War of Independence* (Dublin, 2002).

——, *Green against green: the Irish Civil War* (Dublin, 1988).

—— (ed.), *The last days of Dublin Castle: the Mark Sturgis diaries* (Dublin, 1999).

Hughes, Brian, *Defying the IRA: intimidation, coercion, and communities during the Irish Revolution* (Liverpool, 2016)

——, 'Loyalists and loyalism in a southern Irish community, 1921–1922', *Historical Journal*, 59:4 (2016), 1075–1105.

Jackson, Alvin, *Home rule: an Irish history, 1800–2000* (London, 2003).

James, R.R., *Gallipoli* (London, 2004).

Jeffery, Keith, *1916: a global history* (London, 2015).

——, *Ireland and the Great War* (Cambridge, 2000).

——, *The British army and the crisis of empire, 1918–22* (Manchester, 1984).

——, 'The British Army and internal security, 1919–1939', *Historical Journal*, 24:2 (1981), 377–97.

Kenny, Liam, 'Kildare County Council, 1919–1921' in Nolan and McGrath (eds), *Kildare: history and society*, pp 657–72.

Kinsella, Anthony, 'The British military evacuation', *Irish Sword*, 20 (Winter 1997), 275–86.

Kostick, Conor, *Revolution in Ireland: popular militancy, 1917–1923* (London, 1996).

Laffan, Michael, *The resurrection of Ireland: the Sinn Féin party, 1916–1923* (Cambridge, 1999).

Lawlor, S.M., 'Ireland from truce to Treaty: war or peace? July to October 1921', *IHS*, 22:85 (1980–1), 49–64.

Lee, J.J., *Ireland: the modernization of Irish society, 1848–1918* (Dublin, 2008 [1973]).

Lowe, W.J., 'The war against the RIC, 1919–1921', *Éire-Ireland*, 37:3–4 (Fall/Winter 2002), 79–117.

Matthews, Ann, *The Irish Citizen Army* (Cork, 2014).

——, *Renegades: Irish republican women, 1900–1922* (Cork, 2010).

Maume, Patrick, *The long gestation: Irish nationalist life, 1891–1918* (Dublin, 1999).

McCabe, M.P., *For God and Ireland: the fight for moral superiority in Ireland, 1922–1932* (Dublin, 2013).

McCarthy, Brian, *The Civic Guard mutiny* (Cork, 2012).

McCarthy, Cal, *Cumann na mBan and the Irish Revolution* (revised ed., Cork, 2014).
McConnel, James, *The Irish Parliamentary and the third home rule crisis* (Dublin, 2013).
——, 'Recruiting sergeants for John Bull? Irish nationalist MPs and enlistment during the early months of the Great War', *War in History*, 14:4 (2007), 408–28.
McConville, Séan, *Irish political prisoners, 1848–1922: theatres of war* (London, 2003).
McDowell, R.B., *Crisis and decline: the fate of the southern unionists* (Dublin, 1997).
——, *The Irish Convention, 1917–18* (London, 1970).
McGarry, Fearghal, 'Revolution, 1916–1923' in Thomas Bartlett (ed.), *The Cambridge history of Ireland, vol. 4* (Cambridge, 2018), pp 258–95.
——, 'Independent Ireland' in Richard Bourke and Ian McBride (eds), *The Princeton history of modern Ireland* (Princeton, NJ, 2016), pp 109–40.
——, *The Rising, Ireland, Easter 1916* (Oxford, 2010).
——, *Eoin O'Duffy: a self-made hero* (Oxford, 2005).
McLoughlin, Mark, *Kildare barracks: from the Royal Field Artillery to the Irish Artillery Corps* (Dublin, 2014).
——, 'The killing of Lt John Wogan Browne on 10 February 1922: a test of Anglo-Irish relations', *JKAS*, 20:3 (2012–12), 9–25.
McMahon, Paul, 'British intelligence and the Anglo-Irish truce, July–December 1921', *IHS*, 35:140 (Nov. 2007), 519–40.
Meleady, Dermot, *John Redmond, the national leader* (Dublin, 2014).
Miller, D.W., *Church, state and nation in Ireland, 1898–1921* (Dublin, 1973).
Milne, Ida, 'The 1918–19 influenza pandemic: a Kildare perspective of a global disaster', *JKAS*, 20:3 (2012–13), 301–15.
——, *Stacking the coffins: influenza, war and revolution in Ireland, 1918–19* (Manchester, 2018).
Mitchell, Arthur, *Revolutionary government in Ireland, Dáil Éireann, 1919–22* (Dublin, 1995).
——, *Labour in Irish politics, 1890–1930: the Irish labour movement in an age of revolution* (Dublin, 1974).
Morrissey, Thomas J., *Edward J. Byrne: the forgotten archbishop of Dublin* (Dublin, 2010).
——, *William J. Walsh, Archbishop of Dublin, 1841–1921: no uncertain voice* (Dublin, 2000).
Muenger, Elizabeth, *The British military dilemma in Ireland* (Dublin, 1991).
Murphy, William, *Political imprisonment and the Irish, 1912–21* (Oxford, 2014).
——, 'Sport in time of revolution: Sinn Féin and the hunt in Ireland, 1919', *Éire-Ireland*, 48, 1–2 (Spring/Summer 2013), 112–47.
Murray, Patrick, *Oracles of God: the Roman Catholic Church and Irish politics, 1922–37* (Dublin, 2006).
Murray, Robert H., *Archbishop Bernard: professor, prelate and provost* (Dublin, 1931).
Neeson, Eoin, *The Civil War in Ireland* (Dublin, 1989).
Nelson, Thomas, *Through peace and war: Kildare County Council; in the years of revolution, 1899–1926* (Maynooth, 2015).
——, 'Kildare County Council and perceptions of the past' in Terence Dooley (ed.), *Ireland's polemical past: views of Irish history in honour of R.V. Comerford* (Dublin, 2010), pp 176–91.
O'Callaghan, Margaret, 'Religion and identity: the Church and Irish independence', *The Crane Bag*, 7:2 (1983), 66–71.

O'Connor, Diarmuid and Frank Connolly, *Sleep soldier sleep: the life and times of Pádraig O'Connor* (Dublin, 2011).

Ó Corráin, Daithí, 'Archbishop William Joseph Walsh' in Eugenio Biagini and Daniel Mulhall (eds), *The shaping of modern Ireland: a centenary reassessment* (Sallins, 2016), pp 110–23.

——, 'J.J. O'Connell's memoir of the Irish Volunteers, 1914–16, 1917', *Analecta Hibernica*, 47 (2016), 3–102.

——, 'A most public spirited and unselfish man: the career and contribution of Colonel Maurice Moore, 1854–1939', *Studia Hibernica*, 40 (2014), 71–133.

——, 'Resigned to take the bill with its defects: the Catholic Church and the third home rule crisis, 1912–14' in Gabriel Doherty (ed.), *The home rule crisis, 1912–14* (Cork, 2014), pp 185–209.

O'Day, Alan, 'The Ulster crisis: a conundrum' in D.G. Boyce and Alan O'Day (eds), *Ulster crisis, 1885–1921* (Basingstoke, 2006).

——, *Irish home rule, 1867–1921: attempts to implement home rule, 1914–18* (Manchester, 1998).

Ó Drisceoil, Donal, 'Keeping disloyalty within bounds? British media control in Ireland, 1914–19', *IHS*, 149 (2012), 52–69.

Ó Duibhir, Liam, *Prisoners of war: Ballykinlar internment camp, 1920–21* (Cork, 2013).

O'Dwyer, Martin, *Seventy-seven of mine* (Cork, 2006).

O'Halpin, Eunan, 'Problematic killing during the war of Indepedence and its aftermath: civilian spies and informers' in James Kelly and Mary Ann Lyons (eds), *Death and dying for Ireland, Britan and Europe: historical perspectives* (Sallins, 2013), pp 317–48.

O'Malley, Cormac K.H. & Anne Dolan, *'No surrender here!': The Civil War papers of Ernie O'Malley, 1922–1924* (Dublin, 2007).

Orr, Philip, *Field of bones: an Irish division at Gallipoli* (Dublin, 2006).

Ó Súilleabháin, Adhamhnán, *Domhnall Ua Buachalla: rebellious nationalist, reclusive governor* (Dublin, 2015).

Pašeta, Senia, *Irish nationalist women, 1900–1918* (Cambridge, 2013).

Privilege, John, *Michael Logue and the Catholic Church in Ireland, 1879–1925* (Manchester, 2009).

Regan, John M., *The Irish counter-revolution, 1921–1936: treatyite politics and settlement in Independent Ireland* (Dublin, 1999).

Ryan, A.P., *Mutiny at the Curragh* (London, 1956).

Sagarra, Eda, *Kevin O'Shiel: Tyrone nationalist and Irish state-builder* (Dublin, 2013).

Schmuhl, Robert, *Ireland's exiled children: America and the Easter Rising* (Oxford, 2006).

Scholes, Andrew, *The Church of Ireland and the third home rule bill* (Dublin, 2010).

Sheehan, William, *Hearts and mines: the British 5th Division in Ireland, 1920–1922* (Cork, 2009).

Sloan, Geoffrey, 'The British state and the Irish Rebellion of 1916: an intelligence failure or a failure of response?', *Intelligence and National Security*, 28:4 (2013), 453–94.

Smyth, Michael, 'Kildare battalions – 1920', *Capuchin Annual* (1970), 564–73.

Stewart, A.T.Q., *The Ulster crisis: resistance to home rule, 1912–1914* (London, 1967).

Swan, Desmond A., 'The Curragh of Kildare', *An Cosantóir: the Irish Defence Journal*, 32:5 (May 1972), 39–69.

Synnott, David, 'Diary of a recruiting drive for the British armed forces undertaken by Barbara Synnott, Co. Kildare, 24 January to 2 February 1916', *JKAS*, 19:3 (2004–5), 549–58.

Taaffe, Frank, 'Athy and the Great War' in William Nolan and Thomas McGrath (eds), *Kildare: history and society* (Dublin, 2006), pp 585–624.

——, *Athy Urban District Council: a brief overview of its first 100 years* (Athy, 2001).

Taaffe, Patrick, 'Richard Mulcahy and the genesis of the Civil War', *Irish Sword*, 29:118 (Winter 2014), 437–54.

Tierney, Michael, *Eoin MacNeill: scholar and man of action, 1867–1945* (Oxford, 1980).

Townshend, Charles, *The Republic: the fight for Irish independence, 1918–1923* (London, 2013).

——, *Easter 1916: the Irish Rebellion* (London, 2006).

——, 'The Irish Railway strike of 1920: industrial action and civil resistance in the struggle for independence', *IHS*, 21:83 (1979), 265–82.

——, *The British campaign in Ireland, 1919–21* (Oxford, 1975).

Valiulis, Maryann Gialanella, *Portrait of a revolutionary: General Richard Mulcahy and the founding of the Irish Free State* (Dublin, 1992).

——, *Almost a rebellion: the Irish army mutiny of 1924* (Cork, 1985).

Volunteer, 'South Dublin Union area', *Capuchin Annual* (1966), 201–13.

Walker, Brian M., *Parliamentary election results in Ireland, 1918–1992: Irish elections to parliaments and parliamentary assemblies at Westminister, Belfast, Dublin* (Dublin, 1992).

——, *Parliamentary election results in Ireland, 1801–1922* (Dublin, 1978).

Walsh, Fionnula, 'The impact of the First World War on Celbridge, Co. Kildare', *JKAS*, 20:3 (2012–13), 287–300.

Wheatley, Michael, *Nationalism and the Irish Party: provincial Ireland, 1910–1916* (Oxford, 2005).

Woods, C.J., *Bodenstown revisited: the grave of Theobald Wolfe Tone, its monuments and its pilgrimages* (Dublin, 2018).

Wren, Jimmy, *The GPO garrison: a biographical dictionary* (Dublin, 2015).

Yeates, Padraig, *A city in turmoil: Dublin, 1919–1921* (Dublin, 2012).

——, *A city in wartime: Dublin, 1914–1918* (Dublin, 2011).

——, *Lockout: Dublin, 1913* (New York, 2000).

Younger, Carlton, *Ireland's Civil War* (London, 1970).

F. THESES AND UNPUBLISHED WORK

Breen, Timothy Murphy, 'The government's execution policy during the Civil War, 1922–1923' (PhD, NUI Maynooth, 2010).

Cummins, Seamus, 'A shout in the night: the rise and fall of the Leixlip Irregulars, July–Dec. 1922' (unpublished essay).

McInerney, Anne-Marie, 'Internment of the anti-Treaty IRA in the Free State – 1922–4' (PhD, TCD, 2015).

Ó Conaill, Séan, 'The Irish language and the Irish legal system: 1922 to present' (PhD, Cardiff University, 2013).

O'Neill, Clare, 'The Irish home front, 1914–1918, with particular reference to the treatment of Belgian refugees, prisoners of war, enemy aliens and war casualties' (PhD, NUI Maynooth, 2006).

Ó Ruairc, Pádraig, 'The Anglo-Irish truce: an analysis of its immediate military impact, 8–11 July 1921' (PhD, University of Limerick, 2014).

Ryan, Raymond, 'Farmers, agriculture and politics in the IFS area, 1919–1936' (PhD, UCD, 2005).


G. INTERNET SOURCES


aan de Wiel, Jérôme, *Mgr. O'Riordan, Bishop O'Dwyer and the shaping of new relations between nationalist Ireland and the Vatican during World War One*: http://www.limerickcity.ie/media/0%27dwyer,%20edward%20thomas%2019.pdf

Allen, Gregory, The police and the workers' revolt: http://www.garda.ie/ Documents/User/The%20Wokers%20Revolt%20–20Greg%Allen.pdf

Bertram Portal's ancestry: http://thepeerage.com/p43338.htm

Bertram Portal's diary: http://www.mullocksauctions.co.uk/lot-60736–ireland_easter_ rising_diary.html?p=10

Bertram Portal's diary: http://www.irishmirror.ie/news/irish-news/british-colonels-diary-suggests-top-1860268

Details of Edward Murphy: http://www.glasnevintrust.ie/visit-glasnevin/news/ edward-murphy-1874–1916

Details of Peter Connolly: http://source.southdublinlibraries.ie/bitstream/10599/ 11507/5/Fragment1 916.pdf

Details of the death of James Hunt: https://www.facebook.com/Coolkennohistory/ posts/1560717730892254

Domhnall Ua Buachalla to Shackleton on 15 Sept. 1913 relating to labour difficulties: http://www.lucannewsletter.ie/history/lockout.html

Election results, 1922: http://www.electionsireland.org/results.cfm?election=1922

Election results, 1923: http://irelandelection.com/elections

Kildare casualties WW1: http://www.kildare.ie/Library/KildareCollectionsand ResearchServices/World-War-One/Kildare-Casualties-World-War-1.asp

Lee, Christopher, *A dam good clean fight: the last stand of the Leixlip Flying Column*: http://www.theirishstory.com/2015/01/08/a-damn-good-clean-fight-the-last-stand-of-the-leixlip-flying-column

Matthew, H.C.G. and Brian Harrison (eds), *Oxford dictionary of national biography* (Oxford, 2004), http://www.oxforddnb.com

McGuire, James and James Quinn (eds), *Dictionary of Irish biography* (Cambridge, 2009): http://dib.cambridge.org

Mullowney, Adrian, *Civil War executions, December 19th, 1922*: http://www.curragh.info/articles/executions.htm

RDF website: http://www.dublin-fusiliers.com/Naas/naas.html

Smith, Jim, *The Curragh camp pre-1922*: http://www.curragh.info/articles/smith. htm

'The voice of the Church of Ireland on home rule: resolutions of the General Synod, special meeting 16 April 1912' (Dublin, 1912): digital.slv.vic.gov.au/dtl_ publish/pdf/marc/11/2703855

Ulster Covenant online, PRONI: http://apps.proni.gov.uk/ulstercovenant/Search Results.aspx

# Index